THREE SLATES

DENNIS J. ANDERSON

Table of Contents

One

Crossing the mudflats on the estuary of the Tay was always a great adventure. Scanning well in front for soft spots. Following the Lindy burn to the mouth where the river had retreated to low tide. A set line with fifty hooks was the target. I had a fishing line with me in case I was early, and it looked that way. There were two other people fishing there on the banks. The mussel beds came right into the water as it retreated: Half an hour till low tide. I joined the others on the bank, spreading my line out for the throw. I had a new sinker which I had made by placing a matchbox in the sand, then pouring in the lead and pushing in a stick for the hole. Too heavy, and it wouldn't go far enough, too light, and it would fall short of the hoped for seventy yards. I baited the four hooks with piler crab. Round and round it went, like throwing the hammer until it reached full speed, but careful with it, then smoothly letting go so that it should not cross anybody else's line. I pressed the peg into the mud. Then, with about five yards of line left, I pulled the peg to wind up the slack and then pressed it down again into the mud. I stood waiting for bites. The line tugged, and I felt one on, then there was a big tug from me as another took the bait. This attracted the attention of the others. "That was quick; what bait are you using?" asked one of the other fishermen.

"Piler crab," I replied. I had a tin full intended to bait the sett line, and I was worried now that they could take it from me. I could see the tide had let one of the sett line pegs come out of the water. I pulled in the line, winding it onto the peg. It came out with three flounders on.

"Can I get a bit of your piler?" he asked.

"OK!" I said.

He was already in my tin and took a couple of crabs and told his pal, "Look, the tin is full," so he came and took some too.

"I need these," I said. Worried that they would take the lot.

"Oh, share and share alike." He laughed.

I picked up my can of bait, took the covering sack off and put my line back in the tin, heading up the burn until I could cross. I doubled back to the sett line and started to take the catch off. I had about half the flukes unhooked from the line and safely in the sack when the tide turned. I picked the hessian tattie sack by the top, shook them down tighter, and then swung it onto my shoulder with the bait tin and line in the other hand, heading away from the water as quick as I could. The sand underneath gets full of water as the tide rises. I think that's what they call quicksand?

I had to cross the burn again, too, in order to get to the driest road home. The sack was heavy, and I was sweating now.

"Here, carry my bag, and I will give you a spell," the larger of the two said.

"I can manage," I said, not wanting to let go.

"You're Jackie's boy, aren't you?"

"Yes," I replied.

After putting the sack down, he swung it on his shoulder.

"You need to use a shorter set line so you can carry the catch back. We got a good few with that piler," he said. "We were using worms, but that crab is the best bait I have ever used. Where did you get it?"

"In the seaweed along the braes," I lied, not wanting to give the place away.

Back to dry land again.

They gave me the bag back and took their own catch. I was relieved.

Losing a catch to older guys was something that had happened occasionally. There were many bullies, but not this time. They were nice enough, though very rough diamonds.

I arrived back home; my mum's smile was well worth it all. I had a few people that I sold the flukes to, earning me shilling or a tanner usually, but an occasional half a crown, or often a two-bob bit. I felt great when that happened! Success, a bit like being an entrepreneur, like Andrew Carnegie, maybe? It took me quite some time to discover what an entrepreneur was. I wondered at first if it was a swear word.

I gutted my mum's fish, then ran about a mile to deliver some to Will Doctor and his wife. "Sure, thank you, Dennis, good boy. Sure, Collie will get one too. I see you have given us three nice big ones."

"I am off," I said.

"I must be in early tonight, my mum said." I ran all the way home and was just inside the eight-thirty curfew.

The next morning, I was up at six.

"Where are you off to?" my dad growled.

"To deliver the milk," I replied.

"Forget it," he said. "You are going to court in St Andrew's."

A cold shiver ran through me; I had forgotten all about it. Anyway, the colonel would tell them the truth of it. After all, he was my Sunday school teacher. The truth shall prevail.

About two months previously, Tam, Davie and I had plunked school and gone for a trip up the estate to Jessie Philips dam. We looked down at the bulrushes and wondered if it was haunted by the ghost of Jessie Philips, who had apparently drowned there. We followed the path up to the tower, getting near the estate buildings, past the big house. Colonel Henderson's mansion lay ahead of us, with its magnificent steps down to the policy park where our Sunday school picnics were held. Travelling up there on the horse-drawn carts was a rare treat. He never joined us, even though he was an elder of the kirk.

He would instead make a regal appearance on the landing above the steps for a few minutes and then disappear. Today, however, there was no one to see us slip past the house.

We came upon the old doocot and looked through the bars on the door. The piles of droppings were higher than our heads. The doos were cooing away.

"Let's climb up and see if we can catch a couple," said Tam.

There were flat sandstone copings on the walls about a foot wide. We could climb up easily, but that roof was sagging.

"I wouldn't risk it," I declared. We climbed up and along the side; no one was going to risk the roof bearing us.

"Let's come back with a net and see if we can get some," said Davie.

We were climbing down when we heard, "Hey, what are you doing!"

"Run, it's the colonel!" Tam shouted.

We took off across the field onto the road, all downhill. No pursuit. We began to laugh nervously. The great thing about being chased is not to be last.

The next morning the police came to my door accusing me of having broken three slates on the doo-cote. A lie: none of us had broken the slates. They took a dim view of me calling the great man a liar by saying that I did not break any slates. What's more, I had been charged with malicious mischief a few months before, and I had forgotten all about it.

Dressed in my best clothes, I went for the bus to St Andrew's with my mum, who was looking very worried. Off we went for me to appear in the juvenile court, where Gordon Adams, Justice of the Peace, became red-faced and angry when I refused to plead guilty to breaking the slates. This meant I was calling Colonel Henderson a liar. "I have no alternative but to send you to an approved school," he thundered, "in the hope it will sort you out and teach you not to criticise your betters."

My mum sobbed, and I was dragged off while two policemen tried to comfort her. At the same time, I was taken round to the police station through the two closes crossing South Street and Market Street, to North Street where finally the police station was. I sat for a couple of hours. Police officers there were telling of other unfortunates who had gone before me and subsequently turned to a life of crime. "I don't think the three slates that lying bastard is blaming me for is going to turn me into Dick Turpin," I said.

"You have a bad attitude," one said. "They will sort you out in Oakbank. That is where you are going, son."

I thought about my grandad, glad he had not lived to see me in this position. A thirteen-year-old convict. The shame engulfed me.

"How old are you?"

"I have just turned 13." I said

I was driven to Aberdeen by Mr McNichol, a probation officer, who chatted away to me, telling me that it was not such a bad place and that I would be home in nine months if I behaved myself.

Met at the door, I was put in a room with a stage at one end, a heating pipe all around it. I waited for half an hour when a boy came in and said, "You're the new boy. Have you seen The Gov yet?"

"No, I haven't seen anybody since I came. I thought I was the only one here."

"Where do you come from?"

"Fife," I said.

The door was opened by a man in a kilt. "The governor is ready to see you. I am Mr Wilson, the deputy governor of the school."

I followed him along the corridor to a board room with a big table, and The Gov said, "I will begin by telling you what happens if you run. You will be bent over that table, and we will proceed to apply the MacLeod tartan to your arse." The belt he pointed at me looked fierce. I had had a few at school, but on my arse, the thought filled me with dread. "You will be in Scott's house. There are five houses: Kelvin, Lister, Scott, Simpson and Watson.

"We have a motto here that you are expected to live up to. Be honest, hardworking, and agreeable. Measure up to that, and you won't be here long. Come." He beckoned me to follow him out the door. "Sutherland, show him the boundaries and the rules. Make sure he knows what shefters feel like since you've had a few. Sutherland! Do not forget to mention the pools of tears you left on my boardroom table."

That was my introduction to Scotland's answer to wayward children. Or, in my case, an early lesson in social inequality. George Orwell's Animal Farm was my first taste of the education department here. It completely took over my thinking for the next few months. For the next two years, four months and three days, I took part in gymnastics, education, games and hiking. I turned fifteen and asked to work in the joinery shop, but there were no places, so I opted for the farm. The work was hard, and I loved it. The time flew by. Milking cows that and doing all the other work was most enjoyable. I spent the entire time there dreaming of one of my school friends, with whom I came close to a sexual encounter, except that neither of us knew quite what we were doing and apart from our aroused visual experience. It was a freezing night with a bright moon and stars. The vision of this girl was with me for the entire time at Oakbank.

Free at last, I was picked up by Mr McNichol, who was to be my probation officer for the next two and a half years. Fuck me; when does it end? Three fucking slates that I knew nothing about. The colonel must have had an insurance policy. No trial, no witnesses, only a bad attitude from the JP when I had denied breaking three slates on the great man's doocot.

I was dropped off at my granny's, where I would live and work on the farm near there.

When I went for a walk in the village, I wasn't recognised, being at least a foot taller, six feet in my stocking soles and a pure fighting machine. I felt it too.

Freedom is a heady feeling. I walked with a swagger.

I bought myself a dog and worked on the farm, where my first job was bringing in the hay. With eight horses and three old tractors, it was old-fashioned for 1962. The tractors were from the forties and early fifties.

The hay was in ricks, which were brought into the stack yard on low trailers with a winch and tipping action.

Lifting them off on a pole and a jib, my job was to go back and forwards with the horse, which pulled and closed the grab, then pulled it up to the jib, which was pulled round to the desired spot and about a ton at a time was made into the largest hay stacks I had ever seen.

After the hay-making came the harvest, binding and stooking the sheaves, which kept us all busy till November that year. It was oats, barley, then wheat.

Tatties were made into pits with wheat straw and earth. One the 440 acres worked fourteen men and three women with the eight horses and three tractors.

The stooks were taken forked onto a corn cart and were then stacked into their various grains: much smaller than the haystacks. Tatties were made into pits with wheat straw and earth.

I loved this work, especially the tatties. We had sixty Irish pickers from Donegal. They were great fun, and I went out at night to show the boys how to catch rabbits.

They were quick learners; I was invited to eat with them a big dish of tatties and another filled with a boiled beef rib. It was great. It doesn't get much better, and I loved it there.

McNichol, the probation officer, came to see how I was doing, having heard great reports from Jimmy Butters, the farmer. Auld Jimmy was from another age and a gentleman farmer. Each morning at 7am on the dot, the fourteen of us men and three women met in the stable to get our orders. Auld

Jimmy would joke with the Irish who stayed in the Bothy, Sean Curran and Shawn Gallagher. They would sing rebel songs on the way back from the pub. I loved it.

One of my favourite jobs was to take a horse and a corn cart and fill it with tares or cabbages: Savoy cabbages with hearts two feet across. I would shuck one in half and shared it with the horse. The tender middle leaves were what I loved most. That juicy crunch. The memory of it makes my mouth water. The sheep in question were Border Leicester tups for the ram sales in Perth Milnathort and Aberdeen. We dressed them up much the way of a poodle parlour until they looked nothing like a sheep. Teased and clipped, the wool powdered, legs and faces pampered and fed. They would be bought for around a thousand pounds each, then dumped out on the heather with a few hundred ewes. I wondered how many of them survived the first mating season, which was usually November time.

Who would want to come back as a sheep? I thought.

Springtime that year, I was seventeen and a half, and I joined the army: Scots Guards. I even talked Philip Freelove, who was not very keen, into going over to Dundee and signing up. As comrades, we were signed up for twenty-two years. We went off together to Pirbright in Surrey, training to deal with the wild man of Borneo. I wasn't there long when my heinous past caught up with me, and I was marched up to the commandant's office and put back in my civvies, which was the light blue suit with Hank Williams pockets and a black velvet collar. The winkle pickers were left outside the office so that I could stamp my tackety boots to salute properly. "We are discharging you. We hear you are on probation and have been in a fight with one of our Coldstream's. We will send for you if a war breaks out!"

"Don't bother; I am not coming," I answered. Given my pay and a ticket home, I changed the boots for my winkle pickers and was put on the train.

I got off the train and went straight to the local pub, where I heard words like disgrace and dishonourable discharge mentioned. My temperature shot up. I couldn't put a face to the insults, which was just as well.

I met Ed, who said, "That was a short career, ha, ha, ha." He could not keep a straight face. "It was Mike Moncur that spilt the beans," he said.

"That recruiting sergeant is shagging Philips's mum. She was afraid he would get into trouble being with you, so she grassed you up to him. That's right, she told Sis that," Ed confirmed. "Fuck them, did me a favour. I didn't think they had many fights in them, that army. I should have joined the Paras on my own."

Walking my dog by the River Eden towards the airfield one night, I came across a pile of old rollers. Imagine putting that in the dump, I thought. I gave one a scrape. Bingo, it was copper. I set to thinking how I could get one out to the road.

It was not far to the field, but not easy to get there either. I took the shaft sticking out the end and heaved. I could lift one end, but there was no chance of carrying it. I set it down again and looked around to see if I could be seen from the paper mill across the river. No movement. I would have to come back with help at dark. In need of muscle and transport, I went up to meet my mate Ed, who was working on a farm too.

I was a real peasant to them, a second-in-the-pecking-order kind of thing in their minds. Still working with the horse while they were on tractors. A lot of giggling went on between Ed and his brother on the subject.

I sat on the dyke and whistled. Ed would appear to feed the goose, then nip out to join me. "You should see what they have thrown in the dump," I said. "Must be a couple of tons of copper, and I need a hand to lift it."

"Will we not get seen?" he asked.

"Not if we are careful. We can go in the dark there's nae moon. Let's shoot a couple of pheasants so I can explain being out late then."

Cutting through the field, I showed him, and we took an end each and heaved it onto our shoulders.

"Put it back!" I said.

"No, why, let's just take it?"

"No, we need a van. I know somebody in Dundee. A right gadgie with a van. I will go over tomorrow and see him. You keep your mouth shut, mind!"

"Don't worry. I'll be ready."

I went over to Dundee to talk to Mac, who went out with my sister. His van was broken down, but he put me on to another gadgie with a Bedford van. He wanted to be in on the play. I agreed, and he had a big guy, a good lifter, whom he would bring along his partner, apparently. I was in no position to be choosy, so I agreed. It was Tuesday, and we decided to meet on Thursday with the van.

Thursday night came. Soon as it was dark and quiet, we walked over and picked one up, hoisted it onto our shoulders and carried it two hundred yards to the top of the field and laid it in a tattie drill. The large helper and the van owner could not lift them.

"I am off," said the larger. "This is crazy." He pointed to the bus shelter and asked, "When does it come?"

"Bus there in five minutes," I said.

The driver handed me the key. "Give me something for the van, mind." And they ran over in time to get the bus to Dundee.

"Boozers," I said. "They can only lift pints and talk bullshit."

We worked on sweating. On the way back to get a roller, I noticed movement on the road. A large, young, red-haired woman walked along the road to the bus stop and sat in the shelter. We sat down in the drills opposite, laying low, waiting for the next bus to come till she was gone and the way was clear.

She was joined by an airman.

The bus arrived, and the airman was lit up, pulling his pants up. She had a bit more of a struggle. Neither of them got on the bus, and we were in hysterics. They left in a hurry in opposite directions, and we laboured on through the night, sweating and stifling the giggles. About 3am, we knackered and threw in the towel. We loaded the van, and then I went straight home to bed. Ed shot off to do the same.

Eight on the dot, I got up, had my porridge, got in the van and picked Ed up. "Let's go and see what we can get." We were excited by the daring of it all.

Even with the magnet on the scales, it came to £408 quid. I went over to talk to the dog, a long-haired Alsatian with a bad attitude, who was tied up to a long boundary wire of doubled fence wire with a ring.

"Hello, who has been tying you up like that? Good dog."

"GRRRRrrrr!"

I let him smell my jacket. The tail wagged a tiny bit. I stroked his forehead. The teeth were still showing. "Good boy," I said, and he wagged his tail. I clapped his ears and smiled. He was mine.

"Hey!" came a shout. "You get away from that dog!"

The dog jumped away along the wire, pulling at the heavy iron ring.

"You've been in here at night feeding him," he ranted.

"I have not!" I said.

"Ignore Frank," said another voice. "He can't even go near him, and he is his dog. He feeds it from a distance."

He handed me the wad of notes. I gave Ed his share, and then I weighed the van owner in. I had still half left when I got home. The price was high due to the eight-day Israeli war.

I spent a couple of years married to Carol, a life-changing experience though it lasted just two years. I was madly in love. She had come from

Headington, a finishing or boarding school in Oxford. Then she went to Mauritius. We wrote for a couple of years. She came back to Dundee and stayed with her granny. She shared an enormous sexual appetite with me, and I readily caught up with her. Pregnant, shotgun wedding. Father turned out to be a right shite, only to be outdone by his wife. Made me give up my woodcutting business. Spent the next few years getting up to all sorts to get over the complete betrayal of their agreement with me regarding my daughter. He was a banker, a right wanker, in my opinion. I was from the wrong side of the tracks. There are a lot of songs about the subject, I have noted.

A job as a gamekeeper on the Panmure estate came my way. There were six under-keepers, of which I was one. It was hard to survive on £22 a fortnight, living in a cottage with a pregnant teenage wife. The farmers supplied potatoes and veg. We lived off the land, and Lord Thompson was the main client. Gordon Adams, the bastard who had sent me to Oakbank for three slates, was the other. He could afford a few pheasants and partridge and the occasional roe deer too for my pot. My wife could cook better than I had dreamed of, taught at Headington to take over if the cook died. They were two very tight years for money. When Carol was about three weeks from the due date, the head keeper, Braithwaite, picked me up one morning and drove me down to the factor's office.

"Is there something wrong," I asked.

"We will see when we get there," he said.

"I have found out some things. You can't get a rifle licence because you have a police record. We can't have you here; what would the client think."

"Well, if it's Gordon Adams you are worrying about," I said, thinking he can't think.

"You will go at the end of the month."

Fired!

"Three fucking slates," I murmured.

"What was that?" he said sharply.

"Oh, shut up, take me home before I punch your lights out," I said and left the office.

I had a wife three weeks from the birth of our child. This is Victorian shite, I thought. The head keeper dropped me at the cottage, with me holding back the tears. I couldn't speak. I went into the trees in the yard and let the tears go. I composed myself and went and told Carol the news. She took it badly. We moved into a caravan, and I sold Judy my gundog into the life she enjoyed. I advertised her, and she went to a laird's wife, the best I could do for her.

I got a job as a forester at Kippendavie, which was alright for a time.

I went to the Dunblane hydro and had a go with a fiver in ten-bob chips. I had never played roulette, so I took the odds and evens. I won a few, so I spread the winnings on numbers. The croupier pushed piles of chips. I spread some more and did the 00 and came up. I collected an armful of chips, cashed them in and got £240. I went home. Andy Robbins was working along the road, and I went to Perth and bought two Stihl 08 chainsaws. I got Ed along and went for it, snedding on piece work. After the job finished, I had the phone installed at my gran's and bought an Isaacson double drum winch with a skyline. I did not have enough to buy and mount it on a matador as I wanted, so I bought a Nuffield that did the job, as long as it was well anchored.

My business was moving in the right direction, so I threw everything into it. After the birth of my daughter, I spent a couple of years trying to get it together with Carol. She moved to Glasgow for teacher's training, and then things went wrong while she was in college. She must have been trying to get back to the middle class. Poor girl.

Separated, I was devastated! I sold my equipment. I had stopped working as there seemed little point. I hunted her out, trying to get it on again, without much success. I went to see her in Glasgow, and my aunts looked after the baby, Tracy when I worked.

It was going well, and we were cooking mince and tatties: my favourite. I think she was really trying. We repaired to the bedroom for some steamy sex that I had been missing out on. As I was lying back, feeling on top of the world, Carol jumped up and said, the mince! She opened the door to the kitchen. It was like a blazing inferno. I leapt into action and lowered her out of the window. I went to the door and rang the bell; the landlord came out. "Ring the fire brigade, the kitchen's on fire!" I shouted. He opened the flat to look in as if he didn't believe me. The heat was intense; the window and all the woodwork were ablaze. I slammed the door shut. "Phone the fire brigade!" I said.

That was that. Carol was gone, and I was blamed for being hungry and losing her flat.

"Fancy getting a bit of hash from that pub in Dundee, The Bothy?" asked Ed, who woke me up the next morning feeling flush.

"There is a bus in ten minutes; get up. Come on."

"Alright, keep the head."

We went to the Madras restaurant in Princess Street and had a curry on the way to score a bit of Black from The Bothy. We got a couple of pints and a quarter of Black from a paranoid individual. The music was good, Mr Bojangles and some King Crimson. I went over to the graveyard opposite and had a spliff.

I liked the hash much better than the beer. I started to find that it was possible to get my own for free if I dealt a few deals. Then it was down to London to score a pound of Moroccan hash for £70 and sell it for £12 an ounce. It wasn't long till I figured out that I could sell more than I could get. Black was £110 but sold for £16 an ounce or £55 a quarter weight.

Arty Fogarty and Sammy lived in London. I used to meet them in Earl's Court in the pub. They would let me know where to score.

Sometimes they would come up to Glasgow, and we would do the State bar in Holland Street together, then to the Marylands: a lot safer with the Blue Angels than the State bar that had the police come in and grab someone out of the queue where he was scoring acid microdots from Arty and Sammy at a pound each. Not bad, since they had cost less than 2 bob each. Then Maryland's was burned down. Arty told me about it. I kept doing the hash occasionally runs after that.

I had met a student in St Andrew's that fascinated me. Maureen had a 350 AJS motorbike and used to dress up as Batman and buzz around the town. I used to spend evenings in her flat talking and enjoying a beer. She liked lager and black currant. Yuck! I couldn't stand it, being a Guinness man, the long first draught that the Irish labourers had taught me. Stayed with me to this day. Mausie didn't smoke, so I would have a joint before I called for her.

One day I called, and she was in a real rage. She had been pulled in by the police, who had told her she should not be seeing someone like me.

They threatened to tell her mum when she came up.

Why would they do that? Oh, they stopped me on my motorbike a few times. I was wearing the Batman outfit, tights and all. I told them I had a boyfriend in the police in Brighton. Since then, a hopeful young one has been pestering me a bit.

"Oh dear, what will your mum say?" I asked.

"I will speak to Mumsie, and she will give them what for," she said.

I was worried and didn't hang around for a few weeks, but Maureen remained large in my thoughts. I felt vulnerable. Three fucking slates, and now I am public enemy number one around here. Looked like it was all over with Mausie, and it hadn't even started.

Summer came, and the highlight of that summer was that a finishing school in Gstaad, in Switzerland, had brought a class of American debs to St Andrew's. They were attending a month-long Shakespeare class. They were good fun.

With Desmond, Neil McCourt and wee Peem, I headed for London and got a flat in Cork Street. I had about three months of working nights for a cleaning company that hired the gang, which now included wee shug. I wrote to Maureen and got letters back weekly.

I bought a bottle of whiskey to celebrate, and we all showed up pissed at Marshal Snelgrove's around the corner in Oxford Street. After running around the shop with the kex mops, laughing and getting it done quickly, we headed up to the café. Wee Peem, Desmond and I went up on the roof, looking down at the way home. There was a skip. I took a cardboard box with a bottle of something and chucked it down. It dropped right in. We all looked at each other. Half an hour later, they were dropping Afghan coats, perfume and grub. We said goodnight to the security guards, went around to the skip and had a short sprint to the flat.

One morning there was a knock at the door, and Maureen's dad Eric Muggeridge had called to meet me. He was home on leave from the QE2, where he was the purser. Sounded like a good job. We went for a cup of tea. It was great to meet Eric. I liked him immensely.

"Maureen told me you like a wager occasionally," he said. I blushed profusely. "Try The Clerc in the three-thirty."

I went to the nearest bookie after he was gone, looked it up, didn't like the look of it, so I put fifty quid on it, not wanting to break the bank, and it won at 12 to 1. Spring and summer were coming fast, so I resigned and headed home. What a great feeling.

Christmas 1971, I made some scented candles with Mausie. Boxes of them. I would sell them at ten bob each to make a fortune. We had hundreds. Christmas came, and it was embarrassing: no one wanted them. On the second of February, I went into the sub-post office in St Andrew's and saw the decimalisation stamps were on sale. I bought the presentation stamps, put them on the commemorative envelopes sent one to Mausie and one to my aunt. The guy chucked them into a full sack of mail in its stand.

"Hey, you! I said. "You never stamped the envelope!"

"We are on strike!" he answered.

"I'll fucking strike you! ya twat! Get them stamped."

"They are not getting stamped till the strike is over."

"There is a stamp there. I want them stamped right now so that I can see them. I don't trust you, ya little shite!"

He took them out of the bag, picked up the stamp and stamped them. The incident immediately forgotten, we left.

At my aunt's for tea that night, however, the news was on. It was all about the decimalisation and the stamps, which would not be getting franked until the strike was over, except for a small sub-post office in Scotland where two letters had been stamped by mistake. "Those were mine!" I exclaimed and told my auntie that hers would have the right date. I explained what had just transpired. The strike lasted six weeks.

The electricity board were on strike too. People wanted my candles now. They were big ones and thick, and the price went up. Mausie and I, we transported them up to Leuchars station and loaded them into the guard's van on the London train: £5.7/6d each, and we were on our way to London, where we sold the lot in Oxford Street in record time. The police came to move us, then bought ten and left us, saying they wouldn't last long. They were right. We went down to Hove to visit Mausie's mum and back up the road.

Soon Maureen would be leaving to follow her dream to be a field geologist in Australia. As the time got nearer, I discovered what a large part of my life she had become. We were friends, and it was quite a sad thing for me that it would end soon. After Carol, I did not want a steady relationship, and that suited us both.

We went around together for her results. She had a resit on ancient history set for September. Finding it hard to find a job, which she needed, I got by selling a bit of pot. We hired a couple of vans and started selling potatoes in the new twenty-five kilo bags. I had done well with this the previous year. No competition.

This year, however, there was competition. Every rosy-cheeked farmer's son in the country on every corner of the town was selling bags of spuds, too, it seemed. The Scottish farmer must have alerted them. I eventually got rid of them. The tattie harvest was in full swing now, and I got together a piece work squad. We went for it, as we were saving for Australia. Maureen went down to Hove to see her Mum and Dad and leave after Christmas. I would leave after the New Year. I told her to be in touch by letter. I managed to hold back the tears till the train pulled out of Leuchars junction. I sat in the seat on the platform feeling great loss. Still, I would be on my way to Australia in January.

I continued to work with the squad and went to see a farmer at Dunbog farm who had been let down by his pickers, or so he said. It would take more than a day, I told him, saying I could come on Friday to do the day. We were on another farm for four days, I told him, saying that I would let him know if I was delayed. This suited him, and on Friday, we appeared and picked five of the seven acres. I went for the money to pay the squad.

"I will pay you when you finish it," he said.

"I told you! I needed paid today," I replied.

"I will pay when you come back to finish it next week. If I pay, you may never come back."

I did not trust this big-headed Hooray Hendry, and I paid the squad with my savings.

We finished on the Wednesday and went back to Macrae to see if we could come the next day, being Thursday rather than Friday. I went onto the field rather than to the farm to check the two acres for the time it would take us to pick. To our astonishment, the tatties were gone. A white pickup headed towards us with four farm workers with grapes, holding pitch forks like soldiers.

"What happened to the last two acres," I asked.

"I picked them at the weekend with the local children," he declared.

"Oh well, you owe me 450 quid," I said.

"I used it to pay the children," he said. The workers smirked. I looked at the weakest one with his pitchfork. I knew if I did take him off the back, there were another three, and Macrae would drive off to phone the police.

"Off my land," he said and departed in the direction of the farm.

I was furious. I wanted to burn the place to the ground. "That will just make the cunt more money," said Ed. "You will get the jail."

Bastard. That was my fare and get-to-know Australia money.

Two

I stepped off the plane in Singapore, and the heat blast was amazing. The humidity was quite something too! I went to the Ambassador Hotel to have a long lie. I missed breakfast, went for a walk and had some fantastic Chinese food at the side of the road. Got a massage and had my neck cracked. I was not expecting it. Explosive and wonderful. Not that I would want to do it again.

When I went out to a bar for a beer, a good-looking Chinese girl came up to me.

"Buy me a beer," she said.

"OK," I said, lifted my beer and asked the barman for another.

"OK, thirty dollars," he said as he handed the Tiger beer.

"Not the same price as mine," I said.

"You pay for girl."

"No way, Jose." I drank my beer in a swallow. "Fuck off!"

I put down five dollars and left amid a commotion of protest. I heard a Scouse accent saying, "You tell 'em, Jock!"

Outside I went down the road. The girl came after me, asking, "Where you go?"

"Back to my hotel."

"Which hotel?"

"The Ambassador," I said.

"You go wrong way. Ambassador that way."

I turned back, and a taxi slowed down.

"Where to?" asked the driver.

"How much Ambassador Hotel?"

"Twenty dollars."

"No thanks, I will walk." As I got going, the girl started arguing with him.

"Come," she said, "only ten dollars."

I got in, and she snuggled up closer than I expected. I was light-headed and felt pretty good.

What a smile she had.

I went to the bar and bought us more beer. "I want to change my shirt," I said.

"I come too," she answered. "I don't want wait here by self."

"OK," I couldn't believe my luck.

In the room, she jumped on the bed, full of fun. Took off her dress, smiling and being shy. When I joined her, I was presented with hundred a dollar price tag.

"Forget it," I said. "Free."

"No free hundred-dollar good time," she protested. Good price! Look, nice pussy!" She pulled her light blue panties aside to let me admire her lovely black hair. I opened the door. The manager was in like a flash.

"You cannot take girl to room in this hotel!" he shouted.

"She is leaving," I said.

She left, struggling with him. Very noisy, shouting all the way out and down the road.

Sleep did not come easy.

The next morning, after breakfast, an Australian came up to me and said, "Hi, I'm in the next room, mate. You made some ruckus last night." He chuckled.

“Oh, I never noticed,” I lied. I arranged a plane to Darwin the next day, then went for a walk and came across rubber trees. It was like I had been there before, thanks to Mrs Wetherspoon, my Geography teacher, or Hippo as we called her.

I arrived in Darwin about seven o’clock.

On landing, the entire plane was sprayed with DDT or some other disinfection.

Next, I was interviewed by the immigration officer. He looked positively Irish but had a very Aussie accent.

“Why have you come to Australia?” he asked.

“To get a job and to be an Australian,” I said.

He asked what I did for a living. I told him I worked on a farm. He asked other questions. “Have you been in the army?”

“Yes, I was in the Scots Guards,” I eagerly said, puffing my chest out, wondering if my brief square bashing at Pirbright actually counted as a military career. He seemed very satisfied. “Come in, son, welcome to Australia.” He stamped my passport with a big round stamp: Permanent Entry.

That was it. I got a taxi into town and was dropped off at a guest house and given a room by a six-foot Aussie Chinese girl, a student working her holidays.

After breakfast, I asked her, “Where do you go for a job around here?”

“The dole," she said.

“Can you tell me how to get there?” I asked

I took a bus and got dropped off outside the dole.

I had heard on the radio they were setting up a soup kitchen in Darwin because there was 2.5% unemployment in Australia at that time. I think they were copycatting what was happening in Thatcher's UK. The Poms seemed to influence fashionable behaviour down here.

I went up to the counter and asked the lady if there were any jobs. “Where have you come from?”

“Scotland,” I said. “When?”

“Seven o'clock last night.”

“Where are you staying?”

“I stayed in a guest house last night.”

"Have you got any money?”

“Yes, ten pounds. I need to get a job.”

“There’s Theise hiring at Mataranka. Here is an address. You will get a room there tonight. Here it is fifty dollars. The room will cost you $10 and a bus ticket to Mataranka,” which she handed me.

“The bus leaves at six thirty just outside this door.”

“Where is Mataranka?" I asked her.

“Its thirty miles or so past Katherine. You will be met off the bus by the foreman. Get off at Mackenzie's bar. Good luck to ya.”

“Thanks,” I said. I was still wearing the worsted suit that I got off the peg in Dundee. I had a couple of T-shirts and jeans to change into. I went to the address. They were Italian by the look of them. I was shown my room. I paid, then went to a shop to buy grub.

I left thinking Margaret Thatcher could learn something here! That dole was a lot different than in Scotland, where it would take weeks of waiting and form filling, trying to get £3.50 a week from the dole in St Andrew’s.

I bought an onion, garlic, a green pepper called capsicum and spaghetti, minced beef and tomato puree and some basil. I left some for my breakfast. Nice and full, I drifted off to sleep.

The bus was waiting when I arrived. I gave the driver the ticket and asked him to let me know when I was at Makenzie's bar.

“Find yourself a seat,” he said. The bus engine was running, and soon we were driving south through the bush. I saw my first kangaroos. The 20-foot termite towers looked like gateposts and crowned like sombreros with tractor tyres; they reminded me of Westerns.

I was dropped by the bus in the middle of nowhere. The bus pulled off, leaving me wondering where the bar was. There was about three feet high sandbags. It looked like a machine gun post, with a canvas shelter to keep the sun or rain off.

I investigated, and there was a flight of stairs down. "Anyone there?" I asked.

"Aye, coming, fit like man?"

"Nae bad man foos yer doos. Have you just come out from Aberdeen?" I asked.

"I've been here for twenty-seven years," he replied sharply in pure Doric.

"I am looking for Theise," I said.

"You are at the right place. He will be here in a wee bit. I am just getting the beer ready for him."

"Can I have a beer?"

"What kind?"

"You choose. I haven't a clue. I just got here."

He took the top off a VB and said, "It's a stubby; they call it here. I like it."

He was busy in his gopher hole. I had just drained the beer when the foreman arrived.

"Right, mate, be ready to move soon as I've loaded the beer."

He and Mackenzie loaded the ute till it was a six feet tower of Foster's Lager. Tied it down.

"Good, hop in mate."

Then he took off full speed ahead until we turned off the road. We arrived at the camp—wooden huts with rows of doors.

I went into the dining room.

"Grub's finished," said someone.

"He's come a long way, and he's a new start! Feed him."

"Grab a plate, mate; it's still hot. I still have some late arrivals. T-bone, tomatoes, beans, potatoes."

I noticed there was no till.

"Mug of Billie tea, all for free." I stuffed myself and then was shown my hut. Not much room, with one bunk, a table and a chair.

Work next morning was unloading the trailer of a road train. Bags of cement. Three of us, one after the other, put them down in rows on the sand, which had been graded. One other guy came along, breaking them open with a shovel, then came yet another and poured them out and chucked the paper bags off the road. The road went on for a long way like this. Then the grader came ploughing it one way, then the other. Then it flattened it with the blade squared, and along came a roller, pressed it all flat, and then bitumen tar machine. And the new road went down at the pace we went – I guess three miles a day.

I lay under the truck in the shade. Our drinking water was in canvas bags with a rubber pipe. It tasted revolting, and I spat it out.

"Them's rock melons along the side of this road," said my workmate. "Eat one, and it will help with getting rid of the taste."

I did, and they were delicious. I ate lots of them, but I hated the bore water. Pure Sulphur. The norm was to eat the melon and then spread the seeds along the side of the road. It's an old Abo trick, they told me. They eat the seeds too, but they sow them as well.

After a couple of months, the cash had stacked up a bit, and I needed a break. Staying was tempting, but I wanted to see a bit of the country too. I went back to Katherine and met a couple of hitchhikers, one English and one German: Peter and Hans. They had teamed up, and together we went to the bar at night. We all stayed in a room at the guest house over the Katherine Bridge, right on the river. The other side had Silver City, the Abo camp of shiny corrugated iron shacks.

Wednesday, I walked through the town: one street with a bottle shop, a pub, a police station and some other shops, some houses and a meat works. There was a big queue of Aborigines on one side of the street.

"Something happening there," I asked an old man.

"The government decided they were human," he said, "and gives them thirty dollars dole a week. Used to get two bob for their ears when I was a kid on the stations."

I couldn't help thinking, the dollar 74 pence in the pound; they were getting shot for less than I got for a rabbit. They were getting shot for two bob for their ears to stop them killing cattle to eat seventy years ago. They have come a long way ahead of the British system because the dole is £3.50 a week in Scotland to live on, and it's a fucking disgrace.

Tory bastards to blame for that! Thatcher, I thought.

The pub was fine for a time, and we watched a couple of Aussie cowboys in denim and ankle cowboy boots, hats and all, playing pool.

We had been talking about riding the cattle trail over to the Kimberley's. I'd asked the horse trader what he thought. "You would need to carry plenty of water," he advised.

We priced up three saddles. "Seventy dollars each, mate, but you will need pack saddles as well. The Brumbies are thirty dollars each."

I paid him.

"I will come and get three horses so we can break ourselves in."

I went back to watching the pool game.

"Want a game, mate?"

"No, I've never played pool before," I said.

"Come on."

"OK, show me the moves."

"Put five dollars on the table."

He set them up and broke, sinking half the red balls. Finally, one jumped back out.

“OK. You are yellow. Sink them all, and you've won,” he said with a grin of white teeth.

It was smaller than the billiard table in the institute. So were the balls, but basically the same game as far as sinking the balls went. I sank all but two and snookered him. He tried an around-the-table shot and hit mine. I sank the other two and the black.

He snatched the money off the table and said, “You cheated; you said you never played before.”

“I've played billiards. I have never seen this game except for in American movies. Give me my ten dollars.”

“No way, you cheated.”

Fuck it; it’s only five pounds, I thought. I was pleased that I won. I turned to the bar and laughed to the Englishman.

“Weak as piss,” this loudmouth Billie said. The other Aussies agreed in grumbled mumbles.

I reddened. I did not like this, so since it hadn't gone unnoticed, I spun on my heel. “Alright, give me my ten dollars, ya cunt.”

“You want to talk about it outside?” he said.

He was about six feet, lean and fit looking, probably half-aboriginal. I couldn't back down.

He squared up like a boxer. The pub emptied.

I poked him in the eyes and grabbed his hair and an ear. I pulled his head down and kicked him in the puss five or six times with my £4.50 desert boots till he collapsed on the deck. I was first back in the pub.

“Fucking dirty fighter, mate,” the loudmouth called Billie said to me and the entire bar.

“Scottish rules, pal,” I said.

He kept his head down. He didn't look me in the eye.

“Let's go,” I said, and the two mates followed me out. The ten dollars were now forgotten.

Going back to the Katherine Bridge, we came upon the most unbelievable sight.

It looked like a medieval battlefield. Bodies everywhere.

Hundreds of them on a grass area about the size of a football stadium, perhaps a couple of acres or more. It was dark with some moonlight. There were some women with sack bags on their shoulders, going through the pockets of their bodies. Brings a whole new meaning to dead drunk.

Occasionally a flagon of wine would have the remains of the wine drunk from it. The women were like camp followers moving around the field, emptying the pockets. Every now and again, one would disappear fast. Probably scored well in some way. It was eerie in the light of the moon and stars. This field was a hundred yards from the bottle shop. Silver City was just across the bridge, shining in the moonlight.

The next morning, we were on our way to do some riding in the bush to familiarise Hans and Peter with the horses when a man stopped us. "Fancy a couple of days' work, you guys?” he asked.

“Doing what?” I asked.

“I need to tidy this site.”

There was a couple of shops or something that had been started a few years ago and abandoned, he explained.

“You just bought it?” I asked

“No, it’s in the main street here. Bought it a couple of years ago. I figure it will be worth a lot in years to come, the way things expand here. Did what I could, then went to the bush to make enough to finish it off.” He showed us what he wanted us to do and left us to it.

We cleared all the rubble out and tidied the place up. Met my first snake: we both retreated after stopping dead and staring at each other. There were no windows or doors, and it was on the main street opposite the office where the Aborigines got paid.

On the third day, things were about done when an old Abo and a young girl came in, and he tried to sell her to us for a dollar to buy a flagon. "Get to fuck!" I said. "Who is she, your granddaughter? Get out of here, you auld cunt!"

I was appalled.

The chap came and paid us for the work. "Let's go to the pub?" said Hans.

"You two go. I want to think a bit." I walked down to the sandwich bar, where a good-looking blond one-legged waitress served me terrific roast beef sandwiches. Someone later told me that roast beef was usually buffalo around here.

I was turning around the plan in my head to get those two to ride the trail to the Kimberley's. They had no experience with horses. Maybe they would not manage this.

I walked back to the bar, and the Abo from the fight caught up with me. "Where did you learn to fight like that, Scottie?"

"Scotland. I went to a girls' school," I said.

"Come on; I'll buy you a beer. I owe you ten bucks," he said.

"Keep it. I deserved to lose it for being wound up by that loudmouth Billie."

"Yeah, him troublemaker." I bought him a beer while my two friends were by the bar. I went over to the pool table, handed him the beer, and the four Abos all grinned and nodded to me.

Hans said, "I am nervous about this trip!"

"So am I," said Pete.

"I will sell the saddles back," I readily agreed.

We got drunk and headed back to the guest house.

The next morning, I went down to the station, and the guy agreed to take the saddles back for sixty dollars. "The horses, I don't want them. I've got plenty. You can come and ride them when you like," he said.

I went around to the garage and bought a long wheelbase series three Land Rover truck. I went down to the café and parked, had a Coke, and then went down to the guest house. Hans and Pete were coming out with their bags.

“We paid the room,” Pete said. "We are off to hitch and to get first in case there is a queue.”

“OK, have a nice life,” I said.

I had enjoyed their company, but they were a bit down since bottling out on the trip.

I got another bag and filled it with survival rations for the trip to Queensland that I had been planning while standing with my thumb out for three weeks.

I pulled up when they stuck their thumbs up as I approached. They chucked their bags in the back and climbed in.

“Where you headed?” I asked.

“Anywhere, out of this dump,” Pete said, smiling at me.

By the time we reached the three-way roadhouse, the truck was full. Most were heading south, and we were heading to Mt Isa, then on to Queensland. I picked up every hitchhiker on the way. The hat went around for petrol and beer. We had a few unscheduled stops. Getting near Mt Isa, we found a newly married cowboy and his wife stuck in a creek. We pulled them out. Coming over a sea of mud, I dropped into low four-wheel drive and plunged on. There must have been two hundred cars and vehicles stuck in the mud. They all waved at us. We were moving, but it was touch and go. If I stopped, I would be with them. I saw other stopped off-road vehicles. So I kept going. Tough to do it, but we needed to get through. At Mt Isa, there were outcrops of copper ore all over the place, and men with loaders and a tipper truck were scooping up the ore with them. Talk about streets paved with gold. I shut the others out as my entrepreneurial mind assessed whether I could manage a tipper and a drott. Even a couple of old bangers would do me. The ore averaged about 45% copper, or so I was told by one of the drivers, and I believed this. I fell short on the finance, but where there is a will, there is a way. I kept moving. Outcrops of the green Verdigris rocks were everywhere. That kept my attention as I assessed this situation.

I was fighting against my better judgement here, but I could always come back. I loved this country. I drove on to Townsville and the sea.

I dropped everyone off a couple of miles out as the town grew around us, despite protest.

“Sorry, but I am on my own now. It’s been great travelling with you,” I said to the strangers.

Hans and Pete stayed on, and we camped by the sea beside a couple of others. I soon got myself a job from the paper with the national parks at Mt Speck. While scanning for a job with a mining company, I wanted to get an independent profile of mineral exploration before meeting up with Maureen. There were four of us in the gang, and we did maintenance on Mt Speck, a beautiful place with a river and fantastic swimming pools, giant boulders the size of a three-storey house and crystal clear water. The feeling of complete tranquil well-being that I felt was amazing. Occasionally. I was jolted out of this by my workmate, who was more interested in the coming rodeo season and riding wild Brahman bulls. After a couple of weeks of work,

I was at the beach telling the boys about the job. I told them where to go and try their luck. The national parks didn’t want them.

The couple in a Volkswagen camper was a German artist and Jeanie, his Scottish companion. It was nice to speak without trying to Anglify my accent, which I would otherwise do to allow Aussies to understand me a little better.

We camped on the strip of trees at the beach.

“How are you doing?” I asked them on a return from work. “We are going to hitch down to Brisbane,” Hans said.

“Your surfing friends came around to see if you wanted to go down to Surfers with them,” Pete mentioned.

"Do you think we could get a ride?”

“Ask them,” I replied.

We had a few beers, then drove the camper with Jeanie into town to a place we had been told we could score some weed.

It turned out to be an old warehouse with a goods lift. On the top floor, I spoke to a really down-on-his-luck guy. I was pointed to a group.

I walked over. “Got any weed?” I asked one long-haired individual.

“Why do you think I have weed?”

“That guy thought you might," I said.

“He’s an alcoholic.”

“Oh really?”

“What is it you want?”

“Thirty dollars.”

He handed me a bag with a thirty-dollar deal of Queensland heads, as he told it.

Seedy home-grown, just the job, I thought.

I went over to the rest of them, rolled a joint, lit it up, and then passed it to the alchie, who was well into his cups. “If it’s any good, it might cure him,” I said to the rest.

We shared it between us, and they split off to check out the town. I went back with Jeanie to the camp and my Land Rover, my base's centre. I had a sleeping bag, but as of yet, no tent. It was warm, though required a nightly turn-out of the bag for spider inspection.

I was woken up by the arrival of a couple of utes with surfboards.

"Coming with us, Scottie?” someone shouted.

“When are you coming back?” I asked.

“Monday night.”

“Cool,” I said.

I locked up in the front of the truck and gave the key to Jeanie, just in case it needed to be moved.

“Don’t worry, Scottie, I will look after it,” she said.

Off I went down to Surfer’s Paradise. The waves were about eight feet high. I tied my 5’6” board to my ankle so that it would not leave for shore and leave me having to body surf after it. I was quite new to this and would have been better off with a bigger board and lesser waves. I had made it in quite a bit last time, and I was addicted to the buzz of planning the waves. The other guys could reach the beach without being spun like a washing machine, gravel and all in the waves.

Twice out, and I was knackered, despite having sat on my board and missing a few big ones.

Pummelled a few times on the way in, I got the washing machine treatment in the gravel on my way out. I caught the board as it bashed me on the head and lay on it until shore.

Jugs of beer made the rounds, and I got pretty pissed after all the fun and adrenaline. I got back to Townsville on a Monday.

There was an ad from a mining company, just what I was looking for. I want to do the interview on Tuesday.

I was a little taken aback by the number of applicants there. One big chap with long red hair and a beard said he was overqualified for this job: he had a PhD in geology.

I felt a little abashed because my knowledge of geology had come from looking over Maureen Muggeridge's shoulder in St Andrew's. She was passionate about the subject, and we were inseparable. I learned a lot from her and she from me.

Next, I went into a room where there were four of them to interview me.

I told them where I came from. They said there could be quite a bit of rain where this job is. I said I am from Scotland I am used to rain.

"Oh, it's tropical rain and there is a rainy season. We have not had someone who could stand this yet. It's nothing like your Scottish rain."

"Och, it's warm rain," I replied.

OK, that was it. I realised they were not interested in me.

I took the door handle and said to them with a smile, "Listen, you know what my last job was?"

"No, what was it?"

"I was in the fucking arctic on a trawler, pitch dark for three months. Snow and ice that never stopped, and you think your warm rain is going to bother me."

"Take a seat," one of them said. "We have a few more to see."

I went out and sat down.

The red-haired one gave me a poisonous look when he came out, and after the last one I was called in again.

"Scottie, we are a Canadian company. We know all about the arctic."

They were all jovial and welcomed me.

"You got the job!" they said.

They were all laughing as they talked, and I liked this bunch immediately. I was thrilled and told them I would give a week's notice to the national parks.

"Come on Wednesday, that's ten days 'time."

I shook their hands and left.

Work in the rainforest was great. I took to it like a duck to water. The highlight was the surfing on my days off. Sometimes I went panning for gold, and sometimes filled bags of alluvial tin. I built a banjo on a creek and shovelled for a whole day, filling about two sugar bags of black tin pebbles that fell through the holes. The lighter stones whooshed right off. The black pebbles were easy to separate and fill the bags. The banjo worked like magic, and I would send the harvest to MT Isa mines, who sent back a cheque for $110 for a sugar bag. Five bags was the best I made for one day at this. During my work there, I cut two square sides into a tree and wrote the compass readings and the claim number on this surface. One day, while I was taking samples from this spot, a low-flying plane passed just over my head.

Coming from near Leuchars, I was used to low planes, such as the ones that passed over as I worked in the Kinshaldy woods, so I did not pay much attention.

When I arrived back, they asked me if I had seen the people from the plane crash. Apparently, they had been walking around for days in the Kirima Mountains where I was working. I remembered the plane. It would have been exciting to have rescued them.

I went to Surfer's with the boys and came back on Saturday, then had a few drinks with Jeanie and got pissed. Hans and Pete had gone south, so I was on my own again, something I liked. I find it very relaxing sometimes.

The next stint up at the prospect went well. I had everything ready, and I was to come the next day to bring my samples to the office by 2 pm. I went for a little exploration, looking for gold to the pan, but I tried a couple of streams: nothing at all. To be fair, I only had a few hours, and I had not done my homework on the location – so I was not really expecting too much. Only hoping! On the drive back, I saw an entrance to what reminded me of the quarry at Auchtermuchty in Scotland. I pulled up with a great feeling of déjà- vu. I turned in and pulled the brakes on immediately. It was like the top of a hill that had been torn off a long time ago. I walked over to the far edge, and over the top, I could see it went straight down about a thousand metres. I turned to go back to the Land Cruiser when something caught my eye. It was a crystal formation that looked like square silver blocks about half an inch square. The rock was weather-beaten and had been exposed for a long, long time.

I put it in a sample bag; then I saw another and another. I thought it might be silver. I went all round, picking them all up. If this was silver, I must have had two or three kilos. I had filled a whole sample box full of bags. I got back in the Land Cruiser and headed down the mountain roads to the main road.

The levees were flooded, and I could get through, but others were blocking the way, so I lost time. I pulled a few out so I could get past, then drove over the flooded levees. They were well flooded with torrents of water from the mountains.

I got to the office at 5 o'clock.

"Where the fuck have you been!" asked a man I couldn't immediately place. "I have had the plane waiting since three."

"There was flooding on the levees!" I answered.

"You can get through them in that."

There had been people stuck in them – that was what had delayed me. Then I recognised him as one of the geologists who had interviewed me a year or more before.

He backed his Land Cruiser up to mine, and we loaded them up with my samples from the prospect. I took a few of my own and asked him if he could look at them and tell me what they were. He told me he had no time.

“If I put it in,” I asked, “will they tell me what it is?”

“OK,” he answered, “but write your name on each bag, so it doesn’t get mixed up with the real stuff.”

I did as he said, then he loaded it up, slammed the door shut and off he went.

I changed over to my Land Rover and put the keys through the office letterbox. Off I went to Surfer’s Paradise.

“Yes, it is a bit crazy today,” I declared to no one in particular. The waves were big, and a stronger than usual rip tide left me walking back along the beach quite a way. I gave up when I met the guy I had come with. He suggested we go for a beer, and I agreed.

The bars were packed, and only the diehards were still on the water. “Hey mate, that Sheila with the big blue eyes. She’s had her eye on you, Scottie, since we came in,” said my companion.

I said, “Hi there,” waved and hoped she could lip-read. They came over, and we shared jugs of beer into the night.

Driving back up to Townsville, we sang along to Don McLean: *“Bye, bye, Miss American pie drove my Chevy to the levee, but the levee was dry, them good old boys drinking whiskey and rye.”* I loved the song and the moment.

When we got back, Jeanie said, "These people you work for were looking for you. It seems pretty urgent.”

"Did you tell them where I was?”

“No, they didn’t seem too happy or friendly either.”

“Well done, Jeanie. Thanks!”

"I will see them in the morning. Probably to tick me off for wasting their time with my samples.” I promptly forgot the matter, crashing out in my sleeping bag.

Three

I arrived at the back of the office and parked my Land Rover, locking it since I would be using the company Land Cruiser. I met a Kiwi mate I had worked with a few times, coming down the stairs as I went up.

"You're in the shit, mate!" He signalled behind him with his eyes.

I opened the door at the top of the fifteen-foot flight of stairs.

"Where the fuck have you been? We have been looking all over town," said the boss. "If you've pegged a lease, you will never get away with it.

"We know you have a girlfriend in another company in Western Australia," he accused me.

"You keep shouting at me, you shithead, and I'll punch your puss," I gave him right back. I was feeling the weightlessness of imminent battle as I prepared to attack about eleven people. Up until now, I had had a great relationship with all of them. I was sizing up the onslaught when I realised they had no idea my Scottish ruff was up.

He handed me a map. "Show us where you found them."

"Found what?" I said.

"The samples you put in before you disappeared."

I looked at the paper, turned it this way and that.

"It's not on your fucking map," I said and handed it back. I held my hands out like a glass wall and said, "I am off to cool down because if you keep talking to me the way you are going, this won't end well! You can take my notice as well. I quit!" With that, I left. No one followed.

I passed under the building.

A guy with a Yank accent said, "You shouldn't have talked to that guy like that!"

I stopped dead; my ears pricked up. "This company has made much more from lucky guys like him than you lot, with all your qualifications," he told the bosses. The guy was a big John Wayne type, and must have been my boss's boss, I thought.

I went back to the beach.

"Get fired?" Jeanie asked with a cheeky smile. I smiled.

"No, but I am jacking this in before I put the head on my boss." I laughed, and all the tension was gone. She made coffee. I think I must have found what they are looking for, I told her.

I later discovered that the Yank was actually a Canuck. Gordon Battie, chairman of the board of directors of Noranda, a Canadian international mining company. They had nickel mines and coal mines, and just about every kind of mine there is in plural. They were a big company, alright.

I was surmising this, of course. I let them stew for a bit. I hung out till after lunchtime with Jeanie.

Lunch was a T-bone steak and all the trimmings from a smorgasbord at a hotel for $1.30 each, including coffee. How could they survive, I wondered, charging that? The steaks were huge. I washed it down with a malted milkshake. It was the longest drink in town, with a giraffe on the cardboard cup. Then I dropped Jeanie off at the beach and drove back to the office. I entered, and it looked like nobody had moved since I left.

The Queensland head asked me straight away, with a controlled voice, "Will you show us where it is?"

"I had no intention of doing otherwise, but I have a question for you, however. What is it?"

"Molly," he answered. "Well, I have been looking for this for more than a year, and all I have been told is if you find more than 5% molybdenum in a ton, you would open cast it."

There must have been two or three kilos in the samples that I had asked him to analyse, and he was in a hurry for the plane and wouldn't look at them.

“Looks like I must have found what you were looking for.”

“Dennis, I am Gordon Battie, chairman of the board of directors of this company,” said the big guy. We shook hands.

“I am your most recent employee,” I said, then added with a smile, “I’ve just given my notice. I want my wages ready for me when I get back."

“I am going shopping for stores.”

"How many days?” I asked.

“My wife and three women are coming, and the boss and some others. We will organize our food. See to your own needs for ten days.”

The Queensland head sheepishly handed me a letter from Maureen. The letter had been opened. I contained my rage at this invasion of my privacy. However, he was extremely uncomfortable, so I took no further action. I thought these samples must have had the kind of dramatic effect of the Lloyds bell within Noranda. For him to have arrived here in his private jet, to be in on the moment.

This moment must have come back to them a bit later when the news of the Kimberley strike came out.

In Maureen's letter to me, there was a photo of her posing on top of a mountain with a helicopter in the Kimberley’s, where she later was to persuade Tanganyika holdings’ Rio Tinto to let her continue prospecting (on reduced funding) after they gave up.

De Beers also had tried for years. Turned up nothing. Maureen found the diamonds. She had a passion for being a field geologist in Australia as long as I had been with her.

Mausie must have named the Argyle mine after all the geology trips with Prof. Dreaver and her class to Argyle and Skye. This was the wealthiest diamond strike in the world: three and a half times richer than anything found in Africa. Mausie was motivated like no one else I have ever known.

I went shopping and headed up to the camp, which was a tent with floorboards, a caravan which held the maps, fridge-freezer and other delicate instruments, maps and map-making stuff, compasses, etcetera. You could not travel any distance without a compass bearing in the rainforest, or else you got completely lost. I had overstayed my time, and it got dark and rained. Shutting my vision down, I had marked my way with red tape, and when I failed to find the next tape, I stopped right there and spent the night standing on the spot till morning. I chopped what I thought was a dead tree. Even though I had a rucksack with dry sample bags, I couldn't get my fire to make a light. A lot of smoke which would keep the snakes away, I hoped. I blew and blew a red glow most of the night. My hands were stained with the smoke. Light finally arrived, and I walked to the vehicle. Not much more than a couple of hundred yards. The first thing I saw was my compass sitting where I had left it on the seat. I got in and headed back for some tucker, famished. Porridge was the fastest and best in a situation like this, with evaporated milk even though I had fresh. Full of porridge, I fell asleep until noon.

I expected them to arrive in a couple of days' time, and I had some three-foot deep trenches to dig to take soil samples. There were three of them, six feet apart and twelve feet long – a pick and shovel job for a couple of casual labourers.

I drove down to the road to Cairns and up to Karanda and the hippie commune there. I got talking to a girl there who asked where I came from. "Oh, I live a few miles down the road a bit. I am looking for a couple of casual workers."

"How about me?"

"Digging?"

"I am a country girl."

"Have you two boyfriends? I want three people."

"I have two girlfriends."

"I want to leave after you make me some coffee, if that's all right," I said.

The dark got us about halfway up the mountains on our way back to camp.

"I will fix the grub; you can fix your tents where you like," I said.

I lit the lamps, fried garlic mushrooms and got the loaf out of its tin. Next, I went out and lit a fire under my shower barrel. It was full of water and ready for a fire of dead, dry wood. One thing I found about living in the rainforests with lots of rain, leeches and all the rest of the creepy crawlies and bugs that live here is that a hot shower with two hundred litres of hot water was sheer luxury. The fire was going well, but I would need another fire to get a good temperature.

With mushrooms and sliced tomatoes sizzling away on the stove, I put a pot of milk on. "Will you all drink Milo?" I asked. They nodded seductively with their eyes.

They were beauties, all three of them. They came from different parts of the continent. Karanda was like a beacon for hippies everywhere. Karen said, "You drink your Milo, mate. I will dish out the tucker." She spread the bread and shared the mushrooms and tomatoes between us.

I put on Leonard Cohen we ate to the sounds of "Traveling Lady" and "Suzanne". They taught me to play the game Killer. The one who was the killer was the only person who knew they had drawn the black spot. They would wink at the person to kill them while talking and making conversation. You could not let on when you were killed, either. Karen rolled a spliff, and the game got even more interesting with a puff or two of Sumatran grass. After a little while, I was looking into Karen's blue eyes. They were huge. I felt in love. Her nipples became enormous. I was conscious of the whole universe, and there was only us in it for that long heart-beating moment. I am tripping, I realized. "This is the trippiest weed I have ever had," I said. We all ended up giggling. Karen winked and said, "Got you; I've killed you all now. I put a few gold tops in the mushrooms to make it interesting," she confessed. "I've got a couple of tabs of acid if you would like something stronger?"

"Where did you get them?" I asked.

"I sell them to live," she said. "They are ten dollars each."

"That's expensive," I said.

"No, same as Sydney."

I made another Milo and got some more tapes from the vehicle. Next was King Crimson and the crazy world of Arthur Brown's Fire: "I want to teach you to burn!"

They were the coolest three chicks I had ever met. I could not believe the price of acid and that mushrooms were free. I got up to go check the water drum. It was good with one fire. I got my towel and set the pipes, which were open V planks.

The caravan was at the river, which had blown the bridge away sometime prior to me being in Aus. The last plank had the shower bucket, and I adjusted the top screw to let a decent trickle of hot water from the drum, and that kept running till it emptied. I picked up my towel and went down the side of the caravan and under the water. Five minutes of getting my brain soothed. I began to soap up when I was pushed a little to the side by now four bodies soaking and soaping each other. The laughter echoed through the forest for half an hour or so. They were good crack, these girls. I went to sleep blissfully.

At 11 am, I was awoken by a commotion. “Scottie, who are these people?” Said the voice.

The convoy was stopped by the girls’ hammock tents slung over the road from trees. “The road stops here; what’s the problem?"

“They are the casual labour for the trenches,” I said. “We don’t have women in the camps.”

“Yes, we do, and you have brought some more by the looks of things.”

“Get rid of them now!” said the office chief, taking the lead in an authoritative manner.

Karen was a beautiful sight in her sarong.

“Kiwi, can you give the girls a lift to Karanda?” I asked. “Pay them sixty dollars each, and for two days, we have already done," I lied.

“No probs, Dennis,” he said.

“He told you they are his workers,” said Gordon.

“We don’t employ women in the camps,” said Keith.

“He does and seems to get things done around here,” said Gordon. Geez! This guy so reminds me of John Wayne; I thought to myself, “Want a hand with your gear? In fact, just take my vehicle; it’s empty,”

I said. “This lot have never seen tits before,” I remarked to the Kiwi; he smiled and gave them a hand.

I made some coffee, came back and gave a mug to the girls, Kiwi and myself. They gave me PO box numbers. “I am leaving the company,” I told them. “See you in the commune shortly, I hope?" They all gave me a hug. I felt the world had become empty as I watched them climb the hill out of the camp.

I was introduced to a Yorkshireman and his wife, who would be working with me for this trip. (More of a sheepdog, I thought privately.) However, I would be fair.

The others had important business elsewhere in the area. The Kiwi would be going with them soon. I thought Keith was trying to freeze me out of the limelight as soon as he possibly could.

Tomorrow's another day, I thought, still thinking about pissing off and letting them look for the next hundred years for this strike. I found that thought amusing. Bad Dennis, the menace creeping in.

I thought of our Wullie sitting on his bucket, having Good Wullie-with- the-halo thoughts and Bad Wullie-with-horns in a thought bubble above his head.

"Show me one of the sample sights today," asked Gordon.

I cooked them porridge for breakfast. I filled the big iron pan with bacon, eggs, mushrooms and tomatoes. The door went, and they were all queued outside. I handed out tin plates. A big pot of porridge and the half gallon of milk and spoons then shut the door.

There was a knock. Kiwi was pissing himself. Another knock, and I opened the door.

"We can't eat this," he said.

"Rubbish, my ancestors, have been fighting the English for a thousand years on it," I said and shut the door. Another authoritative knock. I opened it, and John Wayne climbed in and said, "I'll share yours." He had eaten half of the ladle full of porridge.

"You eat this with milk," I explained.

He had closed the door behind him and sat down with us and tucked in. They didn't knock again. Gordon took the pan out with him and said, "Oh, you haven't finished your porridge yet." It's a Scots thing.

"He came off an arctic trawler! We can't eat this," they said. The porridge was completely untouched.

I took them to a lease about four miles from the camp, stopped on the road, then followed tape marks till we got gradually higher. The trees got thinner than the sun got in as we climbed higher and higher.

We were climbing a rock face about forty-five degrees by this time, with a lot of chutes of water cascading down. Then it went into the forest again. "This is the grid here," I explained that it was a square grid that sampled a hundred feet apart. And I showed them the two corner posts of the lease marked with the numbers and compass bearings. Notebooks and maps were brought out, and numbers checked and shown to the big boss.

I stood aside with Kiwi and remarked, "They all have brand new boots on!"

"Dennis, that's because we do all the work," he said. "They all got caught napping this time because you're a surf bum, and they couldn't find you. They would have done a complete presentation to this guy and shown what an asset to the company they were. You would have been sent elsewhere and missed all this. The big boss seems to like you, though."

We were having a coffee from the Kiwi's flask. Gordon came over and asked me whether there was an easier way back or if we had to climb down that waterfall.

No, the road is just a hundred metres that way, I told him. "You said you wanted to check out the scenery."

He smiled and looked me in the eyes.

I hung my head in mock sheepishness, and Kiwi and I had a quiet giggle with the boss. "Dennis says we can go around this way; it's easier," he said as he took over command. "Just follow the markers," I said.

Back at camp with Gordon now in charge, they all studied the maps of the area in the caravan/office.

We were keeping out of the way. The wives talked to Kiwi, but I was getting ignored.

The wives cooked the tea. The plan was, I would show them X marks the spot where the samples had come from, and they would go on back to Townsville. I would meet them and pick up Gordon and be his driver until my notice ended.

I took them to the place where I found the samples.

"I don't see any here," said the Queensland boss aggressively. You need a fucking tranquillizer, you paranoid cunt, I thought. Take a couple of samples from the rock.

"I took over thirty samples from here," I said. "If there had been any more, I would have taken them as well. I thought I had found silver."

The Yorkshire geologist was to stay with me. The big boss wanted us to make a movie of what it is like here. We spent a few days filming some things we thought would be interesting for him on an 8mm camera. I couldn't work it, so I was the main actor.

I picked up the big boss, and we went up to Tully, had a meal with him there, and he tried to get me to stay.

"You've seen what they have become like. They were my friends; now they hate my guts, all over a misunderstanding which was none of my doing. I can't work with them; I would not be able to take them seriously or respect them again."

"Well, if you want to come back, here is my card," he said. "Ring me, and I will get you taken on. I read your report; they see you as a good man, and so do I. We are floating the Jim-Jim mines on the stock exchange, and everybody in the company will get them at half price. We are a foreign company, and the Australian government wants us to float a large part of it on the stock exchange because it's uranium."

This guy doesn't realize I don't have a spare million to invest," I thought. "Thanks, Gordon. I will mind your generous offer. Maybe see you in Canada when I get there."

"Do that." He picked up his bag and left.

I drove down to the office. Picked up my wages.

"There's a letter for you, Scottie," the Townsville head said with a big grin.

"I've just had a letter from Mausie. Are you sure it's for me?"

"Yes, mate, it's your call-up papers."

He must have got in touch with them, I bet. His version of attempted murder. The guy is still thinking I am trying to cheat him out of a strike. Won't be happy until they open-cast it.

I went around to the house in Mitchell Street that I had moved into with some students.

I phoned the consul and explained my situation. "If you don't want to go, you can go home," he said. Apparently, it was much the same as America, white trash first, no offence, just the way it is round here.

In April, I was sitting on the plane on that long haul home, dreaming about daffodils, primroses, birds singing. It was a good time to be back in Scotland. Mind, Australia had been a land of milk and honey. I walked out of Heathrow, and every goose pimple jumped up. Wow, I had forgotten what cold and miserable felt like. I could not stand the cold. Vietnam would be better than this. I met up with my mate Ed, told him about Australia.

"I am going back. It's freezing here!" I told Ed.

"When?" he asked.

"Soon as I can arrange a plane."

"Want to come?"

"Aye, what temperature is it there?"

"Must be a hundred in the shade," I replied.

We grinned, and we were off to Australia the next day.

"Hand your passport to me as I get to the immigration guy," I said. He did. We stood together as I handed them both.

"Where are you going to?"

"The army," I said, "got me papers a couple of weeks ago." In my best Aussie accent. He opened mine first gave us both the permanent residence stamp.

Got a taxi round to the bus station. We took a bus to Townsville and stopped at a garage café. I got off with Ed and another guy. There was an emu streaking towards us. "Quick, back on the bus!" Ed shouted. He slammed the door shut in my face. It was nearly on me.

"It's a seven-foot-tall chicken!" I shouted.

They were all laughing and holding the door. I ran around the bus, but when the owner of the stop held his hand up, it stopped too, looked at me looking curiously, took my cigarette packet, didn't like the smell and pinged it away by its beak.

"They have been feeding it potato crisps," he explained. "It's a young one."

It was taller than me. I didn't feel foolish; I felt angry.

"Some friend you are, Ed," I tried, but they slammed it and held it closed.

He giggled. "What could I do?"

You could have punched him in the teeth, I thought.

I arrived in Mitchell Street. "This is my mate Ed," I announced, then went to bed. I was knackered and a bit jet-lagged. I could see someone had taken over my room. It was still my bedding, though, and I had left without a word.

A couple of weeks went by, and I had still not opened up the chess board that I had made on a visit to Amsterdam, where I had purchased a nice soft kilo of Afghan hashish.

I dug a bit of garden, then got Ed going with the spade. It had not been done for a few years. There was a custard apple tree at the side of the house. Custard apples are amazing, but when you reach out to pluck them, they drop off the tree to splat on the ground. They taste divine: food for the Gods. Passion fruit grew along the fences, as well as various bushes and things I was not familiar with. I planted tomatoes between them. I could water and give them a lot of attention. I made a nice stash there too. One chair, a small table that I used to write letters and read or sit in the sun. I made it clear this was my privacy spot.

I was lying in the grass not far from the house when this guy pulled up about twenty metres away. He was riding a bike and carrying a huge rucksack. It looked like his chain had come off.

I couldn't resist it. I called over. What's that on your back mate, a piano case? He smiled at me and said it was full of steak. He had a midnight cowboy leather jacket, frills and all. I walked over.

“Must be a lot of steak.”

“Yeah, I had a job in meat works. I got fired.” Then he asked, “Do you have a frying pan?”

“Yes, just along the road.”

We took him home. The steak was a big lump, but we took half a dozen slices, and it fried up well.

“Are you a Yank?” I asked him.

"Canadian, Bob’s my name.”

“Steak’s your game,” I said.

We shook hands, and Ed came out with us.

"I’ll just call you Zambezi Bob with that jacket.” That name stuck but got shortened to Zam. The guy came around about the rent.

I paid him, saying, “Sorry, I have been on holiday to see my mum.”

“I’d been wondering why I haven’t seen you. See you next month.” Off he went.

There were half a dozen crashing here now, mostly girls. I took this moment to say to them that since charity is a bad thing here, anyone not paying rent is out.

“This week, I am off to see about a job,” I told them. “This is not a job that I am looking for to pay your rent. So, anyone who does not want to pay a share can evaporate before I get back.”

I was needing a car as I had sold the Land Rover Before I left. I went back to my room to shut myself off. Bob followed me. “I would like to pay my share,” he said. “If I can stay a while, that is.”

“I am away for a couple of days, Bob,” I said. “The rent is not due for a month. See you when I get back. Settle down wherever you can.”

I borrowed a car and drove up to Cairns, where we met up with Sparks and his girlfriend with a broken leg who had just gone into hospital.

I went on up to the commune at Karanda, round to Karen and the girls.

She was cooking pancakes on a stove on the platform. “Hi, Scottie,” she said. “I am not interested in work.”

“Good, I got fired anyway.”

“You wouldn’t miss them, would you?”

“No way, ma’am."

She winked at me and said, "I got some business going right now. Catch up with you later. I am staying a bit back there. Pete, can you show this guy where to rest his head at my place?”

She gave me a pancake with peanut butter and honey. She flicked her head to let me know to be scarce.

The shack in the rainforest was comfortable. I had a nap. Rolled myself a little spliff with the weed I found on the table.

Karen arrived. “Hi, can I crash here with you?” I asked.

“Yes, but I have a bit of a problem at the moment. The girls are overdue. I have collected some money, and they have gone off to score. I am here as security, and one of them has a big mouth who put in a thousand dollars for 120 hits”.

I have some trips, but I left them in Townsville. I didn’t bring it because I had not spoken to you. I have three thousand dollars on me and some Afghan hash for a smoke. Give the guy his money back and tell him to take his big mouth and shut it.”

“Here.” I gave her a thousand bucks.

She left to deal with it while I rolled another spliff of the local homegrown. I walked up the hill to stretch my legs, pulling into the side of the path to let a guy on a horse past.

“What’s up that way?” I asked. “That’s us; we are building a boat.”

“You American?”

"Yeah. You English?"

"No, I am Scots. What kind of boat is it?"

"A ketch," he said. "If you are still there when I get back, I will see you later."

I walked further up. There were no more shacks that I could see, but there were offshoots into the jungle. When I got to the top of the hill, there was a great big forty-foot Ferro cement yacht being built. It looked right out of place. How the hell will they get that to the sea, I wondered.

There was no one around. On the way back, I met the horse. The guy was walking.

"Saw your boat. How you going to get that to the sea?"

"Oh, we'll figure it out," he replied.

I wandered back and sat down in the shack. Saw food in the kitchen, but I didn't want to interfere, so I waited for Karen's return. She arrived with Pete in tow. Cheeky ratbag, that guy. He didn't want the money; he wanted the goods.

"Well, it's people with patience we like around here. Your big mouth needs shutting, I said to him." Her account was hilarious.

"They may end up not getting any anyway," she said. "A few people gave places to try. They might score if necessary. Things change fast in Sydney."

"Karen, would you like to try some Afghan hashish? I have a little." I produced a ball about the size of a ping pong ball which I had been squidging around in my pocket.

She smelled it.

"Wow, this smells exotic."

"It is. Do you have a pipe?"

I rolled a sausage with a thin point that I could heat with my lighter. I let her smell it. "Mmmm! Exotic, all right."

"Erotic too." I smiled.

"Let's keep that till Pete's gone," she said. "Let's not embarrass a guy." We smoked with Pete's pipe.

We were all smiling now and eating the food that Karen had cooked. "Where did you get this, Scottie?"

"Amsterdam," I replied. "I bought a kilo and made it into a chess board."

"Let me see that bit a moment. Smells like nothing I have ever smelled before".

"It smells like Mazari sharif," I added.

"Where is that?" She asked

"In the Hindu Kush."

"Have you been there?"

"Not yet."

"You are a bullshitter, Scottie. Did you make that up?"

"No, I have a couple of friends from Leven that have been there."

"Let me know when you are going; I might come with you," Pete said good night and left. I handed him the pipe.

"No, you keep that. I have another." I handed him a piece of the hash.

Karen beamed at me.

Pete said, "See you tomorrow, mate."

"I hope he isn't your boyfriend," I said to her.

"No, I don't have one, but he is a good friend. I am glad you gave him that. He's a bit down on his luck."

Our attention went back to the hashish. She rolled it out and flattened it, and measured it back and forth.

"I can sell this for about two hundred, two fifty," she said.

“What, an ounce?” I asked.

“I don’t know what an ounce of that looks like,” she remarked. “It was an ounce, but I’ve smoked a good bit.”

“OK, here’s what I propose. You sell that for as much as you can, to set the price high as you can. I will get the rest, and you can drop the price to let someone else get a living, and it will filter out and keep you cool. Me too; I want to keep the house in Townsville so that I can know if the draft is looking for me."

“Have you got your papers?”

I told her yes, but had to concede I had lost them in a pub at home in Scotland.

“Why did you come back?”

“To see you,” I replied, fluttering my eyelashes at her. She laughed.

“The truth is I couldn’t stand the cold. I will have to go back, but I am going to choose summertime," I explained.

“Cold weather and warm beer. Pommie land sounds like a shit creek to me.”

“You would like Amsterdam, though,” I replied.

We went to visit some of her friends. We had more gold-top soup, and we were tripping again. Nobody ever seems to mention the fact, but reality has subtle changes.

“I can’t understand why people would want acid here with all these mushrooms?” I asked.

"The season is about over. They come with the rains.”

“Why don’t you dry them?” I asked. I have seen it done at home with the wee ones Gold-tops look like the kind you see in supermarkets. The golden-brown ones are very similar.

We rolled a joint for her friends and smoked some hashish too.

We all walked down to the river and took off our clothes, hanging them on the greenery and branches. About three hundred people were swimming and sitting in the river, at a guess. It was full of beautiful people all trying to live a better way. Pools and waterfalls.

"Are there crocs here?" I asked.

“Only you, mate.” She said. I smiled at that.

When we got home to the shack, Pete showed up, and between them, they had eight hundred dollars they had sold the ounce for. Amazing, they had no idea what an ounce was. They made deals.

“Almost everybody would like more,” she said, then handed me the lot. We had a bit to smoke. I handed her two hundred dollars back, and she split it with Pete.

“Make a stash with large jars, kilo jars with lentils in them, because I will bring some acid with me too. It’s to keep it dry.”

I stayed for another two weeks and then returned to city life to pick up more clothes and return. Hash is the same: it will go mouldy in this kind of climate if it’s not kept dry.

Pete asked me to bring some Glad bags along – plastic bags, he said they were, from the supermarket. I agreed and asked if I could stay with her when I returned. I was feeling a bit guilty since Mausie was in Western Australia.

I had not mentioned the army to Maureen, but I knew what her reaction would be. It was an unpopular war, although I don’t think any war is popular. Only the arms dealers like it. Demonstrations everywhere. Hundreds of people over there were dodging the draft: Americans hiding out too, and two years in jail if you got caught. Better than being forced to kill some poor people who were fighting for their plot in their own country. Way better than being shot for something you don’t give a shit about.

The Australians, like the British, follow the Yanks wherever they go. Terrified of the yellow peril, as they called the Chinese in Aus. If China wanted a big empty continent, they would have moved in thousands of years ago.

Of course, getting their Western asses kicked like in Korea did not go down well. The Chinese were their allies. These countries were all part of old China. Korea is why Britain said no to Vietnam. The death toll was horrendous in Korea and just after the Second World War. It couldn’t have been the Tories in power; they would have grabbed it with both hands. The warmongers would have made millions again. I thought about this on the way down to Townsville, arriving after dark, which came quick. Wham! Night fell with a clang-now-it's-dark kind of thing. Especially when it was cloudy. Night got starry by the time I was home. The rainy season would end now. I took the car back and asked what I owed. "Tank of petrol will do it, mate," he replied.

I gave him a hundred dollars and thanked him.

"Any time, mate, I have my ute, remember, so I am not grounded."

I liked Australia because they were easygoing, unlike the uptight, small-minded people I had left behind me. With home still in the dark ages, long hair and hippies were detested. No wonder there was an alternative society. Thatcherism and government wars against their own people for this and that. Love and peace, IRA, Baader-Meinhof, the red army, ban the bomb. The movements against the most grotesque things. Killing people in greater and more horrible ways seems to be where all the money goes.

Back in Mitchell Street, everything was crazy, as always. Ed had taken over the kitchen.

"This guy eats everything," Zambezi Bob said.

"I need a joint and some peace and quiet for a bit while, I think."

"What's for eating?"

"There is not much left," Ed said.

"Where are the girls from the other house," I asked. "I thought they were staying here?"

"They come and go," said Ed. "Go to the shop on your bike, Zam, get mince and potatoes, carrots. Black pepper and garlic. I will cook, but I need a shower first."

In football shorts and T-shirt and flip flops, showered and feeling fresh, I cooked the tea.

I knew they liked it. There was not a word as they polished off the grub, and we shared the rest between the three of us.

"How was Cairns?"

"OK. Met some friends from work," I lied unless I meant Karen. "Lot of draft dodgers up there."

"Septic tanks?"

"Some Yanks, some Aussies, some that are just trying to stay out of touch and invisible. Snuck up on me unless that bastard from the mining company put me up for it."

Four

A week went by, in which I mostly hung out with Ed. Then I arranged a lift up to Cairns the next day. I got half of my Afghani and a thousand micro dots. Pink ones. They were all the same, though the colours varied. Dropped up near the commune, I walked the last bit myself. Pete was cooking chilli, and Karen was sleeping when I arrived.

“How’s things?" I asked.

“Shhh! Let her sleep,” came the reply.

"Up late?”

“No, she is anxious about the girls."

“Still not back yet?"

“Nope,” Pete said, biting his lip a bit.

“The waiting is hard. I know what you mean, but I used to do this at home, and if I had other people’s money, they’d freak out as soon as you are a minute late. You got rid of our problem for us. He would have been in the nut house by now,” said Pete.

Karen woke, stretched and smiled. “Hey, you came back then, Scottie.”

“How could I stay away?"

She hugged me, and we had a cup of herbal tea while Pete dished up chilli and rice.

“Have you brought a bit to smoke?”

"Yes, we can have a smoke after our tea."

"I'll sprint and get the pipe. I left it in my place," Pete said.

The chilli was good. Pete went for the pipe. I produced the hashish – about a pound or so.

I took a bit to smoke for me and said, "Here, sell it like you did before.

I won't have any more of this, but I will have something else."

"Weed?"

"No, acid."

"Do you have some now?" she asked.

"Next time," I said, not wanting to complicate things.

The days rolled by, and we were at the point when she produced all the cash. She gave me four thousand dollars and kept a good wad to herself.

"Are you happy?" I asked.

She nodded. I had rolled a joint and lit up; she wouldn't touch it because of the tobacco.

The girls arrived back – excitement and tears. Seemed like they had been ripped off by someone they knew. Lost half the cash. Finally, they scored some orange barrels from someone who had got them from California.

Have you tried them?

"Tried one before I bought them," he said.

I asked how many, and she said seventy-two.

"Is that all?" I asked.

"We got ripped off. I went to my mum she gave me a thousand dollars.

She didn't want me to come back. I showed her all my pictures, and she relented. I promised to go to college. When I go back."

We had one each while listening to music. It was a mild trip, and as people turned up, she told the tale of woe from the Sydney trip and shared them proportionately with them and got cash back too.

I got fed up and went to Pete's. He let me in, showed me my comforts. "I must get back in case she gives me a hard time," I said eventually. "What is mine is yours, Scottie. Help yourself."

I sat listening to the sounds of the forest at night. Six hours later, I was dozing off when my two conspirators came back.

"Is it all sorted?" I asked.

"Yes," she smiled. Pete smiled too!

"A six-hour mild trip," I said.

At least it was real.

I smiled and went to sleep, leaving them sitting talking. Pete had a slow, low laugh that came through to me while they chatted about the pros and cons and how like mushrooms, it had been as I drifted in and out of sleep. Then morning came.

"What's for breakfast?" I asked.

"Toast and Vegemite. OK?" said Pete.

"How about bacon and eggs?" I suggested. I hadn't had that for a while.

Pete agreed to go and get what we needed and said he would be back in an hour or so.

"You can wash up these dishes," he said.

"Fair enough, no problem," I said, smiling.

Karen intervened. “I’ll do the dishes,” she said. “You need elocution lessons, Scottie.”

“Try this,” she said, “Stone the bloody crows, mate.”

I did, with a few fair dinkums, and she’ll be right, mate.

"See, you can speak in God’s language after all,” she said.

Funny, I always thought about Scots as being God’s language, I thought to myself.

“Do you have a car?” I asked.

When she said no, I asked her if she could drive, whether she had a driver’s licence.

She said yes, and I suggested we buy a car.

"I don’t want a car,” Karen replied.

I dropped the subject, but I had to do something to get moving. I needed wheels.

The whole idea of staying invisible is to not register. No job, no car. No dole, just get a bit of pot now and then and survive.

I was saving all my seeds from the weed. I was going to sprinkle them along every creek or watercourse I found. Johnny Appleseed revisited. A regular Dennis weed seed, I thought.

“Have they ever raided this place?” I asked.

“No, I don’t think so,” she said. “There will probably be politicians’ kids here. It’s a haven of some kind. Just like America, white trash first along with the blacks,” she said.

We were the blacks of Europe, in Germany at least, I thought. Long may it last!

I let another week go by, with the beach as a favourite hangout. Not a wave in sight, but beautiful beyond belief. Thought about fishing. I did not feel like buying the gear, but I did like the fish. Bought some fish too.

Cooking them over hot coals was my favourite. I had a thick piece of wire netting that I used to lie the fish on, stuffed with whatever I could get: capsicum, tomatoes, and chillies. The girls ate a lot of pumpkins, but I did not like this veggie much. Rice was a staple here.

"Karen asked me, would you like to do some business?" I asked one day.

"Yeah, what do you think I have been trying to do while acting like a tourist? Well, what are you thinking?"

"I am thinking about sending down to Sydney with this guy Paul."

"How well do you know him?"

"Why don't you send him for some weed? There is always a bit of weed. See how he does with a little amount; if he is no good, then you won't lose it all. I have a thousand trips right here, and it's good, not like the last crap."

"Same deal as last time?"

"OK, let's do it, Scottie." Karen smiled now at this surprise. I gave her three hundred pink microdots.

"They are small," she said. "I will ask the girls if they want to test them."

"They are strong," I said, "try a half first."

"You are kidding, right?"

"No, I am not. This is the real deal."

She halved one, and they took it. I showed her how to put them in clear plastic and fold it over till there was a long line. You can cut them off with scissors, which makes it easy to keep them in a Tupperware or a spool case to keep moisture away from them. By the time they had them done, the girls were flying.

"Wow, it's amazing. Try one, Karen."

"No," she said.

"I have the stuff to do."

We got out some spool cases, and she put fifty in each, and they went to different people.

"Let's get out of here for a while," she said.

We drove down to Townsville; I picked up more clothes, my bag and my sleeping bag. Ed and Zambezi were out, so I cooked a meal with what I could find: spaghetti, mushrooms and garlic, and left some for Ed. I hoped they would be back soon.

On the way back, we stopped off to check out a creek where she had planted some seeds. Most of them had been eaten. The kangaroos and wallabies like it, she told me. We checked three spots, and all we could find were the chewed-off stems. Then we found two patches that were much better: thick stalks and ten feet high. The seeds were quite green; we gathered them anyway, filling about four carrier bags. The next move was to head back and to drive to the commune without stopping

Back at Karanda, we hung hessian sheets up and spread the weed out. "You stay here, Scottie," she said, "and I will do the same at Pete's gaff." Off she went, I went to bed to catch up on some sleep.

I longed to get another job. Mineral exploration was in my blood. I thought about going over to Perth to Mausie, but the thought of being delivered to an army barracks did not appeal to me at all. I was haunted by the thought of having to shoot some poor person that I didn't know. I was a good shot: all the poaching I had done saw to that. This would not end well if I went. So, that was that, I was stuck there whether I liked it or not. I had to survive, and I was not going to the army.

"We are invited to a party, Scottie," said Karen.

"I don't want to meet anyone new," I said.

"It's the Yanks. Come on, they are OK. I want to give them a bag of weed to see if they like it; they may buy some. They do their own, so they don't buy often, but I know they are pretty dry at the moment."

I relented, and we went. They were nice people. The guy with the horse I knew, having run into him a few times. He was their seek-it-out guy when they needed something, and he sold their weed. They had a couple of guitars and sang anti-war songs, which got me going.

"One, two, three, four, what are we fighting for," they sang.

I loved it, and Karen rolled spliffs, which I lit and passed on. They never came back. There were quite a few people: some Aussies and others. Most of them left home as soon as the draft papers arrived so that when they checked up, the papers were unopened.

The horseman asked me if we had anything for sale.

"No," I said. "I don't!"

Karen said, "I have a friend who has an early crop. How much were you thinking of?"

"If it's like this," he said, "as much as I can get."

I knew he had the market cornered off from Karen's mention of them a few times.

"I have some acid, too," she said.

"I know, it's crap!" he said. "Does nothing."

"Oh really? Try one," she said.

"How much?"

"Fifteen."

"Nah! Too much."

She opened a spool box, pulled out a strip and cut one off with nail scissors.

"Try it. If you are not impressed, don't pay me," she said. He picked it off the tape and put it on his tongue.

Food came next: cornbread and Mexican beans and cheese, along with a fiery curry. There was plenty, and a girl from Guadalajara came over and said, "You are no stranger to Mexican food, my friend." She smiled into my eyes. "I always watch strangers. The Aussie guys don't like the spices."

"I'm Scottish, and I like an Indian curry," I said. "I do know what you mean, though. Are you dodging the draft too?"

"No," she replied. "I came here to be with my man. He's from Texas. This was his R and R stop. I thought it would be Europe or the USA. I was all ready to take him to Mexico. I have had two children since I have been here. They are Australian. I officially live in Bundaberg; I have an address with an Italian family for mail, but of course, we spend most of the time here. When school comes, I will go down to Bundaberg and get a job."

"What job will you get?" I asked.

"Oh, steel mill or cooking."

Steel mill made me think of Ravenscraig.

She read my mind and flexed her biceps up. It was as hard as a rock. "Wow, got any sisters?" I kidded.

She smiled. "My mother would not thank me for more foreign grandchildren. She can't wait to see my kids for real. Photos only upset her."

She went on to help others get food.

"Let's go home," Karen said. It was near morning, and she wanted to get to sleep before it got dark.

"Why are you in such a good mood?" I asked.

"Sold them all for twelve dollars, and they want more."

"They will want them cheaper," I said.

"No, I told them I had paid a lot."

"Good girl."

"Makes life easy, and they are well established."

"Ha-ha, they want weed too." Great stuff. It gets better. Life was easy for a few months. I went down to Townsville and back a few times; sometimes, I stayed there for a while. On one of these visits, Zambezi and I went for a trip round town on old bikes that seemed to be there for the using. We got talking to some girls, who asked us if we would like to come and smoke some weed. A couple of guys ran past us, gabbled something and kept going. We parked our bikes at the bottom of their stairs. Upstairs there were a couple more guys and four girls. Typical house on stilts. I had a little pea of hash and started to roll a joint. They did the same. There was an explosive entry, and a stocky bull of a guy came in, shouted something and threw the opposite end of the big table up in the air, so all the bits and bobs of the makings landed on the floor. I shot my arms out mainly to save myself but also to take the guy out. It slammed down and nearly got him. He started on the rest, who were made to sit on the floor.

"One at a time, do you work," he shouted, then grabbed them and slapped them. Next came a girl. "You're on opium or something," he shouted. "Look at your eyes!"

"I'm half Chinese," she said.

He got to the next guy and asked, "You, are you working? No!" He gave him a slap on the side of the head.

I was glaring at him. "You," he said, "are you working?"

"Yes, I work!" I said. "I work for Noranda Australia ltd. I'm from Scotland, and if you think you are going to slap me around like them, you are fucking mistaken."

"What are you doing here?" he wanted to know.

"We met these girls outside and came in for a cuppa. These are our bikes outside."

"Did you see any other guys come in here?"

"No, but someone ran past us when we were talking to the girls." He said to Zambezi, "You, Goldilocks, are you working?"

"I'm with him," Zam said.

"OK, you two can go. You are in bad company here, mate." He gestured to the door.

Other police were arriving as we were getting our bikes. We were nearly taken back in, but the aggressive cop said, "These guys are not part of this."

We got on our bikes, waved goodbye and left. We headed home.

I made a trip up to the commune, taking all but two ounces of hash and five hundred trips.

Karen and Pete did their magic again, and the cash was high. I had brought a few bottles of wine. The girls are going on the bus the next day to college to make a better life for themselves.

Karen said, "We are having a small party with the girls, Pete." It was a bit sad, with tears and hugs and kisses. "We are going to miss you all," they said.

"I will miss you too," I said. "When they burned the bra round here, they burned the T-shirt too."

With that, one got me from behind, while the other flew into my arms, and I was forcefully kissed and cuddled with much giggling and tickling.

Next morning, I awoke late to nobody there. With their rucksacks gone, I presumed they'd gone for the bus. I lay back and thought it was time for me to move along for a while, back to Scotland. I would stay here the rest of summer until the weather was a bit better in Scotland. June was my target. I wanted to head south.

Karen came back and jumped on me, kissing and tickling. I struggled hopelessly.

"What's got into you?" I asked.

"I am about to head for India," she said, "what's the best way to carry my money?"

"American Express card and traveller's cheques," I said, "leave some with your mom."

"Can't; she would spend it on booze."

"Someone you trust."

"You?"

"No, I am heading to Scotland after Brisbane."

We drove down to Townsville that evening.

"Hi Zam, Ed. How's it going here?" I asked.

"Pretty quiet, really."

The girls from the house with the police situation arrived. "Can we stay here?" they asked.

"Why?"

"We got chucked out of our last place. The police told the landlord to chuck us out."

"I could go along with that, but if you are talking about the guys that stole an orange from the shop ... Well, we would be getting pushed out of our own place. We are not a democracy here."

"It would only be until we get a place."

"Where are the guys?" I asked.

"Where were they last night?"

"They stayed with their mates."

"OK, I can give you a week. We will feed you too, but you look for somewhere else. I don't want your friends here. Clear?"

"OK."

"Give it an hour, and the guys will be round," said Karen. "They've been sent in," she said quietly to me.

I agreed.

Ed and Zambezi liked the idea of the girls being there and were already sharing a spliff with them.

I joined them and started making some spaghetti but did not join in the smoking.

"What was all that business with police about?" I asked. "One of the boys got seen pocketing an orange."

"Well, they nearly got us busted, all busted, so the answer to them moving in here is no. We like a quiet life, and they will be round here shortly when you have made yourselves comfortable. So if and when that happens, just go with them."

They arrived sure enough before the meal was eaten. All smiles, they walked in and asked, "Got any left?"

"No!" I said.

"Aw, there's some in the pot," one of the guys said.

"That'll be mine," Karen said. "Touch it, and I'll break your fucking fingers." She had put on her war paint. She was six feet tall, beautiful, physically very powerful. I had never seen her with makeup before.

"You can stay the night, but you are out by nine tomorrow," she said. "All of you!"

"Yes, Ma'am," the leader said.

"That sounds good to me," I said.

A crestfallen orange thief said, "I didn't know your lawyer was visiting. Thanks for the night anyways, mate."

I held my hands out in submission.

"How did you know she's a lawyer?" I asked.

"Look at the clothes she is wearing, and the perfume is expensive."

"She's a good lawyer," I said.

I had noticed she was dressed to kill. So far, I had only seen her in the bush gear, but I liked it. She is a stunner, I thought.

We ate, and then removed ourselves from the rest by going to my room and shutting the door with a do-not-disturb sign from a hotel in Europe.

"I am going shopping tomorrow," she said, "for travellers' cheques and a ticket to Bombay. Want to ditch them blokes and come with me, Scottie?"

"No, I have another plan, but I will give you my contact address in Scotland. I would really like to show you Holland and Paris too." I felt a bit of a fool, but Mausie was still in my head.

She would take a plane to Brisbane and get more travellers' cheques, and then she was flying to Bombay and out of my life. Both of us shed tears at the final parting.

It had been good. I was going to miss her, but that was how it was as a draft dodger, I supposed.

With Vietnam hanging over my head, I couldn't get too complacent. We went to Brisbane on the train, having passed the house over to the girls. The train journey was worth it. We all dropped half a tab, and the scenery and sunset were amazing, a big red orb that made everything red, then slid into blackness.

We got a taxi to an address in Redhill. Just before we got there, as we passed a big Ford Falcon standing on the side of the road, Ed asked two girls if they wanted a hand. The car was stuck, grounded with a back wheel in the ditch. He did his party trick and lifted the car so they could drive out. They parked about twenty yards further down at the bottom of a steep dip, right opposite the number I had.

When we knocked, we didn't get an answer, but a girl came out of the house, and we assumed it was the girl's house.

"Looking for someone, mate?"

"Yeah, I am looking for Peter," I said.

"Aw, he's not here at the moment."

A girl from the car came from the back and asked if she could help.

"They're looking for Peter," the first one told her.

I said we would come back; I had been hoping to stay there, but we could get a hotel.

"He goes off for a few weeks at a time," she said and asked where we had come from.

"Townsville," I said.

"We won't be back for a couple of days," she said. "You can have our flat behind here. This house is split in two. That lot are moving in the morning. If you want, I'll have a word with the landlord and get you in there before he advertises. They never gave notice till yesterday. Be handy in case we get stuck again, too," she added with a smile. She kissed Ed on the cheek as she passed him.

"I didn't realize you knew these guys," she said.

"Well, you know now!" she retorted.

"Come on, what's keeping you? We are gonna be late," she called out. Her friend caught up, they piled into their car and off they went.

Zambezi smiled and said, "Well, that's sorted. We have a place to stay tonight."

We went around the back into their flat. There were two single beds. I booked one, and Ed claimed the other. He laughed and told Zam he could have the chair. Zam sighed. "We need three beds," he said, "but I will manage tonight. If they move out in the morning, then we move right in. I will help them with their bags."

"I am having first pick of the beds," I said.

"One of the blokes said the landlord is coming at nine when we leave. He knows about you, so if you come, then he will talk to you." We were knackered, and I hit the hay.

Next morning, I was awakened by a rough voice. "Come on, mate, up you get!"

I rose. Zambezi was still fast asleep. Ed had been on the floor. He got up quickly. We approached the door, and there was this apparition in a ragged boiler suit, gruff and looking down at heel, to say the least.

“The girls said you wanted to rent next door,” he said.

“Yes, that’s right.”

“It’s $240 a month, all right, one-month deposit and one month in advance.”

“Let’s see it,” I said.

We went next door, and I said, "Mate, this is a bit rough. Needs a good paint job.”

“Paint it, and I will take it off the rent.”

“Two bedrooms. We will paint the whole place for four months’ rent."

“That’s a bit steep,” he said.

“Stone the crows, mate,” I said in pure Aussie, “it’s a lot of work, and the next guy will pay more.”

“OK, you got a deal.” He shook on it.

"You will have to supply the paint and brushes,” I said.

“I will bring it here next week. See ya later,” he said, and off he went.

I got my gear, moved in, and made my bed with my Indian Navajo blanket. I told Ed to take the other bed. Zambezi was still fast asleep. We checked out the gas stove. It worked but needed a good clean.

They were mingers, so we set to giving the house a good scrub. Ed was the most industrious. “If I am painting this house, I am giving the lot a wash,” he said, asking me if there was any Dettol. I said I would check, adding that there were a lot of sheep here. "Perhaps Jeyes’s fluid will be what’s required, judging by some of the bugs I’ve seen so far!”

“Have you been in the bog yet?” asked Ed.

“No."

"Well, you are in for a surprise. I’m calling it Hendry.” He chuckled away to himself.

We were settled in, and the girls were back next door. Turned out they worked in the topless bar in town as barmaids. They did have big tits for sure, so we said we had best look in for a pint sometime.

Next day the girl across the road arrived. I went over to ask her if Peter would be back soon.

“I don’t know. He comes and goes,” she said, asking if I knew him. “No,” I told her, "but a friend gave me his name and asked me to look him up.”

"Who would that be?” she inquired.

“Karen, her name is from Karanda.”

“What do you want him for?”

“Private matter," I said.

She was so distrustful for a hippie chick in her long sarong kind of skirt and lace bodice. I was dismissed, so I walked across the road.

“Did you find the guy?” Zam asked.

“No, and I don’t think she likes me either. Very distrustful. You can’t win them all, I suppose.”

A week went by, and we treated it like a holiday. No, Peter, I was going to have to think of something else or dump it. We were smoking our way through the hashish. It was a pleasant spot, though.

We were playing our music and sitting dreamily, having a spliff, and generally feeling good about this town.

In walked a stranger.

"Hi, I'm Marie's flatmate, Peter," he said. "She told me you were looking for me."

"Hi," I answered. "Karen gave me your address. We were looking for you when we fell into this place. What is Karen doing these days?"

"She has gone to India, intending to do some travelling. She said you might like some of the hash I have. Smoked a lot of it, though." I gave him an ounce to inspect and handed him a joint. He spluttered and said it's got tobacco in it.

"Sorry mate, a Pom habit, I'm afraid."

"No worries, mate. I have a pipe." He disappeared and came back with a pipe and Marie.

"Sorry I was so suspicious. He grows a couple of plants in his office. I thought you might be the police."

I laughed. "Scotland Yard, eh?" We all had a good giggle.

Brisbane is a very pleasant city. Walking home one evening after a nosh in a Japanese restaurant, conga and everything. There was a lot of music and a couple of aborigines sitting on a seat by their front door. It was high off the street. He made the smoking signal with his hands and pointed to some big white trumpet flowers.

I went over to talk to him. He waved me up, so I went up some steps. When I looked in the door, there was a card game going on inside. They made gestures to come and join them. They were a rough-looking bunch. I remembered my game of pool in Katherine, so I declined. The old one was saying the flowers were the same like smoke.

"What, you smoke them? I asked.

"No, put three in a pot with water. Boil up, then drink the water."

He made the smoking sign with two fingers, then turned a circle and spread his hands to depict being stoned.

"Take some," he said, so I picked half a dozen and made my way back.

Walking back, I could see these big white trumpets hanging over walls and fences all along the way. Sparks had shown up with two girlfriends from Cairns. One had a broken leg. The girls next door gave them their flat, so they could move out. They were going to Melbourne, so they and Sparks became our neighbours.

We boiled the flowers, three of them, and put the mixture into five cups. We were Sparks, Zambezi, Ed and me. The four of us took one each. I sniffed the pungent smell and decided against it. Ed smiled into my eyes and waited to see if I drank it. We both put it down, Zambezi said cheers, then downed his, followed by Sparks – in one go.

No, I'll go to bed, I decided, and with that, I was off.

Ed woke me later. "Come and see this," he said in a conspiring tone.

"Tell me?"

"Sparks is in the toilet, cuddling the lavvy pan. Zambezi is as bad, but he has gone for a walk."

"OK, keep me posted but don't keep wakening me," I said.

Some hours later, I woke. The light was on, and Zambezi was still gone. Sparks was there, talking in a language that sounded like sleep talk. He came into the room and tried to pick up bright bits on my blanket. Then he put his hand out to the shelf above my bed, picked up my wallet, opened the zipper and started taking notes out and dropping them on my bed. He dropped the wallet and left the room.

Ed laughed nervously and followed him. I got up and into my clothes and started to question Sparks, who seemed to be walking around with about a dozen people and dogs. Their description was weird. Normal people about six inches wide and dogs with long pointed noses. I was finding it hard to make out his words at first, but it got better. "Don't let him out of your sight," I said to Ed. "And if Zambezi comes back, keep them here." I went back to bed, wondering what we had done.

Morning came: no Zam, but Sparks could talk now, although most of it didn't make sense. By midday, Zam came back. He had a swollen temple and head. He had been arrested and thrown in a cell. They were trying to get him to admit he was on something, and he got punched a bit. He had been standing by a shop window where he backed up to them: A Canadian kids' game to piss people off, I gathered. He beat the window like a drum with the palms of his hands, and it vibrated in a scary way. The cops thought he was on something and took him away. The drug police beat him, then chucked him out in the morning. He was still on this weird trip that lasted about thirty-six hours, but they could talk coherently after about twelve hours. Ed shepherded them throughout to keep them out of trouble.

Marie came back from night shift in her nurse's outfit. I waved, and she waved back. I waved her over. I was in my underpants, so I got into bed again. She came just inside my doorway, and I said jump in. She looked at Ed snoring and pointed to her house, and said I'll put on the kettle. I put a towel round me and joined her across the road. This was the beginning of a passionate love story.

Time came for me to go back to Scotland. I planned with Zam and Ed that I would go over and send him a thousand tabs, and he would sell them and send me half the money in travellers' cheques, in his name, signed by him. Then we would up the ante.

Marie went off in her little car to play tennis one afternoon. Half an hour later she came back, walking with the tennis racquet. Where's your car? I asked her.

"Wrecked. It was your fault!" she snapped. "I was thinking about you when I drove over an intersection and into the side of a truck."

"Are you OK?"

"Yes, but the car is wrecked," she said.

"Well, I am off home to Scotland for a couple of months or so," I told her. "I will write and let you know where I am." I gave my gran's address. She gave me her Indooroopilly address.

Next morning, I was on a plane watching Australia disappear underneath for a long time.

I arrived at Heathrow. It was not warm as I would have liked, but I managed this time. When I got home to Scotland, I went to see my mum and slept for a long time, mostly dreaming that I was still in Aus.

I went to see Ali Ruff to score. I told stories about Australia but don't think he believed a word of it. We smoked hashish and listened to The Byrds, The Grateful Dead and Pink Floyd. Ali was good on the guitar and was right into Jimi Hendrix. He would sometimes give a wee concert when he felt in the mood. I told him I had given his number to Ed, who was still in Aus, in case he needed to talk to me. "I told him I would visit you on Tuesday at seven o'clock. Are you OK with this?" I asked. Ali agreed.

"Are you going back?" he asked.

I told him I was not sure and that I could end up in their army if I did and be shipped off to Vietnam.

"That's scary, Dennis," he said. "I wouldn't go back if I were you."

"I love it there, Ali, but we will see."

There was a knock at his door. It was Sherrie with babe in arms. She came in and spoke. Ali nodded to the door, so I got up. I needed to get a bus to St Andrew's, so said my goodbyes and left.

Staying with my aunts was great; getting fed regular meals. I went down to London on the train. Could not find Arty and Sammy, but I did find one guy I knew, Teddy. Or at least one of his mates. He was a paranoid guy called Graham who let me stay in the flat and told me not to answer the phone. Teddy was off somewhere, and all I could do was wait. All he did was sniff coke and shake whenever I was there. He kept offering me some, but I was not interested.

Teddy would be back in a week. He had finally talked to him. I went out every morning, took a tube to Earl's Court and had a pint in one of the two pubs. At the King's Head, I met people I had met before with Arty and Sammy. I noticed the king's head was that of a Stuart, and I wondered if that was anti-Scottish. I noticed that even the lowest of the low seemed to assume superior status above me because I was Scottish. I called them little Lord Nelsons to give this syndrome a name. They had to have been taught this in school because there was a lot of it around. One of Sammy's Irish mates showed up, and I had a drink with him. He said that it was possible that they were in the nick because they had been missing for some time. Nobody cared, really. That was the way it was.

Graham gave me the spiel that he had a big dealer coming around, and I was not to talk to him. The door went, and in came the Paddy from the pub. Graham was taking him into his room for secrecy. I was down below in the sitting room. I looked up and right into his eyes. "Hi Dennis," he said. Graham tried to get him into his bedroom, but he said, "Relax, man, Dennis is a friend of mine." There was a bit of banter between Graham and us. Sold him an ounce of coke, and we had a joint. When he went, Graham said, "You should have had the door shut."

I said, "Listen, mate, you left it open, and anyway, I know him from Earl's Court. He's my Celtic brother."

There was a lot of little Lord Nelson strutting around on his flagship in his weird mind. Teddy arrived back with a lot of foreign notes. He was high as a kite on what he had been doing. "Can you phone Eric and tell him I want to speak to him?" I asked. He said I can only get him on certain days.

"Tomorrow evening," Graham said. "Dennis can't stay here; he knows too many people."

"Get me, Eric, and I am gone," I said.

One day they were both out. The phone rang. I answered. "Teddy and Graham are out at the moment. Can I give them a message?" I asked, but the person said he would phone back later.

"Eric?" I asked. "Hi man, it's me, Dennis. I've been waiting here for weeks to see you. Can you drop by, or will I come to you?"

He agreed. "OK, not today but tomorrow morning."

That was just what I had been hoping for when I answered it. I went out.

When I came back, I was met with a "Did you answer the phone?"

"It rang for an awful long time," I said. "I thought it was your mum. Don't worry though, it was an old mate of mine anyway. You know him, Teddy. It was Duncan's mate Eric!"

Touché! I thought privately. Eric came around and said hi.

"Can I have a word with you?" he asked and took me into a bedroom. "I am not going through them, Eric. I have never done business with them," I said.

"Send me to Russ if you don't want me, or I will just wait for Arty and Sammy to appear. These are not my kind of people, nice as they are," I added.

He handed me a piece of paper with his number and said, "Before ten in the morning."

"Thanks; see you in a couple of weeks."

Back in the living room, Eric said, "He had a message from a friend of mine."

"OK, job done. I am off to Scotland. Thanks for putting me up."

The train ride home is always quicker for some reason. I sent the goods to Zambezi and Ed and waited a long time for the return from them.

"They were broken; send more," came the reply.

What the hell was this? I thought.

I went to all the bother to do this to make some money, not to get a lame excuse and a game. They would still manage even if it was powdered.

I got into Scotland again, dealing bits of pot.

There were many calls from Ed and Zam to Ali, who was getting annoyed and somewhat abusive.

A telegram arrived for me. They were always treated as bad news. I opened it with my aunt looking on. It was from Marie. "Arriving Schiphol ten thirty tomorrow. Be there!"

My head spun. I was elated and thought, I have not much time.

I booked on the early flight, arriving at Schiphol well before Marie's flight from Aus. I saw the flight from the deck where stood among the waiting relatives and friends. I saw Marie's mum and dad and stayed back away so she could greet them first.

I was eagerly looking for the long blond hair. There was one I kept going back to, wearing a cat suit with a bolero jacket. I had never seen her with makeup and so well dressed. When she walked out the gate, she looked around and headed straight for me and into my arms. I recognised her as her dad was moving forwards for a hug, but she side-stepped him. Then I was wriggling free. "Your mum and dad," I hissed.

She introduced me, and we went for a stand-up coffee. They were going on a trip to Scandinavia. "I am going to Scotland with him," she said. I persuaded her to go on the trip with them. It would be a wonderful opportunity, I told her.

"I will still be waiting. Get a plane to Edinburgh. Book the ticket before you go, or else it will cost a fortune. Last-minute flights cost more than double," I explained.

She went off to Zeist, near Utrecht, with her mom and dad to see her grandmother. They were all Dutch. Her dad had been the Dutch Ambassador in New Guinea and had retired to pineapple farming in Queensland.

I returned to Scotland. Marie was off for a few weeks. There was a knock at the door one day, and I opened to find a grinning Ed and Zambezi. What mostly surprised me was that Ed had come back. All these years of wanting to go there and he came back.

They told me they had been to Cupar, where they phoned Ali Rough from around the corner where Zam had said, "I have a collect call from Edward Skotnik. Will you pay for the call?"

Ali shouted "No!" and slammed the phone down, and they went around and knocked on his door.

Ed said, "He near had a heart attack when he saw me."

"We smoked his pot," Ed said, then they came to see me. I laughed at their story. I had a house in mind to go with Marie, but we moved in, and instead of solitude with Marie, the pantomime came along with us. I did a bit of hash to keep us going, and we were enjoying having friends from Methil and Leven and the rest of Fife. Thrust was a caricature of fat Freddie from the Freak Brothers. His friend Gruesome a dead ringer for freewheeling franklin, one a mass of red hair and the other dark.

We were raided by the police while they were there on one such occasion. We managed to get the inspector to hand up the search warrant, and I ate it with the help of fat Freddy. We were on the second storey of three. I told them they would need the fire brigade to get us out of here – it had three storeys, and every door had a security lock.

"Ah, I've wasted enough time here," said Inspector Nairn. "You will all be dead shortly, smoking that stuff." The inspector and crew left. We could not believe our luck. We vacated the premises post haste.

I moved farther away from my home area to another house.

About a year later, I decided to return to Australia. I had met a social worker with a friend from Dundee. She would score hashish and was a bit of a mover. We went out for a Chinese meal at lunchtime, got pissed and got to know Angie a lot better after I had a passionate moment with her in the gents' toilet.

She liked the stories of Australia that came out of us all the time. I told her of taking acid there, and she was right up for it. We came to an agreement that she would take some in a cigarette carton, so I arranged it that way. I was worried about the Army situation. When would this unpopular war end? If it had any merits like the Spanish civil war, I could justify it. I would not feel at all bad about shooting a few fascists. The wee man in his paddy fields defending his country from foreign invaders. No way, mate!

We arrived in Sydney armed with the address of Peter, who was a friend of Zambezi.

He put us up, and we got his balcony with a mattress after a few days on the couches. His girlfriend was nice and had a baby. I asked him if he would like some acid. He took it and gave me half the money after two days.

Then he brought a guy who looked more like a tramp than a hippie. He had a photographer in town where he could sell the rest of what we had. I said four thousand and kept the rest, and Peter had four thousand, and another nine thousand stashed in the ground in the garden.

We agreed next day, to meet his friends from Melbourne who wanted to buy them.

Next morning, we were up at the crack of dawn with the tabs in a cigarette packet after breakfast. The tramp came and asked us to come with him to meet Peter.

"You want to just hang around here in case something goes wrong?" I asked.

"No, I'm coming with you," Angie said. I relented.

We went to a photographer in Sydney. It was a poor business, I thought. The guy was very tall at six foot four. He said they were coming from Melbourne and would meet us in the restaurant in the airport to exchange the money for the goods.

We got in his car, the five of us. His driving was fast and nervous.

"Fucking slow down or let me out," I said. It went unnoticed. I had a great desire to punch him in the back of the head. They are nutters, I thought.

We pulled into traffic that slowed us down. "Pull up there. I want to walk in," I said. Ignored again. The guy next to us said that this was the airport now, only a couple of hundred yards away. I wanted to get out and stash the acid and proceed on foot. They could park the car. Angie was sitting in the middle with the cigarette packet with four thousand micro dots and her lighter in her hand.

At that moment, plain-clothes men with guns pointed at our heads ran onto the road, and the driver pulled up. They stood there. Nothing moving. "Try to drop that as you are getting out," I whispered.

We were sat cross-legged on the pavement with a gun pointed at our heads, all five.

"Relax," I said to him. The gun was shaking like a leaf. "Just relax; it's not going to happen. You won't die today. It's over; stop fucking shaking." There was no comprehension. They must have been wondering if I would pull out a machine gun and spray them all with bullets.

No, instead, just peace-loving hippies. I wondered what this would do for my imminent army career. If they asked me, I would tell them I want to get stoned with the Viet Cong. Fraternize with the enemy. The Yellow Pearl that the Australians were so afraid of. Shower them with love and apologise for ten years of bombing.

We were taken to the police station, where they questioned me. I had nothing to say.

"You must give a name, address and date of birth," said a cop.

"My lawyer will give you that. Where is he?"

"You will get one, but I need your address in Sydney."

"I haven't got one."

"Where do you live?"

"Karanda Cairns in Queensland."

"Yes, but where do you stay in Sydney, mate?" He was getting pissed off now.

"I just got here," I said.

"From Cairns?"

"Yes."

He got up and left me on my own.

I was remanded to Long Bay jail. It was primitive, Botany Bay kind of architecture. A wall with armed guards. A big yard, three wings: one of them was the cats' wing where the homosexuals went.

We baked in concrete yards all day and were fed the worst food I have ever had in my life. Porridge with weevil skins that got stuck in your teeth. We played paddle tennis against the wall. I had one visit. Pumpkin was not nice either.

I played chess with Tivi Molov, a Yugoslavian who was on remand for blasphemy. I doubled up laughing. When I could keep a straight face, I asked, "What did you do, Tivi?"

"I stole a gold chalice from a church," he told me.

"Are you sure it is blasphemy you are charged with?"

"Yes."

"Was it a Catholic church?"

"Yes, I think so."

"Are you a Catholic?"

"No, I am Muslim but not practising."

"Then you cannot be charged with blasphemy unless you are of the same religion," I said. "I would not say anything to anybody until you are in court at the trial. Tell your lawyer to submit that at the beginning of the trial."

"Play chess," he said.

"No, you beat me too easily."

"I give you dam," he said, pointing at his queen on the board.

"No."

"OK, queen and castle."

"OK."

He played me without a queen and a rook and beat me again so easily; this guy could beat Spassky or Fischer any day.

Next, we played a couple of games of draughts he called dame, where you got a queen instead of being crowned. It was a waste of time playing when the outcome was certain, no matter what I did. He would teach me defences that would be great if I played someone else.

I was sitting cross-legged when this guy backed in and squashed the plastic chess pieces. "Look out!" I shouted and got a kick for my trouble. The gate opened, and he went out. He went over and asked a question at the office, came back to the next yard and stood at the gate to get in, telling his friends what he had done to this Pommy bastard.

The guard was at our gate, opening it to let somebody in. I nipped up and said, "Officer, he let me through, and I grabbed his hair and kicked him in the face." To my astonishment, I had a handful of hair. He punched me in the eye. I dropped the hair and went in, punching and kicking till I was dragged off. He went on and on about me being a dirty fighter to his friends in the other yards. I was thrown in a cell on the second landing. There was a foam mattress and a blanket. They stank! I threw them out of the window between the bars. Half an hour later, the door opened. It was an angry PO, Gillespie, who sounded like pissed-off Belfast.

"What the fuck do you think you are doing throwing the bedding out the window?"

"It stinks; go and smell it."

"You're Scotch, are you?"

"No, Scotch is whisky. I would have thought any Irishman would know that. I'm Scots."

"Sure, ye get no whisky here, that's for sure." Chuckling, he said, "Bring him fresh bedding. Ye, behave yourself; I give ye a warning."

With that, I was locked up for the rest of the day, and that was that. Life went on as usual.

Back in the yard, the other half of the fight had gone to the cats' wing. "You fight like a Yugoslav," Tivi said, smiling.

People were called for visits morning and afternoon. I had none. Even my lawyer seemed to have no interest. After six months passed, I was called for a visit. I wondered if Ed or Zambezi had come looking for me.

To my astonishment, it was Angie. "Why are you doing this?" she asked.

"What?"

"Pleading not guilty!"

There was a guard between us in a passage he could walk through. The passage was lined with chicken wire. The guard sat on a stool at the end, reading a newspaper.

“What do you want me to do?” I asked.

“Plead guilty and get me off.”

“If I plead guilty, they will go for you.”

“Where are you living?” I asked.

“With another girl,” she said.

“Are you working?”

“Yeah, up the cross,” she said. That blew me sideways. Was that the deal for the bail?

She nodded. “One of the girls helped me.” I felt very guilty at that moment. I supposed a bit of prostitution might be better than sitting on remand in Silver Water women’s prison.

It played on my mind. I wondered if she had made it up to get to me. I couldn’t do anything in any case. If I changed my plea, then they would go for her, and she would be well shafted.

It was heavy on my mind, even though you take the money and you take the chance, and if you fall, you fall alone.

Her working up the cross was a mind-boggler for me, from middle-class social worker to hooker. It may all have been a police ploy. Perhaps she was taken from the prison to the visit to try to get a result. Now, they needed her to get me, as I saw it.

I was taken for a bail application before Judge Goran. How are you pleading? He asked.

“Not guilty, and I would like bail.”

“What’s he up for?” he asked the prosecutor, who seemed to be taken by surprise.

"Oh, er ..." He scrambled and dropped papers. "Marijuana, and quite a bit of it."

"He obviously knows nothing about it, my lord. It's LSD, and it would be a very small handful," I said.

I was asked if I had a lawyer, and I said no, that I would represent myself. "We have a saying in Pit Street, our street of solicitors," he said, "that a man who represents himself has a fool for a solicitor."

"We have a saying in Scotland," I said, "the truth needs no advocate. I am not expecting to meet Cardinal Richelieu here. He said, 'Give me six lines that any honest man has written, and I shall find enough to hang him with.'"

"Richelieu!" cried the judge, slapping his thigh. "I'll take this case."

"You are fully booked," the prosecutor hastily added, still looking flustered.

"I fix bail at five thousand dollars." He tapped the gavel, and I was taken away.

I had no way of paying that from my present position. I had not expected to get it. I was bowled over, but I could only think of getting that money for my x marks the spot. There was a big stash in Drummoyne at the house about the remainder of the seventeen thousand we had brought. The worms would be having a party.

There was no one I could get in touch with from there, really, and five thousand dollars was still a lot of money in Tory Britain. I was unreachable to anybody that I could ask.

I wondered what Angie must be doing. The words "Working up the cross" echoed in my mind. I hoped she was working as a barmaid rather than the obvious.

Five

The trial finally took place thirteen months after our arrest. No one heeded the call for my bail. I did ask a few, more in jest than expectancy. The first judge I had been given was called Cameron-Smith. I objected to him on the grounds of prejudice. He assured me he was not prejudiced. I said, "Well, you should see what it is like in Long Bay. They are terrified to go up in front of you. I would be so nervous it may affect my defence."

The trial judge I had now was Judge Leslie. My counsel came and spoke to me in the corridor just before I went in. I said to him I had one instruction I would like him to follow.

"Yes?"

"Do not prosecute Miss Stephens in any way."

"If that is your instruction, very well," he said.

Angie sat next to me, on my left in the dock. The trial was quick and boring, police witnesses. No mention of the other three persons in the car. Suspicious by their absence, I thought.

Angie was called first. She gave her account of innocence. She talked of her haemorrhage that exuded a tiny bit of blood during sex, saying that I didn't care about it and kept shagging away regardless, which was the opposite of the truth. I was concerned, but she was not and said she had had it for a long time. So, I kept shagging away, I suppose. A funny thing to have brought in. Perhaps as a social worker, she might have been inferring abuse.

It was turned over to my defence for examination. No questions.

"What?" Judge Leslie exclaimed.

"I was instructed by my client not to prosecute Miss Stephens," he said.

"Does your client wish to give evidence?"

"He will give a statement from the dock."

I looked around the court since I had the floor. The jury looked like I would hang. I said, "My statement will be short. I know nothing about nothing," and sat down. The silence was long and deafening.

The summing up was short.

The judge said the fact that we had turned up on Commonwealth property at the airport made it look like the Commonwealth bureau of narcotics had orchestrated this, looking pointedly at my counsel.

The jury was not out long enough for a cup of tea. We were ushered into the court again.

The jury found me guilty and Angie not guilty. Angie kicked me in the shins as she left the dock.

"You are a clever bugger; you got your girlfriend off," said a detective.

"I don't think she is aware of that," I said.

I went back another day for a sentence and got five years with a minimum non-parole period of twenty-one months. It was obvious to all of them what I had done here. Otherwise, I would have got more, I thought.

The counsel who defended me asked me if I was happy with my result. "It could have been a lot worse if you had not been seen to be saving the girl. Judge Leslie thought you would have gotten off if you had fought either the police or your co-accused.

I spent time on Milson's Island in the middle of the Hawkesbury River. This was an easy-going place; a shark-infested estuary with currents made a swim out of the question. Life there was perfect for me. Fishing with a line and some bread made into dough and put on a hook would get you a mullet of between one and two kilos. A Fiji Indian called Jack Singh was my fishing partner. We would put a piece of wire netting over the coals of a fire and cook mullet stuffed with peppers, onion, tomatoes, cooked potato and most important: chillies. We felt almost free. Jack would talk about Fiji, and I would wish to go there. It was a good existence on Milson's Island. We had our little crew: a Fijian, one Polish and one Scottish. Watching the kookaburras was amazing. They were always catching snakes and lizards. Just one kookaburra in a tree would laugh at you, and it sounded like the tree was full of them. What a shock the first time.

On the top of the hill above the buildings was a reservoir with the water. One particularly warm day, while having a dook in there, I saw a head with a hat on come over the edge. "Right, you lot, down to my office."

The Irish deputy governor was taking a dim view of our ingenuity, shouting to the rest of the hundred and fifty or so inmates in his very Irish accent to incite them to give us a hiding. I said to him, "Forget it, Paddy, that bunch of paedophiles and bent solicitors couldn't fight their way out of a wet paper bag. I thought you might like a bit of Scotch in your water," I added.

For my trouble, I was on my way back to Long Bay, Shanghaied straight away in one of these budgie cadge trucks for one prisoner. The only drawback about Milson's Island was you almost needed a safety belt so the mosquitoes wouldn't fly away with you. I wouldn't miss all the splotches of blood that the little buggers left where they had drilled through to get blood. Thankfully there was no malaria in Aus.

Back in Long Bay, Noonan was still the chief, and it was still familiarity There were a lot of wisecracks about me arriving back.

I worked in the bake house. I spent a few more months in Long Bay working there on the night shift. There were big old ovens where we made bread for the orphanages and some police stations, but we were never allowed to know which was which. One exception was a special order for an event the police were having. There were mouse nests thrown in it. Good roughage, I thought. Some were sent back, and when we opened the loaves, there were little round slices of baby mice in some of them. Nobody had noticed this, and there was great laughter amid the denials.

The other exciting happening was McLoughlin and Danny Rice climbed out of the bake house by dismantling a fan to get on the roof and escape. No one had noticed.

They spent the next three months robbing banks all over Sydney. The shootouts with the police were being commentated on the radio each time. They were a prolific pair of bank robbers, and we cheered them on every time. 2 SM was the radio station that played some music but not really what I was into. It was loud, which was quite good.

After a while, I was sent to Newms afforestation camp. That was good. You could leave any time, but you would need water containers, and they were nowhere to be had. We would go out on a truck with Happy. He was driven nuts by silence if he misbehaved, but if he behaved, the bookie would sit in the truck and talk to him about horses. It must have been his passion. We dug ditches at the pace of slaves. If you have ever seen Cool Hand Luke, you would have seen what this set-up looked like. We didn't have shackles; they didn't need them. You could not make it to water on foot.

Working near the prison, we came across a big pumpkin patch with maybe forty or fifty big green pumpkins ripe to pick. Happy Jack went off to get a cook. I took a long-handled ditching shovel and went crazy and smashed the lot of them.

"I hate pumpkin," I said.

The guys laughed. Two cooks arrived with a big, galvanised bath and knives.

"Who did it?" Happy cried.

"It was a big fuckin' emu!" I said.

"An emu came and done them in," someone else put in.

Happy was not convinced. The cooks went back to the kitchen to tell the story of the destructive emu.

We spent a day on lockdown, and nobody knew why. About three-thirty, we were let out.

We were all called to the parade spot where we were counted, and the deputy governor was going mad about something.

"OK, who is responsible?"

"What's happened," I asked the guy next to me.

"It was on 2JJ radio; someone said if you get bust, Newms is the place to go; they have a marijuana plantation there."

"Nice guy," I added.

"So, the New South Wales police descended on the place. That's why we were left in while they searched the area. They were walking through the trees up there and noticed it was cultivated. Hundreds of plants, that's it all in a couple of semi-trailers."

"Come on, admit it! Who is responsible?" the dep cried in vain. I laughed out loud.

Who would admit to tons of marijuana? "You are in for drugs," he said.

I thought about the slates. I had a feeling of déjà-vu.

A car drew in, and two guys in white shirts and shorts got out. "I have come for Anderson with a deportation order," said one.

"We are having an investigation," the dep said.

"I can get you the Minister for immigration on the phone if you want, but he is going with us right now."

"OK, that's him," he pointed at me. "Get your gear," he said. I filled a pillowcase and went with them.

Back to Long Bay. "When am I going to leave?" I asked them.

"Soon as they can organise the travelling bureaucracy. Probably a week or so."

I was back in the remand wing because of the deportation order. I was lying there on the concrete, getting my suntan primed for leaving the sun, listening to the Eagles on 2JJ when they came for me about three months later.

I signed the order, which banned me from Australia for five years.

I was handed to an armed Qantas security man, who put me in handcuffs and was told by the air hostess to take them off. "Yeah, I am free, so what's the problem?" I asked.

"Would you like anything to drink?" she asked. "Yes, can I have a wee bottle of wine?"

"He can't have alcohol," the guard said.

"They must have told you I am not a terrorist. Where is my money," I said. "I want a beer, at least."

"You will get it when I hand you over."

"Hand me over to who? I am free. I don't think beer is going to make much difference. You're right; all I did was get stoned and have long hair."

She ignored him and brought a beer. "It's on me," she said. After the guard had a few, he lightened up.

I told him a couple of poaching stories from Scotland. Gaffing salmon from waterfalls and mill races around the falls. The crays at the bridge of Alen was a favourite.

I arrived at Heathrow with a hangover, had my passport handed to the immigration, who handed it straight back without looking at it.

“You are free to go,” the immigration official said. “Behave yourself now you are home.”

That put a smile on my face.

The summer of 1976 the best summer in living memory. To me, it was like winter.

Home again, I worked on a farm doing twelve-hour shifts with my brother Tam. We took turns for six weeks keeping a grain drier going. The barley had to dry at the correct temperature. Too hot, and it wouldn’t germinate since most of it would be malted. That was important. The wages were not great, but we were paid cash.

I met a ballet dancer from Alsace and spent some time with her, which reminded me that I liked girls. I needed to make some money. The dole was no use: The Government had decimated the Scottish economy. Jobs were hard to come by and paid very little. The North Sea was as bad as a prison, I decided. I wouldn’t try it.

The sea was not an option after my brief encounter with a hurricane in the arctic. I had worked for a summer on the Day Dawn at Anstruther with Ronnie Macbeth. I went to Hull and signed on to the St Romanus. In January, a hurricane off the coast of Norway had beaten the ship up, and we ran for shelter to Tromsø. The decks were under the water: We were sinking. Tied up at the pier, they came on with pumps, and we spent a week there for repairs. The skipper landed the fish and took on stores. At least he took on potatoes and ice. The crew was disgusted that there would be no meat, which turned the next thirty days until the boat was filled with fish, a meat-free and fish and potato diet. The snow was up to the roofs of the houses; I got whiskey and cigarettes from the bond and sold them to Norwegians at a tidy profit. When I finally got back to Hull, I got off the ship at the lock gates and picked up my wages at the office. I got a train home, although I had wanted to stay at least six months until I could get a seaman’s book, and then into the merchant navy to see the world. However, it was not for me. Four boats went down that year, the women from Hull marched to London to complain about the conditions their men worked in.

I got a telegram threatening me to be back for the next trip, as I had signed on and had a bond bill that my share in the catch and liver money did not cover.

Next thing, on the news a few days later, the boat had sunk with all hands. I thought about the repairs in Norway and wondered if they were temporary. That was a close call. That was when I was sixteen or seventeen, before my distinguished military career at Pirbright. It sent me back to farming and woodcutting.

I felt that I could probably get on the oil rigs. But the North Sea was not a good memory for me, so I did not consider it.

After a few attempts at getting employed without success, I got back into selling a wee bit of pot, and before I knew it, I was off to London to see if I could find Arty or Sammy.

I could not find them.

I did find one chap, Duncan, who knew the guys I was looking for. He told me about Operation Julie and that acid was a thing of the past. I did, however, turn up a few pounds of Black and a bit of Lebanese hash. It was hardly the lucrative thing it would be in Aus. I spent the summer in Inverness and the Black Isle. I had gone to an address where Sherrie lived, selling both Sherrie and Sean some of my pot.

I met Alan, who sold most of it for me. Not such a good relationship as I had with Karen in Karanda. The prices seemed meagre; it would do for a time, I thought. Alan and I soon became great friends. We drank and played with many girls. The tourist board would have been proud of us entertaining many foreign girls to history as I knew it. We should apply for a grant from the tourist board, I joked with Alan.

I enjoyed visiting his mum and dad on the croft, meeting his many brothers and sister. They were in a very remote part. They loved it there. I loved my many visits to the waterfall we used to have a shower in. It had a ledge where we stood. The water in the summer was low and warm. We could soap up and stand under the water, and it was exhilarating diving into the pool where you could see small trout going about their business.

I returned south and got a cottage. I wanted to write a book, or at least try.

I stayed with a couple, Will and Fiona, who were friends of a friend. I was selling him some Moroccan. He said he would buy an ounce.

“Give me a knife, and I will guess you an ounce,” I said. Will instead produced a set of scales, and we had just got it balanced when a motorbike arrived outside, and the rider's leather jacket and jeans knocked on the door. “Stash it,” I said.

“It’s cool; I know him. It’s John T. He will maybe want a bit too."

The guy came in. He looked and saw what we were about, he asked for a quarter, so I sold it to him. Will was rolling a joint when John T said, “You must be careful around here; there is a guy called Dennis. He will rip you off.”

“Has he ever ripped you off?” I asked.

“Yes! He ripped me off for some acid.”

I said I would be careful. Then I looked him right in the eye and spoke quietly. “I am Dennis. I have never set eyes on you, and you have never even met me before.”

“Right,” he said, then fled out the door got on his bike, revved up and went. Will and I were rolling about on the kitchen floor, laughing and giggling at what had just taken place. We smoked a joint, and Will’s wife came into the kitchen and said, “Was that John T?” Fiona said. Which sent us off again.

I produced Ed, and we did a bit of work there. I got a farmhouse, Potty Hill, in Glenfarg for a very reasonable deal, so I moved there.

I was up in the Black Isle; it was mushroom season, and we would go out and search for magic mushrooms. Sherrie's farmhouse was where a few people crashed out in a guest room. I noticed when the mushrooms were hard to find, all you had to do was eat a couple. They would be very easy to find after that. We all did it. I found about twenty was about the right dose for me, but some of the crew would just keep eating them into the hundreds. I found that keeping to twenty occasionally was fine. Sean, on the other hand, ate an awful lot.

Six

I was in Inverness and having a pint with Alan when Angie came up and asked us if we could get three pounds of hash for her. I could, but I would need to go and get it, I said. Alan cut in and said he could get Moroccan in London. I said I could get Black for that price. She decided to go with me. Angie gave me her cash, and off I went, getting off before Alan, who was pissed off and heading for character assassination in all quarters. All's fair in love and war was his way of looking at it. I liked Alan very much, but he had a few failings, and one was that he was a bad loser.

I had better be quick. I collected a bit more cash and took the train down to the smoke. Everybody I went to was all out of hash, telling me of a big bust, and everyone had left town or was unavailable. Apparently, some Moroccan boat called the Eagle had been caught with a lot on board.

"Why don't you get some in Holland? I remember these famous chess boards of yours," said Sid.

"Some of them had two kilos in them. Remember that Canadian in Amsterdam that wouldn't believe there was two kilos on the board. You opened it up and had to do it all over again. Yeah, I kept half a kilo out for his cheek and the extra work," I smirked. "I put a bar of chocolate in it. He wouldn't pay twice for the job."

"Serves him right," said Sid.

"I might just have to do that," I thought. I took a bus to Amsterdam.

I got much the same story here; all the big ones were on vacation due to some big bust of tons. I was screwed. My wee, poorly connected entrepreneurial pursuit was failing me. I was looking for a cheap ticket back.

The trouble with failure is the expense is all yours.

I passed this office or travel agency advertising something called The Magic Bus. I went in, and it was full of hippie types. I saw a map on the wall behind the staff. It went to Delhi in a red line from Amsterdam.

"How long does the bus take to get there," I asked the guy behind the counter.

"Ten days," he said in a positive voice.

"How much?" I asked.

Two hundred and forty guilders. I counted, and that amount came to about seventy quid.

Before I had thought it out, I said, "Give me a ticket," and paid in pounds.

"What is this?" he asked.

"It's Scottish notes; it is the same as English. Look, it tells you sterling."

"OK," he said but looked uncertain.

"Look, man, I am not paying for a taxi round to the bank. Live a little."

One of the others said, "It's OK. I got my ticket and was told at eight o'clock tomorrow morning the bus leaves. Right outside here!"

I went and stayed in a Christian youth hostel off the Oudezijds Achterburgwal, near Torenzicht, right in the middle of the red-light area. I reckoned ten days would be a case of bread and cheese; it would be tough but worth it. I bought a cheap sleeping bag and a German army parka that would take care of any cold or wet periods on the journey.

Next morning the bus was there. It was an old Bedford with a pile of spares, fuel pipes, brake pipes and many other parts. The drivers were a pair of ex-cons, I guessed from London; one was six, two with quite a pleasant nature. The other, who did most of the driving and talking, was five-four and was a complete asshole with a real loudmouth.

I got on the bus that did not follow the route I saw on the map in the bus office. It went to Paris to pick up more freaks. One was a Canadian girl about five foot two on her way to Thailand, where her dad was working for the United Nations.

When she joined the bus, I had my rucksack in the seat and me in the window seat and a mean don't-sit-near-me look on my face.

"Can you move your bag?" she said.

"Listen, why not grab one of those empty seats like I've done? It's a long way to Delhi."

"I want to sit there," she said.

I put my bag on the rack and hers too. It was going to be cramped by the time we got very far along. I gave her the window seat, so I could stretch my legs a bit in the aisle. We picked up more in Italy. The bus was filling up. We went along the international highway in Yugoslavia and headed for Greece. As we pulled into the Yugoslav border, check lane marked "cars and buses" we drove in, and it wiped out the top planks, which were loose. They charged the bus driver four hundred dollars for the damage and said when the morning crew came on, it would be more expensive. The driver cursed but paid, and on we went.

I said to the French-Canadian girl, "They will put that top right on again and wait for the next sucker, I would bet."

We picked up more freaks in Athens then Alexandropoulos. We stopped there to get some lunch.

"How long are we stopping?" I asked the big guy.

"About an hour," he said.

I saw a fish stall and bought a kilo of something that looked almost like sardines for very little. I picked up some dried wood and a bit of netting wire from an old fence. I got a fire going, and I asked the girl if she had some bread. She produced some, and I had butter from Paris. It was soft but OK. We slathered it onto the bread. The fish were sizzling, oil spluttering out of them.

There was an American couple with their two dogs. They had passports and let me see their papers. This was new to me, being able to travel with your dog.

"Are you not worried about the dogs in the streets in the East?" I asked. "Where are you going?"

"Delhi," was the reply.

"There are a lot of stray dogs there."

"Oh, they're street dogs; they can take care of themselves," he said knowingly. "They were fat and pampered like the Yanks, who were Ivy League from California, I'd say."

We ate as much as we could. The fish was delicious. I turned to ask if anyone would like some. "No way," the yanks said. Others did, all of them licking their fingers and enjoying the snack. We met more of the bus people. There was not much socialising due to the continued movement, sometimes into the night. We got off the track a bit between Greece and Turkey and were escorted back, then put on our way again by the Greek army. We entered Turkey, crossed the Bosporus and parked at the Blue Mosque. We checked into a room in a guest house on the square next to the pudding shop. We would be there for four days. The room was sparse. With the door shut, we tore our clothes off and had rampant sex. Both of us had a good head of steam being on the bus for a few days respecting each other's space. It was great to be sleeping in a bed that did not move. We made it creak a lot, though. More empty seats were filled on the bus. I missed the incident of the dogs with our hurry to get into a room. What happened was the Yanks, and their dogs got off the bus, and Istanbul's local strays had grabbed them and tried to tear them apart. The drivers and the owners had driven them off. They had opted out for Crete instead of Delhi. They left on another bus.

On the way to the Iranian border, still in Turkey, we were getting into the mountains. The driving went into the night, the bus careering round the bends. The driver had been drinking whisky and was snarling at anyone who suggested stopping for the night. He wanted to get to Tehran, so we could stop there for a day. He finally pulled off the road and stopped for the night.

Next morning, we awoke to a shock. We were on the edge of a precipice of a few hundred feet. One of the front wheels was more in the air at the edge of a sheer drop.

The driver, who had been shagging his mini-skirted American conquest on the dashboard, freaked out and started shouting to get on the other side of the bus. We did, and he reversed back to safety. It blew our minds that he had not been aware of it.

When we stopped for breakfast, there was a café of sorts. The driver, his mate and the American girl went over to the café, and they brought a table and three chairs out. She minced about in mini-skirts and felt important. They were drinking ouzo, I think, at ten in the morning. We went down to the river where it was golden sand. I walked along the bank a bit, and we discussed the rest of the journey and how they were obviously nutters. I came along to the rest of the passengers; they were complaining about the treatment the drivers had given them. One guy and his wife from Yorkshire said he had worked in a steel mill to save his fare, and this was turning into a nightmare. "Will you lead us and tell them we want the crazy stuff to stop?" he asked.

I said, "I don't want to be left at the side of the road if you don't back me up. You lead, and I will back you up. I'll tell you what to do. That pile of spares and things. Walk over to the bus; there is a three-foot tyre lever. Walk over to their table smash that little cunt's glass into smithereens, like it's his head. Poke him with it in the ribs and lay down the law. I will back you up. That is what they understand."

"No," his wife said.

"Just grin and bear it then," I said.

Half measures are no good. Love and peace are great but not good for backup, I thought.

What's more, the drivers were into loud music, with Stairway to Heaven and Peter Frampton playing repeatedly. We were near Tehran when I had had enough. I put my boots on and packed my rucksack. It was three in the morning, with us trying to get some sleep, when the poison dwarf driver rolled in with his sweetheart on the dashboard, playing his loud music. I got up. "How do you switch this shit off?" I asked the tall one, who was built like the Jolly Green Giant with a heart like a pea. Suddenly it went off – my fumbling had got it right. I went back to my seat and said in a loud voice, "People have been saving up for a long time for this trip of a lifetime, and you are making it fucking miserable."

The poison dwarf got his drunk head out of the tangle of sleeping bag and wench. "Who turned the music off?!" he shouted. "Turn it back on," he said to his mate, who replied, "I don't think we better."

Silence prevailed. I didn't sleep sitting with my arms folded and ready for any development. Things got better. I slept with my boots on. Yorkshire's wife whispered to me. "You are my hero, Jock." I was red in the face, but I enjoyed the moment. I wished Ed was with me in a situation like this. He has a real calming effect. The big guy was a decent sort. The short, stocky one was the danger, I figured.

We stopped in Tehran and saw all the big silver statues of the shah in his uniform. The iron-fisted ruler, with American help. A teenager came up and asked me if I had a Playboy or Penthouse.

I said, "No, sorry, you are out of luck."

He said, "I will give you thirty dollars for your Levi's."

That sounded good, but I would have felt naked without them. I was tempted to sell him my spare pair, but I needed them to be able to wash the ones I was wearing. I rotated my clothes because my rucksack was small, and all I had was my changes to allow washing: two shirts, two T-shirts, half a dozen pairs of socks and one woolly jumper. My sleeping bag went on top. My footwear was a pair of desert boots (camel creepers). I had a fork and knife that joined together like a pen knife. My wallet and passport lived in my front jeans' left-hand pocket. No hand goes near my Charlies without my knowing it. That summed up my travelling kit, except for the string bags, of course, that usually carried food or were stashed in my rucksack pocket. I felt free. The music on the bus had changed from the three tapes the driver liked. That was a relief. Not that I didn't like Led Zeppelin, because I do. We stopped by a café, but it was Ramadan, and they would not sell us any food. Sundown, and there was food everywhere.

The Arab food of the Persians was nothing short of amazing. We were invited to try this and that, and I did. The yoghurt drink with herbs in it was the best I have ever had. I told one Iranian that, and he said if one had this drink every day, one would live to 120 years or more. I don't doubt him.

Tehran's population were paranoid about speaking to us about anything. Secret police were everywhere, whether imaginary or real. The women were very Western, in short, Western dresses, and they were extremely beautiful too. There were quite a few burkas too. The journey from Tehran to the Afghan border was a long and flat desert. We were told stories of the "Black Museum", where lots of different smuggling techniques were displayed with a warning that anyone returning with contraband would be caught. We were, however, not given this display of good advice.

We had many things to check going into Afghanistan: a stamp for each one. I got off the bus and stretched my legs. I had no afghanis, as the money was called. I walked over to a building, and there was an official in an RAF-coloured greatcoat. I said, “Excuse me.” He turned around; his hat had a gold salad bowl. Christ, he must be the chief, I thought.

I asked him where I could change money. I noticed he was filling a chillum with small bits of hashish.

"Do you smoke hashish?” he asked.

“No,” I lied.

He said the bank was “over there”, and he pointed the way I had come. I thanked him and left.

I went by the bus and told the people still on it they wouldn’t believe what just happened. I told them of the encounter. They mostly all immediately headed for him. I did not join them, but the rest of the way to Herat, the bus was in a haze of hash smoke.

When we arrived in Herat at a campsite or caravanserai on the outskirts, we built a big fire and laid out our sleeping bags and gear. The bus driver said to take what we needed for five days: he was having the gearbox stripped and rebuilt, or we wouldn't get far. It was dark, and I needed water, so a few of us went into town, walking down the street looking in the shops and stalls. We were offered food as there was plenty, it being Ramadan. A lot of sheep and goat meat, deliciously spiced.

The Aussies were in a clothes boutique, arguing about hash price. They bought it and left very loudly, going into a stall a couple of doors down. I went in and asked the chap whether he had hashish. He showed me the same as the border guard had. No, I said, I was looking for something better. “Flying saucers,” I said. Doc had told me about them in Methil.

He opened a brick out of the wall and took out a discus-shaped piece of about half a kilo, and let me handle it and smell it. This was what I wanted.

“How much?” I asked.

"Fifty dollars a kilo. How much you buy?"

"Ten kilos," I said.

"I will have to go and get it," he said.

As he put the hash back in his stash, I told him we were there for four days.

"If you give me money first, I can make forty dollars," he said. I looked him in the eye.

He said, "I will make more money because I will pay more if the hash is given, and I must take money back."

I understood this, so I decided I liked him and was counting out the money into his hand when I was startled when one of the Australians said, "You mug." I had not heard him behind me and did not know how much he had heard.

"Mind your business, mate," I said in a pure Aussie accent. "I never danced at your mother's wedding." I gave the out sign with my thumb. He left. How much did he see?

"He came in same time you. I thought you were friends."

"No, I don't really know them. Only from the bus." I had lost count, so I took back the money I had given him. He looked worried, but I counted the four hundred dollars and gave it to him.

"My nephew will meet you tomorrow," he said.

Back at the camp, the Aussies were loud at taking the piss out of me for giving all my money to a guy with a turban on his head. I had to stop this dead. I got up with the intention of attack, to get out of the way things were going.

The Jolly Green Giant said, "I think you have bitten off more than you can chew. Come on, Jock, I'm with you, mate." He smiled.

"We don't want any trouble. We were just having a laugh."

"I don't allow fights on my bus, but I would put my money on Jock here against the four of you sheep shaggers."

I laughed and said, "Come on, mate? There's some good-looking sheep in Australia."

The circle of people around the campfire were smiling at the outcome of what might have been a very nasty experience.

I went into town, and before I got very far, a voice cried urgently, "Firangi!" This means foreigner, so I turned around and saw a well-turned-out young man. This was the shopkeeper's nephew, who was a student at Kabul University. He was on a bicycle with another in his hand. "Come on, take this."

I did and took off after him. We went to get his friend, and we three went cycling, seeing the sights. Ramadan must be finished, I thought. There was food getting cooked all around. They were given food for free everywhere we stopped. They must be very well known, I thought.

"See you tomorrow," he said.

"I am spending the day with my girl," I said.

"OK, next day then."

I went into a clothes shop looking for something to wear. I was not so interested, so I wandered into the next shop. I heard, "No, no, no!" Then, she called, "Dennis!" I went in. "What's wrong?" I asked.

"His changing room is this curtain, then he wanted to come in with me soon as I was undressed!"

The primitive little shopkeeper was cringing.

"Come on," I said, and she put her trousers on and threw the thing she was buying on the ground, and we left. I wonder if he would have lived if I were an Afghani.

On the fourth day, my friend came to the campsite and signalled me to follow him. I did, and we went to a leather shop where the bag I had described to them was ready to be filled. The flying saucers were red as I have seen the very best of Lebanese. They were wrapped in plastic, and the inside was smeared with glue as I had asked them to seal it. The ten flying saucers were attached to each end of the hand-stitched leather, leaving enough space for the zipper. They finished stitching. I went out and bought Afghan products and filled the bag up: Long socks, hats and other items that took my fancy.

The bag was stuffed full to keep its shape and was a bit longer than a five-gallon drum and just as round. It was pure white camel leather which was quite thick as I had asked them if it would be thick. "What you want," had been the answer. I paid the man a hundred dollars – twice what he asked. Everybody was happy. The bus came back and sounded just as healthy as it had when it left.

"How much hash did you buy?" asked the Jolly Green Giant with a knowing smile.

"A few kilos. Not nearly as much as you pair have loaded up," I said.

"Three hundred kilos, Jock."

"I intend to get off in Kabul. Mine is not nearly as well stashed as yours is," I said.

"That's very good of you, but I wouldn't mind if you stayed."

The next stop was Kandahar, a caravanserai nearby the town. There were trucks, camel trains and other people doing business from bundles, cars and horses. It was a busy throng. I sat on a rock watching some curry getting made in a big cauldron. A whole sheep was chopped up along with onions and some veg. Rice was cooked in a big pot right next to it. I was waved over by the vendor trying to make a sale. He offered me a bowl from the top: green-looking fat. "No thanks," I said and went back. A pile of naan bread was put on the bench, and people started to move in. I could see the greasy three inches from the top was a delicacy. It was halfway down by the time I went, so I paid five afghanis for a bowl full of only gravy and lamb and rice. It nearly blew the top of my head off. The wee round chillies were demonic. It was great, so was the lamb that clung to the bones. I had been vegetarian due to my economy. The ten days was now five weeks and still a way to go. I went back to the bus to let the girl eat as we were taking turns watching the bags. "Try the lamb curry; it is great," I told her. "Hot and good."

"I will stay veggie," she replied.

I fell asleep. Kabul was tense, people were leaving, the communist government had asked the Russians for help, and they were coming down the nice new road they had built to Kabul with the Russian army invasion.

I had waved goodbye to the bus and the nice people on board. I hoped they made it, I said. We spent a couple of days in a hotel. I went out one day and was offered a shoeshine by a boy of about ten years old, I would say. He made a good job of my boots, and I paid the two afghanis he asked.

"Wait, I have one more," I said.

"I will come back in five minutes, OK?" He agreed.

I went and back and got the camel bag.

"How much?" I asked the young boy.

"Two afghanis."

I agreed. He put the polish on it, and we saw the dry white leather sucking it in. I said, "Three afghanis." He smiled and kept going. After he finished, I gave him the three afghanis, inspected the bag and pointed out bits with no polish in the joins at places. I took the bag and scraped it on the dry gravel to rough it up, then I gave it back to him and said, "Do it again." He giggled at the crazy firangi, living up to all he had been told about foreigners.

I saw a tall Afghani watching me from a doorway, smiling. I became more eccentric as he smiled at the antics of my game. I had scraped it on the gravel a few times and started over once again. I gave him a note, and he gave me some change. I told him one more polish with no scraping. The bag looked amazing like it had been looked after well and passed down from the last generation. I went back into the hotel. He stayed put, hoping for another fool like me to come by.

I went into the town to find a travel office that had been recommended. It had a lot of disappointed people hanging around. I was still trying to get near the door. It felt pointless, but I went through the motions. A familiar voice said, "Firangi". I turned to find my friend from Herat.

"Come," he said, and I followed him along the street. "I saw your bus leave, and you were not on it. I am visiting a friend," he said. "Your bus stayed three days, but I could not see you. What happened?"

"We left them but did not know about the situation here."

"I am glad I found you. I can get you on a bus tomorrow morning. I will meet you at your hotel at seven this evening."

I embraced him, and we went our separate ways. I met him down at the lawn on the slope from the hotel.

"Here is your ticket for two on the bus," he said. "It will leave at six sharp. Pay on the bus."

"Thank you, my friend."

He smiled, we hugged and parted.

Marie was waiting. "Did you find out if there was a plane?"

"I have tickets for a bus through the Khyber Pass to Peshawar," I told her. "We must be there at six sharp."

"I will set the alarm," she said.

There were bed bugs of enormous appetite. We slept on top of the bed in our sleeping bags. At the bus, there was a throng of people. It was not easy to make our way through them until the guard on the bus spotted us. He barged through to usher us to the bus. I handed him the ticket.

"I must pay you," I said.

He threw our bags on the roof and said, "Later. There are two seats at the back."

There was another European couple I noticed on my way through to the back. The bus moved off. The crowd was silent now and sadly watched us leave. "How much?" I asked the guard when he had counted everybody from front to back. Twenty dollars each, he said. I paid.

We were travelling through the pass about four hours later, and we were all more relaxed than the last few days had allowed. It was nearly all men on the bus, and it was like a matador that I used to have, with a crane fitted on when I worked in the woods in Scotland. Big well-treaded tyres.

I noticed words on the cliff on the other side of the pass, perhaps a kilometre wide. I asked the Afghan in front of me, "What does that writing say?"

"Iskandar," he said.

"Iskandar, what does that mean?"

"Iskandar," he insisted.

It dawned on me suddenly. "I said, you mean Alexander the Great."

"Iskandar Grik," he replied.

I smiled. He might be Alexander the Great to us, but to an Afghan, he was just a Greek.

After all, they were the descendants of Genghis Khan and Temujin, who had sent four tumens of cavalry to attack India. They were in Afghanistan on their way there when the Great Khan died. Instead of going home to claim their position or contest the throne, they decided to stay there and went on to attack

India and return with wives and probably slaves. The Mongol practice was to kill every male over the age of twelve so that they could never attack from behind. They took the women as wives and slaves to produce many Mongol children, who were trained to be experts with the bow, horse, sword and lance. They joined Alexander as friends on his adventure to India.

These are the only firangis that they did not fight and throw out.

Fighting firangis has been almost a sport for hundreds of years. They are a proud nation, never defeated, and I like them very much. They have a quality and sense of honour that is often absent in England and the West.

We arrived at the border with Pakistan. With the road deeply rutted, the bus was low down, and we had to go to several offices to clear through. We were higher than the bus immediately below us. There was an awful wailing and crying going on. I think the crying woman was Pakistani, and a customs man in an RAF-coloured great coat was attending to her. This went on for twenty minutes, with me looking down through the window of the bus. Finally, she handed him ten rupees. It was like turning off a very loud radio. He turned and got off the bus. Then he decided to go on the roof where most of the baggage was. He looked through a couple of the bags from a standing position, then he looked at the rucksacks and pointed to them. The Guard said something; he disagreed and pointed at the one bag I was hoping he would not see. The guard pointed to his watch, tapping it. He snapped something and again pointed to the bag. The now annoyed bus guard grabbed him by his collar and the seat of his pants and propelled him off the back of the bus, and signalled to everyone to get on the bus. We did, and the bus drove off.

After a hundred yards up the hill, I looked back; he was still lying on the ground. About four miles further, the guard turned and said something over his shoulder in Afghan. The men on the bus all laughed and chuckled. I was expecting the army, but no, it did not happen.

Peshawar was full of life. This was another border town that the government here did not control: Tribal lands where they are a law unto themselves. We got off the bus, and the baggage was handed down by the guard. I got Marie's rucksack and mine. Then the round camel bag. I handed two hundred rupees up to him in a handshake, and it was palmed discreetly. He looked in his hand and beamed back to me with a smile that said he had guessed right.

We took a train to Lahore, where I expected mail from two friends with a cash order. One was money owed, and the other was to honour an agreement where I had fulfilled my part, and his was the repayment. The second was a procrastinating little shit. I had backed it up with the second who I had given credit to. The tickets would take us right through to Lahore. The train journey allowed us visit to all the towns on the way, and there were a few. The infuriating thing was when we got on the train, nice and early, the seats were all taken already by babas – older gents – who sat in them to reserve spots for commuters from the towns. Standing was the only option. When we tried to sit down, we were told, "You cannot sit there; that is Mr So and So's seat."

I told one of the babas, "Show me your ticket!" But would hear, "Mr So and So's has his ticket. I am keeping his seat."

We kept butting heads. I would say, "Well, you did not do a very good job because the seats were not filled when I got here," with him saying, "No, be a good fellow and go away" as I said, "But, no buts, fuck off!"

Two hours later, two businessmen came. They were appalled that this long-standing arrangement had been scuppered. They worked in the bank and were miffed that their seats were already filled. Marie looked at me. I was speaking back in Indian English. I had friends in Dundee from Pakistan and could flit in and out of accents at will as I could with Irish, Dutch, and with anybody else, I spoke to for a time. Usually, one conversation was enough. They squeezed along. By the time we were at the destination, we were afforded offers of a night's lodgings and meals. For me, this was difficult to refuse. However, I was on a mission, so I declined.

We got a guest house in Lahore. It called itself a hotel, but that was too much of aggrandisement. There were bed bugs for sure, so we slept on top in sleeping bags, which helped but were not foolproof. I slept like a log. The next day I went to the American Express office: closed. Open the next morning, I was assured. Marie said I was getting nervous. "Well, I don't have enough for my fare home," I said. She offered to lend me some, but I wouldn't compromise our friendship like that. I was pretty sure Kenny, my contact, would come up trumps.

Next morning, there were two letters for me. I opened the first one: from Kenny. A tale of woe, it was, saying things had been happening there. "You are not popular," it read, and went on, "I know where you are and could put it to rest, but that mad bitch from Methil has a bee in her bonnet about you. Anyway, things are not cool here right now. I can't move, so I am not able to send you the five hundred."

The next letter was an aerogramme, which spelt bad news before I opened it. Yes: another tale of woe and poverty. I handed Marie the letters, then tore them up and binned them.

Friends in need are a bloody nuisance, I said.

She asked how much I needed, and I told her two hundred would do it. She told me she could manage that. "You can get it back to me. I will come via London on my way home."

"Great," I said, "come to Scotland and visit me for a while."

"That will be nice," she replied, "but I will be going back to study. It will depend how much time I have left."

We arranged Marie a ticket to Delhi. I was on my own again, and I felt the loss of her company. I would have liked the journey right through to Bangkok with her. She was an amazing travel companion. I thought about the journey on the bus and cheered up. She had told me that she had pinched the tapes on the bus. Stairway to Heaven and Peter Frampton and one other. What did you do with them? I asked. She told me she had put them under my seat. "It was both the girl from Yorkshire and me," she said. The memory put a smile on my face. If it had gone wrong, I would had to have taken the Jolly Green Giant apart and his poison dwarf, too, with no guarantee of the outcome.

"That could have turned out bad," I said. She fluttered her eyelashes at me playfully and said, “You’re a resourceful kind of a fellow.”

I recited Dangerous Dan McGrew to let her know that I knew of a resourceful Canadian, and they should have called her Lil. I knew the excitement of what I was doing was the only thing that kept tears away at our parting.

Marie went on to Delhi, and I spoke to a young chap at my hotel who asked me whether I wanted some charas.

“What have you got?” I asked him.

He showed me a piece as soft as well-chewed chewing gum. I said, come into my room. I went in; he followed but did not shut the door until I took it and had a pipe full. I asked.

“How much? A tola?” he said.

“No, for the whole plate,” I said. He said he would ask, but he thought about ten dollars. “OK, I told him, if it is ten dollars, “but more than that, forget it and don’t bother to come back.”

He came back about two hours later. I was lying on the bed thinking this was an incredible piece of charas. He came back and said twelve dollars. I gave him the money and asked him to find some glue. He came back with a bottle of UHU envelope glue with a rubber top with a slit in it. I thanked him and went out looking myself. I could not find any other glue. I came back with another two bottles and half a kilo of sesame seeds. I caked the bar with glue and seeds. I could still see the hash. I gave it some time to dry, but it moved when squeezed. I applied more glue and seeds, left it overnight and next morning, it was less squidgy but did move when I tested it. It looked edible, however. I was booked up the following day to Karachi, then on to Amsterdam. I went out and got a couple of paper bags and a solid dry-looking samosa. Then I placed the sesame bar into the double bag and the samosa with it, turned over the corners twice to keep it shut and carefully put it in the left-hand pocket of my parka.

My bags went on the plane at checkout, and I went through the pass control. I was moved through a walkway and searched in a small wooden room by an army officer who went over me with a metal detector. It buzzed, and he asked me what was in my pocket. I took the bag carefully as I could and handed it to him.

He lifted it open a little with his finger and said, “Ah, your lunch.”

I nodded with relief.

“OK, you are cleared.” It was a terrorist search for guns and explosives. I had never heard of such things.

Karachi was terrible. I had to wait until ten o’clock before the flight was called. I went forward with my bags and boarding pass. Same thing but here my bag was put in a box, which was shut, and a television monitor above showed the X-rayed contents of the bag.

The camel bag was next. I could see the faint outline of the ends compartment, and I was ready to hold my hands out for the inevitable handcuffs. However, there was no gun or grenades, so I passed. Place your bags there, he said. He pointed to a line of baggage for the plane. I then went through a metal detector, which went off. "You are very dangerous man,” he said.

“Why?” I asked, thinking I was a goner.

“You have a very big knife on your belt.”

“Shit, I am sorry,” I said.

I snatched my belt and felt it, then unbuckled the belt and slipped off a buck knife in a green leather carved pouch.

“Put it in your bag,” he said, smiling at my discomfort and pointing to my bag.

I put it in my rucksack pocket.

After midnight the plane finally arrived: Thai Airways from Bangkok to Amsterdam and London. Couldn't be worse, the Golden Triangle and all that. I was worried because the chances of fog were great in Amsterdam. Then this flight would make me go through customs in London. I did not want this. I had heard accounts of folk dumping the bag and could see myself taking the tags off and leaving it spinning on the baggage collect escalator.

Sure enough, we were told by the captain that there was fog in Amsterdam. Pity I didn't have a parachute, I thought humorously.

The captain put a smile on my face because he did land at Schiphol.

I collected my bag and was invisible, walked out into the throng of the outside barrier and onto the tube to Central station, where I went straight to the left luggage to put my bags in with different tags. My buck knife was missing. I went to the bottom of the main compartment. I still had some dollars but not enough, but my French knife was there. I put the camel bag in the left luggage and went to the toilets to cut a piece off the sesame bar to get some guilders to buy a ticket to Scotland. Next, I went to a canal boat where some freaks I knew lived. It had changed hands, and the new tenant was a long-haired giant with a great red beard.

"Hi, would you like to smoke some hash?" I asked this perfect stranger.

"Come, I have a pipe," he said.

I went on board his houseboat, which smelled lovely from incense he had burned a short time ago. I asked whether he knew the last tenants. He told me he had seen them but didn't know where they went.

"Pity," I said. I burned the hash into the pipe, and he lit it, then asked if he could buy some. Sometimes things just work out right.

"Fifty grams here," I said, "I need a ticket to Scotland and some food to eat."

"I can give you food," he said and cooked a mushroom omelette with plenty of garlic. I ate, and he smiled at the rate I put it away.

“Your hashish is the best I have tasted,” he told me. “Come, I will buy you a ticket.” He gave me ten guilders and said, “You can get yourself a broodje. The way you ate that omelette, you were very hungry.” I did buy milk and demolished the carton in the shop, put the carton back and picked out a cultured milk, then paid for it.

“I know an office for cheaper tickets,” he said. He got me the ticket, paid for it. I presented my passport, and the girl thumbed through the pages of stamps. "You have been around the world,” she said, amazed. When we left, I said I had one other thing to do before setting off.

We were near the Leidseplein, and I was heading to the Dam square to the Magic Bus office to take up the matter of ten days with guy who had misled me.

“When are you back in Holland?” the bearded one asked. “About a week or two, I guess.”

“Come and see me,” he said. “You have a place to stay for a visit if you like.”

I mentioned I might have a friend with me. “Two Scottish!” He laughed and told me we were welcome. Then we went our separate ways.

I went into the Magic Bus office, and I looked at the people behind the counter. "Where is the tall guy with black hair?” I wanted to know, adding that he had been there six or seven weeks ago.

“There is only who you see here,” he said.

“Listen, I bought a ticket to Delhi here, and he told me ten days to Delhi. Well, five weeks took me to Afghanistan, and I was pissed off with his advice. He acted like the chief of this office, so where is he?”

“Oh, you are talking about Hans. I think, and he left two weeks ago to Delhi, driving a bus.”

“I will look in half a year or so, and when I catch him, I will pull his tongue out," I said and left. As I walked down to the station, I smirked at the exchange I'd just had.

I picked up my rucksack, left the bag and headed to Schiphol. I thought I had plenty of time, but the plane was being called, and I had no time for duty-free. I got the plane and bought my duty-free on the plane. I had a sleep for the duration of the journey, and soon I was home in my own bed, catching up with myself. My dollars had run out, so I decided to visit Thrust.

"Come in, lad, there has been some shit going on about you lately, I have to tell you. I don't believe a word of it," I said.

I went into his room, which was warm, and four others were there, including Gordon and Cherri. I nodded, and they got up and immediately left without a word.

"What's been happening?" I asked, passing a bit of Black to him. He started to roll a joint.

"There was a guy from London got bust, and the Gibsons have been putting it round that it was you grassed him because you were nowhere to be found."

"When did this happen?"

"About four weeks ago."

"Really? Well, I was on my way to Afghanistan then." I handed him my passport.

With a big grin, he said, "I knew it was shite." He smelled the joint like it was a Cuban cigar and said, "This smells like you got from the man with a two-hump camel and a magic carpet." We rolled about laughing. Pipers at the gates of dawn played, and we indulged in a good smoke.

"Was that Gordon?" I asked.

"Aye, but they are disgusted with you because of what they have heard."

"Chinese whispers," I said.

"Put the story like I just got back from Australia or something. Don't mention Afghanistan."

"I will keep it cool," said Thrust. "Give me a bit, and I will sell that right now. It's like gold here."

I gave him a couple of ounces, and he left and when he returned twenty minutes later. He weighed me in. "Top dollar," Thrust said. "I hope you have a bit for me."

I sold it, the lot. I gave him a bit for his trouble. Had another joint, and I was a stranger in a strange land listening to the Floyd. I needed a car, but I could not buy one, so I went to the girl who had sent me the hard luck story. That part I did not doubt.

"I am not here to complain," I told her. "I do need a shot of your van."

"That would be OK," she agreed if I got it back in three days. "I must do something then, so please, don't be late," she said.

"Thanks for letting me know with the letter," I said, then I told her of the journey and smoked a joint, breaking off a bit to give her something to smoke.

Then I went up to a garage on the way to see Kenny, the other person whose hard-luck tale I had received in Lahore.

I stopped for some fish and chips and a bottle of Coke. It was early, so I went around to Ali Ruff's pad. I was welcomed with a big smile and sat down on some cushions. I gave him a bit of Black to sniff, and with a big grin, he bought an ounce. He smoked. However, I was trying to straighten myself up before the next visit, so I refrained.

I was comfortable and warm in Ali's flat, with the warmth coming from the folk downstairs. They must enjoy his music because it was out of this world. I fell asleep listening to the Byrds. Byrdmaniacs was one of my favourite albums.

Ali woke me. "What time is it?" I asked.

"You have been asleep three hours. How much of this have you got?" he asked.

"A few ounces," I said.

"I will come back to you. I have some things to do right now."

"It's very nice, man," he replied.

And with that, I was off.

I drove up to see Kenny. His wife let me in.

"Where did you come from?" she asked.

"Kabul," I said.

"What's all this shit that has been going on with that mad bitch?"

"Well, she has a thing about you, alright."

"Listen, they went behind my back to my landlord trying to get me chucked out of my house so they could be near you."

The laird had asked me if I wanted to stay. They said they know me and that I am all over the country, avoiding people.

They seemed desperate to get the house, making up stories behind my back. The guy was a bit agricultural and had children. "I think we could let them have it," I said to the laird. I would go at the end of the month, which I had decided on the spot, and now I wished I had not been so generous to them.

Kenny arrived, and I asked him for a word in private.

"Yeah, come through here," he said, leading the way. We had just sat down when Kenny asked, "Got any blow, man?"

“Yes, I have a little,” I said. I took out a chunk and made a pipe, passing it to him to light. He vaporised the lot in a series of puffs. I filled it up and asked why he hadn’t sent me money as promised.

“There were all kinds of shit went down here, man,” he said.

"What did that have to do with me?” I asked.

“The man we were scoring from got bust with twenty kilos coming off the train from London,” he said.

“Well, he seems to think I had something to do with it. What’s his name?”

“Don, he is called.”

“You knew where I was. Why didn’t you tell them it couldn’t be me?”

“If I had said that, she would have grassed you. She hates you.”

“Because I don’t sell her hash when I have it? Kenny, we had an agreement. You should have sent me some money, and now all this shit-stirring with your friends.”

“What was I supposed to say? That you were away trying to smuggle hash in.”

“No, but you could have said something else,” I said. “You can tell that guy he better shut her up. You go and let him know that I am pissed off about it, and he had better let them know it's not me.”

“I have some mates in Perth at the moment. I will deal with him, and he won’t like it. He is a nice guy. I will get a message to him,” Kenny said.

I was really pissed off with them. I gave my house to them at Potty Hill, even though they’d been going behind my back with character assassination. I gave them it. He asked me if I had wanted to stay on. I wish I had now, the fucking lowlifes.

“I will come back in a couple of days and see what’s happening to right this sad fucking business," I told Kenny. "You could have nipped it in the bud." I was raging inside; sure, they were profiting from this and had probably blown on the flames.

"Did you bring more of that back?" asked Kenny.

"Yes, ten kilos!" I didn't mention I had left it in Amsterdam. "Here is a half-ounce for Geoff," I said. "He gave me a bit when I needed it. I will ask him, so don't milk it,"

I said, then left. I went home to roost and rest for a couple of days. I was recharging the batteries. Had a trip into St Andrew's for a new pair of desert boots. There wasn't a hole in mine, but the soles were thin. Desert boots, or camel creepers as they were affectionately known, were the uniform of the hippie movement round here. Most of the people I know wore them. I looked at a pair of South American riding boots with longing, but I had to watch my cash. Keeping the head here, I got my £6.50 desert boots. I was so close to a hole in the last pair that I wore the new ones straight out of the shop and binned the others. I still preferred the boots I'd worn in Auss: buckaroo boots. I sold the rest of the hash to Ali then took the bus to see my pal, Ed.

"Are you working," I asked Ed.

"No," he replied. "I have signed on the dole."

I asked if he wanted to come with me to Amsterdam. "I have a bag of hash I brought from Afghanistan to Holland, and I met a guy from Germany who told me if I made it back, he would buy it for a good price. He lives relatively near Schäffer."

"How much?"

"A grand, OK."

"Aye, if I make it."

"Well, it's a case of paradise for a while or misery," I said.

“Can’t be worse than the dole £3.50 a week. The fucking salt mines would be better than that. When do we go?” he asked.

I told him we could get on the London train that night.

“I need to take my dog out for a walk before he forgets me," I said. “I’ll take the gun. See if I can get a pheasant. Let’s get the tickets at the station. We can book a seat in case it’s packed.”

“I am skint. Can you sub me a few quid?” I gave Ed a hundred.

“Don’t spend it all. You will need some cash to cross borders.” I paused. “My long hair and beard won’t go down well with the Gerrie’s,” I mused.

“Just put some cream on your face, and the cat will lick it off.” Ed chuckled at his joke while I ignored the jibe.

We bought the tickets which I showed to auld Berwick.

“What are you two up to, noo?" he asked. "Must be good if you have bought tickets. You usually just jump the train.”

“Only when we have no money. We are the victims of Maggie Thatcher, like the rest of the country. I see Tam’s at Dobbie’s joinery," I said. I tried them too, but no Masonic connections, so I was not considered.

“See you later,” he said.

“He is sound, but maybe he will tell Sis if he bumps into her. This place lives on gossip.”

“Well, if they think we are working in London, that will do,” I said.

I took the dog out for a long walk. We had to run for the train in the end. Jumped on just as it started moving. Arriving at King’s Cross early, we bought tickets to Amsterdam. There was time to spare, so we bought some breakfast: Two bacon rolls and a coffee each. We talked to a couple of whores trying to sell us a taste of paradise. "Let’s see your tits then,” I said. She looked around, then moved right in front of me, lifted her skirt and flashed her great black bushy muff right in my face. "You're a piebald," I said. I was giggling at the combination of blond hair and big black fanny. I couldn't get my head round that.

"A tenner," she said.

"Listen, it's free where we come from," I told her.

"Ten, and it's yours."

"I've no money; I spent my last on the rolls."

We were dropped like hot potatoes.

We crossed on the ferry and on again to Amsterdam.

"I thought it would take longer," said Ed.

"You slept a fair bit," I said.

OK, we will have a night in Amsterdam. We booked into the Torenzicht, put our bags in the room and carried all valuables with us. We were looking for a good kebab on the way up to Dam square when I remembered there was an Egyptian. We had two each, filled up a pita bread and topped it with mayo and pickles and loved every bite. We walked up to the pub on the corner near the Ousel. It was nice listening to the people from all over talking and laughing. This was a Dutch pub. We had a couple of beers and went for a walk. We went into a coffee shop, bought a bit of Moroccan and smoked a joint with a coffee.

Next morning, we got up and ate well. Drank tea, ate toast and jam, cereals, milk and orange juice. We headed for the station. I got one ticket to Darmstadt and one ticket to Frankfurt for me. I did not want Ed taken for my travelling companion in case I got pulled. He had short hair and looked straight, whereas I looked like I had just walked from Afghanistan with a camel.

The Germans got on the train and went through the compartments, took one look at me and asked how much money I had.

"Not much," I said. "I spent it in Amsterdam."

"Which is your bag?"

I pointed to the rack above my head. "Are you together?"

I said no. Then they asked Ed whether the bag was his, and he answered yes.

The train had stopped.

"Come," they said and took me off the train. They were very interested in my passport. My bag was emptied, and then they told me to fill it up again and said hurry. Two minutes later and I was still in Holland.

I got off the train and phoned George and asked him to send me a couple of hundred guilders or more if he could so I could get the next train. A friend of his arrived at the station about two hours later and gave me six hundred guilders so that I had the means to support myself. I got off at the next station the last train had stopped at.

No, Ed waiting for me. I wondered if he would have gone to the end of the ticket and waited there.

I phoned Sabina, one of the German girls that I had spent some time with in the summer. I told her I was on the way, and she did remember Ed.

When I got there, she was waiting and had met every train, but no Ed.

I went to her flat, and she made some food: very German sauerkraut and sausage. The music she played was all my music from Scotland that I had in my van. Plus some others. I was chuffed because she must have liked them – the Eagles, Hoyt Axton, Cories, Isla Sinclair Floyd, Neil Young. That was the music from my van. She and her sister had spent a couple of weeks travelling around the highlands with me. Yes, I listed them all, she said. About thirty taped records. I kissed her, and then we rolled about on the floor.

Next morning, I went to Dieburg to see if Ed was there. Schäffer was the only person Ed knew. I was a bit apprehensive. We had a difficult parting in Scotland. Instead of staying with me, Ed had asked them to drop me off and took them to his house.

His father was Polish and spoke German, and he had been conscripted into the German army during the war. His father had refused to have a German in the house. Schäffer had gone to St Andrew's and stayed in a guest house. He came around in the morning about to leave for Germany and told me of the events. He was not pleased. I had come out to say goodbye and brought out my copy of Lord of the Rings, which I had not read yet and gave it as a parting gift.

"Pah! A fairy tale," he scoffed and threw it in the glove compartment.

I walked into his farm. It was the holidays, and he had his girls who would be in college. They were babes when I knew them. They were up on some bales working together. I walked in, and Michael said, "Dennis!" He slid down to the ground and embraced me. "Can you stay for a while?" he asked. "You know that book you gave me. I was angry at Ed's father. It lay on my bookcase until my friend from Canada stayed a couple of years later. He saw it and read it. He couldn't put it down. It was a wonderful present. We have all read it now. Please stay!"

"I can't. I have to find Ed. Merry Christmas and tell your wife I still think of her cooking," I said, and then we departed.

"I am glad you didn't stay," said Sabina. Katherine is looking forward to seeing you. Come home with me?"

I had planned to be home by now. I had been a week in Germany. Still no word. I was worried about him. I left it until after Christmas with the German girls, which I enjoyed immensely.

The big celebration was on Christmas Eve. I liked the sugar cone over spiced wine, which they poured brandy over and set it alight. It burned and melted into a great bowl of red wine, which we drank with about a dozen of their friends.

I phoned Ed's mum. "Is Ed in?" I said again like I was just around the corner.

"What have you pair been up to?" she asked. "He is not telling me, but I can tell there is something."

"Put him on," I asked.

"Are you alright?" I asked. "Did you leave my bag somewhere?"

"No, it's here," he said.

"Where?"

"In my wardrobe."

"Fuck's sake, take it out, put it in a poly bag and bury it. See you in a couple of days."

I hung up. All was well, except that it was now devalued quite a bit. He was alright, and that was the main thing. I was so near Friedrichshafen that I couldn't resist a visit to Monika. However, she had a boyfriend who snarled some insults angrily from a distance. "Come a bit closer, you fucking Dummkopf!" I responded. "We will see what your shouting is all about."

She spoke to him across the way in German. "Come," she said, and we continued to the station to get a train to her mum's. "Such violence," she said. I quietly seethed but kept it to myself.

"I am going to Berlin University in the autumn," she told me. "I will go travelling first, though. Will you send me shillings when I am in Berlin?"

"Yes, remind me nearer the time." I had a couple of pounds' worth with me. I had discovered how to change shillings into marks in the vending machines. You could buy almost anything, but especially cigarettes. I spent a couple of days with Monika rekindling our friendship. Then I hitched up to Amsterdam then took a plane home. I collected the bag from Ed and brought it home too.

I phoned Thrust and asked him if he wanted some Afghani. "I will be in tomorrow if you come," he said.

"Can I come tonight?"

"OK, but you will have to be before midnight."

"I will chap your window if you want to sleep," he said.

"Aye, OK then, Bud."

A chap roused me at 2am Thrust and four of his pals.

I had one flying saucer out ready for them. I showed them with a flourish.

"What's that?" he asked.

It was the kind of hash I went for, right out of the great book of hashish. "Looks like Moroccan to me," he said. "It looks a bit like red Leb, right enough. How much is it?"

I told him sixty pounds an ounce. "Fuck off, that's ridiculous."

"Well, it is better than that Nepalese you had, and that was sixty quid."

"No, I am off," said Donald. "I can't afford that."

"Smoke half the amount, then," I said. "Naw, it's too rich for us."

"Here, Thrust here is an ounce. Take it away home and have a smoke of it, and you can pay for it if you change your mind."

"I wouldn't hold your breath," was his parting comment. I slept late, awoken by a returning Thrust.

"Menace, I rolled a joint at the foot of your road, and we got lost. Lost in Fife, I couldn't believe it," he said in amazement.

"We have never had better. Gordon was for coming right back. You have blown my mind this time. Put it about you got it in Glasgow, would you."

"Aye, what can you give me?"

"I will clean up."

I gave him a kilo and said come back when you need more. "How much is there?"

"A fair bit," I said.

"I won't be long. Will you come doon to me? Aye, I love your music, Lod. Tell Gruesome that I am asking for him."

"Aye, I will see him when I get back."

One unfortunate thing I had to deal with was the fact that Angie's brothers had been down-threatening people and kicked Ed's mum's door in. It was unfortunate that the ten days had turned into six weeks, and the following fiasco turned into even longer. When I did catch up with the little loudmouth, his sister had gone to Australia to live, so I gave him the money she had given me and told him it would have been a lot more if they hadn't taken the course of action they did.

This was the last I saw of them. Alan had stirred them up. All is fair in love and war.

The pot ran out after about three weeks. I went down to Methil for a smoke with Thrust. He was not in when I called. I walked round to Gruesome and had a joint with him and his brother. We listened to some sounds. I left and walked round to see Bob McCrindle.

"These chickens you sold us are all cockerels," Bob's wife said when she opened the door to me.

I saw them as I came in. Fearsome. There was one on each gate post, more like eagles than cockerels.

“There’s ten of them; look out the back,” she said. “Not one egg. You are a fucking menace right enough.”

They were in the back garden of a Council house.

“That’s unlucky,” I said, “but how can you tell when they just hatch?” I knew fine well the colour code. “Bob took all the yellow ones,” I said. “They are big, though. Rhode Island and Light Sussex crosses.”

Bob arrived while we were looking out the window. “Beauties, Bob.”

“Aye, they are just ready for the pot. I hope you have come to sell me a bit of that Afghani.”

“Who’s got it?” I asked, all innocent.

“Menace, it’s me you are talking to.”

“I have none left, but I am thinking of going back. Do you want to come with me?”

"Count me in,” he said.

“It’s not to here. It’s to Holland.”

“So much the better.”

“Alright,” I said. “I will come and get you when I am ready. Two or three weeks.”

“Skin up then. You must have a bit of it left,” he said. “Aye, I still have enough for a smoke.” I gave him a bit too. BMC’s bairns were plentiful and good fun.

“Make sure your passport is valid.”

“It is; see you soon,” I said. "I cannae wait, Menace,” he said, rubbing his hands.

I went around to Thrust and asked him to give a further half ounce to BMC.

"When will I get some more?" Thrust asked.

"When you have weighed me in for the last bit that I just gave you."

Then I continued: "I went up to Inverness and talked to Alan about the fact that Angie's brothers had caused me a bit of bother. I can only think that you must have had a hand in telling them where to go because they got information that only my friends have, and you are the only one who had the knowledge. What do you say about that?"

"We all thought you had ripped them off. I was with them and thought the same," said Alan.

"Alan, we are the same, you and me; I would have backed you up to the hilt."

"Dennis, I told them you were an honourable man and were probably busted or something."

"OK," I said, "I just wondered."

Alan said, "I heard you gave half an ounce of Afghani to let them taste what they could have had."

"I gave an ounce and their money back," I said. "We are talking about people who are kicking in friends' doors; lucky I didn't kick his teeth down his throat."

"That wee one is a nutter," said Alan.

"Alan, I am a warrior, not a bullshit artist like yourself," I said. "You are not bad at that either, Dennis."

"Alan, I left to get Afghani. That's where it comes from." He grinned. "Let's go up to Slapbuie."

Fine, we finished our beer and went to his cottage.

I met Alans' friend Stornoway John, who looked like a cat weasel with no teeth. Made me think of Para Handy's crew on the Vital Spark. He gave me his Edinburgh address.

I thought of Fat Bob. He was always asking me to do something with us.

I walked round to a phone box at the station to use the phone. George picked up. "Is fat Bob around?" I asked.

"Yes," replied George. "He has a painting job. I see him in the evening for beers or something else."

"Tell him I am over in a week or so if he wants to do something with us. I don't know what, but we will talk about it when I get there, OK?"

"See you then too."

I still had a bit of Afghan, so I had a smoke with Alan and his mum and dad. What a place to get high, on the croft, swimming in the pool. We were eyeing up the salmon in the dam around about Agas area. There were monsters there. One was about five feet long. "Look at the thickness of that one, Alan. That's the biggest by far that I have ever seen, and I worked a season on the Tay salmon fisheries. That's a world record."

"Aye, but we have nothing to catch the bugger with," said Alan. We left, probably both of us intending to return without the other.

"A swim in there with a harpoon gun would have done it," I said.

"Fine, if we had one."

The only time I had used one was in Mauritius once, and it would have done the job easily.

We went to Inverness, pubbing, and forgot about it. I slept in the van outside the town with the two German sisters, Sabina and Katherine, that I had met earlier. Getting sober for morning was a matter of intent, so we slept late, then made the journey south in good company.

I would buy some clothes, and my next journey would be to the sun. I still had Australia in my head, at least climate-wise. I did not want to settle back in Scotland; I enjoyed the freedom of the hippie life and meeting people. I got a couple of European contacts from George to deliver to from Amsterdam a while back. They bought in Holland but took delivery in their own land. I flew to Holland, relieved, and rested.

"The money sounds good and all cash, you say."

"It must be," he said, and told me tales of Greek and Pakistani, Indian, and other ships that sail the moment they are out of the dry dock, then the cheques will bounce.

"We have an agent whose job it is to collect the days' pay every day. We collect from him at the end of the job, then go on to the next one," he said.

"Can you get me on it?" I asked.

"Yes," he said, "if you can weld well enough."

I said I could. If I had a week to get my hand in, though, I thought the first day would probably do it.

I worked with three others.

"If you are good enough, it will be good for us," he said. "If not, you get fired." He wrote down his number and told me to call him. "I am a friend of George," he said. "Not when he is drunk, though." We laughed. "I have to go; see you when you get there."

"Cheers," I said, then went off to join George. I told him I wanted to go and get some sleep.

"Come on," he said. "Have one drink."

I agreed to have a Coke.

"Oh, come on, man. Have a beer. Or a whiskey. Wi tippeny we fear nae evil, wi usquebaugh we face the devil." George always remembered that toast from a visit to me in Scotland.

I spent a few years on and off working in Holland. It was hard, gruelling work, mostly overhead wet and miserable. The money was amazing. The other guys went to Spain four times a year. I went to Scotland to relax and see my mum and the family.

I had some real pantomimes in Dover, as the customs would pull me every time I went home for a break from honest toil. I noticed that all I had to do was be mildly threatening or loud and Weegie, and they would shut the other bays and come to help their colleagues.

Give a dog a bone.

I would come next time prepared with a couple of friends.

We loaded two cars in Holland to just blag it. "You better be right, Menace," I was told pointedly.

It was Bob and Mr T and me. Off we went, and they boarded right behind me. I was waved forwards, and then the others were waved another way. We met in the canteen as strangers eating.

"What happened?" they asked.

"I was the last car in that bay," I said.

"Just don't worry and remember to smile,".

I was late off and in a great queue of cars, so I couldn't see them. I passed the lot right up to before the immigration. The car at the passport control started moving, and I jumped the queue with perfect timing, showed my passport and was waved on.

Booth 1 was operating like clockwork. “Anything to declare, sir?”

“Aye. Every time I come through here, I have trouble with you. I am fed up with it. Come on, you big creep. Let’s see what you have got.” I started shaping up like Muhammad Ali.

Sure enough, the others closed the barriers and came to their friend’s rescue. I got madder and argued with them all about the fact that I got this shit every time I came through. The second car went by, and Mr T had a big smile watching as he drove out.

“Wait a minute, this is crazy," I said. “Let’s begin again. Let’s just be pleasant.”

Calm down, I said to myself.

“OK, ask me if I have something to declare.”

“Do you have anything to declare?” one of them said.

“In the words of Oscar Wilde, ‘Only my genius,' I said.

They pulled the car to bits. I asked for the man in charge. “Oh no, not you again,” he said.

I was taken to a room with two customs men who looked like clerks to me. I was pacing about when one of them said, “Why don’t you just sit down? This will take a while. If you don’t calm down, we will put you in handcuffs. If you don’t believe I’ve got them …,” He flashed the handcuffs at his back.

I could not believe this Boy Scout. I smiled, wondering what would happen as there was an open door beyond them. I felt confident that I could handcuff the pair of them and make a run for it. Instead, common sense prevailed. I asked for a cup of coffee. He obliged, and we all became friends and talked about my work in Holland. They saw Holland as Sodom and Gomorrah. Probably did not believe a word of the truth. Released, I drove the car round to the garage in the terminus and checked the oil. Good, just as it should be. The gear oil was missing. Nothing on the stick. I bought the amount I needed to fill it from empty and whoop-dee-doo. It was exactly the right amount. I'd read that right, but I had been here before.

At home, I had outgrown my hometown, but I was a country boy at heart, so I needed the fresh air. I was tempted to join a couple of woodcutters I knew to go contracting. Hard work was something I needed. The fresh air appealed to me, but the money welding in the shipyard also kept me focused. I hated the fumes, though.

I listened to some music with Thrust at Gruesome's house. We rolled around on the floor. I was laughing and smoking a bong they had brought out until I decided it was time to go. I wanted to head up to the Highlands and Snekie. I met Alan, had lunch in Castle Street and got drunk after. He was doing business with some folk he knew. "Let's head off and sober up for an evening session," he said.

"No, I am on holiday," I told him. "I am going back to Rotterdam in three days."

We slept until seven.

"Let's go to my mum and dad's. Plenty of scenery there for you," he said.

I agreed, and then Alan went to roll a joint.

"Got a pipe?" I asked.

"What have you got?" he wanted to know.

"Kashmir twist," I said, and he threw his Moroccan down with disgust and filled up a wee pipe. We bathed in the swimming pool. The water was cold. This was Scotland; the numbing effect of the cold water seemed to make it bearable. I soaped up, dived in for one last swim around the pool and got out. I felt exhilarated, as I always did when I walked back down the hill.

We ate bacon, eggs and mushrooms.

"These are bought eggs!" I remarked.

“Yes,” said Val. “We had a pine marten visit us. It took the lot and terrified the hens who have gone off the lay for nearly a week now. However, I did get two this morning. John had them for his breakfast,” she said.

John was a forester, and the croft a great place to bring up his children.

Being a bit of a forester myself, I enjoyed his stories.

I gave Alan a lift to Snekie on my way south again. I always felt great when I spent time here; the hills, the trees and the lochs gave me a great sense of being. I loved to drive to the strains of Dysart and Dundonald pipe band, Ry Cooder, the Doors, the Byrds, Pink Floyd and Janis Joplin, Arlo Guthrie, Snooks Eaglin and many other blues men and women. I listened to the Cories, the Ozark Mountain Dare Devils and many, many others.

The Vietnam War had ended, and Australia beckoned, but I had been banished for five years. I did not really want to be unacclimatized from Scotland either. BMC had persuaded me to lay on a couple of kilos of good Black and shot the crow with it to places unknown, owing me two grand. One of the friends let me know he was back and staying with his friend Ross. I picked up Stornoway John, and we went down to Ross’s pad in Largo.

Bob opened the door.

"Oh, here you are,” he said. “What a surprise. Come in,” he said with a big smile. “Where have you been?”

“Texas,” says Bob, who had developed a southern drawl after three weeks. “I just arrived home.”

“You owe me a couple of grand,” I said. He gave me it as though he were ready.

We were entertained by Bob’s tales of America and his stay in Texas.

“Did you play poker with them," I asked.

“Oh, aye, all the time.”

"Teach us how to play it," I said.

Bob explained seven-card stud to us. Five-card was the one I'd played a couple of times. It's simpler.

I said, "Are you in, Ross?"

"Aye, count me in."

I stripped the pack down to fives with two discards, which was right for four people. It meant the hands were much better and made a lively game. I played it most days in Long Bay jail in Aus. Kept me in tobacco. The game was exciting and brutal. The fifth hand came, and Stornaway John gave me a tap with his leg to tell me to get out. I stayed in. Ross asked to cover the pack.

"Fuck off; this is poker," I said. "You pack or brag. There is five grand on the table. I'm sure Bob will lend you some if you want to stay in."

He threw his cards down a full house. I kept it going a bit, then I decided it was too rich for me, with seven grand or so now on the table. I made a big thing of packing the winning hand.

"Let's see what you have got then," Ross said.

"It costs money to see me," I said and shuffled my cards into the pack.

I had nothing: two pairs.

Bob went another five hundred and smiled at Stornoway John, who saw him and paid the five hundred. BMC put down three jacks, then put down another with a big grin. "Sorry, John, but that's the way it goes," he said.

"Hang on!" Stornoway slapped them down: four queens. "Wow, you both beat me," I said. "I thought I packed the winning hand," I lied.

"Let's go to the Crusoe Hotel and get a drink," said John.

"Will they be open?" I asked.

"Aye, it's a hotel. Breakfast time."

"I sold your two keys in Texas," said Bob.

"Swapped it for a suitcase full of weed. So, I am pretty flush at the moment."

We had a few drinks in the Crusoe, then said farewell and headed along the coast to Anster and the Dreel Tavern. I went in, and the pub was just opened. We sat at the table with a drink each and laughed at the events of the last few hours. We split the proceeds from the card game. I was seven grand richer than when I had got up that morning and Stornoway five.

We played slot machines and Space Invaders. I knew one of the barmaids; the other I had met on a couple of occasions. A real beauty. That I could hardly take my eyes off when I saw her.

"Let's get out of here. I will be finished in half an hour," she said, and we left in her Fiat 500. Just as well. I was beyond driving.

After a long walk talking and holding hands, we were in Dunino, an ancient place of our Celtic ancestors. It was dark, dry and warm, midnight with a good bit of cloud cover. Our arms held each other, and we slid to the ground. Our passion matched each other's. We lay there panting and realised that time had gone by. I had the keys of my car in my pocket. John would be locked out of the pub and the car.

We returned to a mightily pissed-off John trying to force my car door. I unlocked it and drove home in silence. I was in heaven, and I intended to get back as soon as I could to the arms of the bonniest lass in the East Neuk.

"What's that song you are singing?" asked John. "I am trying to sleep."

"Pittenweem, Pittenweem, bonniest lass you've ever seen, guts the herrings on the quay, saves her kisses just for me," I sang out loudly.

Next morning, I awoke to nettle stings. My legs were stung to bits, and I had a hangover. It took two days until the itch from the nettles totally subsided.

I went down to Pittenweem to see Elaine, who was living with Lorna at the honeymoon hotel.

She opened the door with a big smile. My goodness, she was a beauty. I felt tongue-tied; she put her arms around me and kissed me on the lips. The great red beard made that the only safe place. We went in, and Lorna made some tea. I stayed there for a week.

“I am going to Greece next week with Lorna and Peter,” Elaine said.

“I can’t come. I have a trip to Holland for a bit of work planned around then.” I had said I’d do a job welding in the docks in Rotterdam in two days’ time. It was a great visit, and I had not been so in love in my life, where it was returned with interest. She would be gone for three weeks or so. What if? I thought. I reprimanded myself for this kind of thinking. What was it Rose had said? Too good looking for you, Dennis!

I worked around the clock for a few of the ten days of continuous hard going: Paid and finished.

I met John and BMC when they came over. We went up to Amsterdam in my car, into the Torenzicht for a kip. The rest of them left to tour the red-light district and have a spliff and a beer. Me? I was shattered and went to bed.

I woke in the morning when they knocked me up. “Wild night, was it?”

“What do you think, Menace?” BMC laughed. “I will lend you a hundred each, pocket money. I have a friend to see, then I will talk to you in the evening. Six o’clock in the bar. Make it your survival for about a week. I will get the grub.”

"Can we get the cash now?”

“No, in the morning. It’s not for having a piss-up.” Next morning, I went up to George.

He pressed the buzzer, invited me up, and we had coffee. “Did you speak to Fat Bob?” I asked.

“Yes, he is not at work this week. Waiting for your arrival.” He said he would call him on the phone, and then we drank coffee and smoked Georges's weed until Bob arrived.

“Hi Bob, how’s the painting?” I said. "Will the Guy give you a reference?”

“Give me the sack, more like,” he said. “He wanted me to work, but I came to see you. What is it that you are proposing?” he asked.

“Carry a bag from Delhi to right here," I said, smiling.

“What’s in it for me?”

“Five grand.”

“What’s in the bag?”

“Hash,” I said.

George said, “Don’t worry about him, Bob; he won’t touch anything else. He’s a hippie; they all hate hard drugs.”

“That’s a big share when you put in nothing," George said. “That’s right,” I said.

“OK, I am in. When?”

“Next week. How is your passport?”

“Two years to run,” Bob replied. “I have one problem. I have 450 quid’s worth of parking fines outstanding. Can I get an advance to square them? Or else I will get pulled when I come back.”

I agreed and gave it to him in sterling. I asked for his number; he said he didn’t have one.

"I can meet you here,” he said. “I see George every evening.”

“OK, well, I will see you Thursday morning 10 am. I plan to leave Friday.

Bring your passport. We will need it for the tickets."

I left them and walked back to the Torenzicht. We went shopping for the biggest rucksacks we could find, plus big, wide, padded sleeping bags and a few bits of jingling mountaineering gear and crampons. No ropes: they never bring ropes back, but ice axes were a must – to decorate the rucksacks. We got rolls of tape, scissors, Stanley knives and large freezer bags in copious amounts. Plus toilet paper in case we got the shits. Delhi belly is the worst dysentery imaginable; I remembered from my last trip to Manali with Ed.

"BMC, you keep Fat Bob's rucksack and gear for him, then I will know where it is," I said.

"No sweat, Menace."

Next morning, I went around the bucket shops looking for cheap flights.

Kuwait Airlines had the best one, which meant we went back through Kuwait. Fuck's sakes, they chop your hand off in the square there. Nobody in their right mind would carry a joint through there.

"How does it all work?" I asked the travel agent. "I would not like to go through customs in Kuwait. They would charge duty on booze."

"No, your luggage is checked right through," he said. "Yes, but can we be there for twenty-four hours?"

"Ah, yes, but you will be in transit."

"OK, hold the tickets for me," I said. He refused, saying I had to pay right then. I gave him my money and told him I would leave my passport with him until I returned with my two friends on Thursday morning.

I went back to the Torenzicht. John and Bob were getting pissed. I joined them, and when we lit up a joint, we were asked to leave. It was full of Hell's Angels from England, looking and acting like Vikings. The president was a cool dude, smarter than the rest, I would say. His bodyguard looked like a berserker.

“I could take that cunt out,” said BMC.

I didn’t doubt it after seeing him fighting miners in the bars of Methil and the rest of his escapades. Bob was a good six-four. I laughed as I remembered the time he had a whole tattie squad chasing him after their wages. Thrust had told me about this with much glee. Since they were after his blood. Aye, he was well made, with hands like shovels.

We wandered round the red light pretending to chat up the whores. “What you want, what you want?” they would ask.

“I am looking for the perfect woman," I replied. I had just met her in Pittenweem.

“I am perfect,” she said and flashed two beautiful well, shaped tits.

“I don’t think my mum would approve of you," I said.

“I approve, out the road, Menace,” said Bob.

“Get a grip; I’m hungry.”

We went for a shawarma.

“I’m going back there,” he said.

“Save your money,” I said. “Let’s get an early night!”

Back at the Torenzicht, the Hell’s Angels were a noisy bunch. They filled the bar. I smiled and nodded to the president and his monster. He nodded back. Upstairs we went to our rooms. The clothes we wore in India would be discarded. I didn’t want a pocket used for pot attracting a narcotics dog.

I lay back, thinking of anything I might need. Fat Bob asked where he could put his gear. “Go back and leave it with George,” I said.

“We are ready to ship out. We will meet you at Schiphol. This is your rucksack and sleeping bag – only one change of clothes with your underwear and wash bag. Nothing else.”

BMC said, “What a dope you have here, Menace!”

"Well, I hope not, or else he is on his own.”

The flight went via Kuwait, where we spent a few hours and then on to Bombay.

“That gives us an idea of how it will be on the way back,” I said.

“It’s just as you figured it would be, Menace, nothing to worry about.”

We came through passport control and went to a hotel by the airport that I had stayed in on the trip with Ed. The plane Ed and I were on had crash-landed, and we had spent three days in this hotel.

The café there did not open for a couple of hours. There were beach beds all around the pool. We lay there getting hot when the sun came in. I saw the café had opened. Stornoway was fast asleep, lying, sweating with a sheepskin jacket his mother had got him for Christmas. I stretched a foot and gave BMC a tap. He woke and looked round at me. I held a finger to my mouth for silence and pointed at John. We crept up and took and ended each and tipped him in the pool. John hit the water and came spluttering up to the edge. We were rolling around on our sun beds, giggling like the children we were.

We took a plane to Delhi and went to Mrs Calasoe's guest house. I got it from the book India on a Dollar a Day.

I wanted to meet some freaks, and that was where there were a lot of them I had read.

There were a couple of very tall Hooray Hendries, I thought, with the public-school accents they sported.

They were a couple but looked like brother and sister to me. They got talking to me and said they were selling some precious stones. I looked, and there were rubies and emeralds and cornflower sapphires. They looked pretty good, I said, but without testing them, I wouldn’t buy them.

I could have done a Mohs scale of hardness test on them with a diamond if I had one. I said they were very nice, but no, thank you.

We had a bit of a walk. Stornoway John had bought some samosas in a basket made from leaves. I pointed at an eagle bearing down on him from behind. "Duck!" I shouted. It closed its wings as it passed his ear, deftly lifting the samosas from the leaf bowl and flying up into a tree to feast. It was hilarious to watch John's distress. Our laughter was splitting our sides, but John did not see the funny side.

Two days had passed, and still, I had not cracked a light to any of them as to what our purpose there was. I liked one guy, Peter, who seemed a decent chap. He was playing his guitar. I joined him and listened for a while. He offered me the guitar. I played a few riffs then gave it back as he was much better than me. I went to our room, where BMC was sitting on his bed.

I told Bob I want to make friends with this guy and asked him to come with me. We went next door and skinned a joint, then handed it to Peter. He took it and gave me the guitar while he lit up. I handed the guitar to BMC, who went right into the tune of "Alice's Restaurant,"

Following it up with a couple of Neil Young numbers and a couple of others after that. We were all friends by this time, and Bob went into the full miner's club repertoire.

"Who are your friends?" I asked, and he told me that they were with the guy with the precious stones – which belonged to a Nepalese family. He had persuaded them to let him sell the stones on their behalf.

"I wouldn't trust him as far as I could throw him," I said. "Where do you live here?"

"Macleod Ganj," Peter said. "We are heading for Manali to buy some of the best hash". Manali is practically the next valley to Macleod Ganj," he told me.

"Tell me something," I asked. "Do you know a man who would manage to get me a few kilos of the best there is?"

He answered yes. "Come up with us and introduce me to this guy," he said. "My wife is about to have a baby, and I should return home soon. Can you leave without telling the rest what we are about?"

"We are leaving in the morning," I said.

"I have a taxi arranged 9.30 outside the Imperial Hotel. We will give you a lift," he said.

Peter was at the hotel when we got there. Our driver ushered us out to his taxi, and off we went. He would take us to Chandigarh, where we would change to a mountain driver.

He told us of the reason he was in Macleod Ganj was because they had had a child in Thailand that had died. There was a military hospital in Dharamshala, just down the mountain, about four miles from them. He had learned that a lot of Europeans that lived in India went there to have their children in case of complications. Macleod Ganj is a bit like Scotland, he said.

"Really," I remarked.

He went on to tell me it was founded by Macleod, at the time British Governor General of India. He found it too hot in Delhi, so he made off with the whole Indian government elephants and all up to where the temperature in summer was to his liking. Anyone going to New Delhi with urgent business for the government had to go another four hundred miles into the Himalayas.

Bizarre, but that was the British?" said peter.

"Yes, and now they are all on the dole in the UK. Can't pay the Yanks for the Second World War. The Royals and all the hangers-on require all the money, and they never ever give it when the country needs it. That's when the population of serfs get screwed even worse. Tories, They are all the same."

"There's some talk of oil in the North Sea," I said. "That will be a right royal fuck up if it happens."

"Doesn't seem to be much," he said. "All negative rumours surrounding it surely must be a very small strike."

We stopped at one place for a break and to relieve ourselves. I walked up to a wooden shelter where an old man was smoking a hookah. He nodded quite vigorously to me and offered me a smoke. It was green: fresh tobacco leaves, different to what I expected. I offered him some of my drums, and I put a little in his hookah. I gave him the rest of the packet. When I left, I could hear him coughing his guts up as I descended the wooden steps down to the road where the taxi driver was waiting impatiently.

On we went: Up and up and up with some down as well. McLeod Ganj, at 6,831 feet, is situated on the Dhauladhar range, where the Dalai Lama now lives.

We arrived at the Green Hotel. We got rooms and enjoyed the mountain air. The hotel was on the side of a precipice, and it was a long way to the bottom. They had a café that served egg drop soup, which I liked. We drank Chang in the evenings in a hut with a very old lady serving us bowls of liquor. It was milky, pleasant to drink, and after a few mugs, I felt pleasantly intoxicated.

On our second visit, all of us were present. The large Hooray Hendry from Delhi appeared and asked us if we would like some hashish.

"Depends on what it's like," I said. He replied that he would bring some in the morning. "It's Chamba, the best you will get." He had a young Indian chap who was his gofer.

I left and went to bed. I was asked very discreetly by the two Tibetan children whose father was in the army, based at Dharamshala. "Hang on," I said. They asked for two rupees for fireworks, for it was the Chinese New Year.

I had only a hundred rupee note. I went around the rest of them and collected rupees. I got a hundred, so I added my hundred and gave the kids two hundred rupees. They came back with a big box of fireworks and wanted to give them to me. I gave them a box of matches. I took a bunch of rockets; they were the only fireworks that fascinated me. I noticed the jumping jacks were much bigger than ours at home and quite painful if you didn't jump out of their way. They were letting them off all day. In the evening, we let off the rockets: Wheeeeeeeee! An erratic circle round and round, screaming upwards. Next one, I pointed out and downwards. It expired long before the bottom. The kids had a great time.

Next morning, I was up early and eating breakfast, hot tea and toast. I walked up the steps to the road. Stornoway and Fat Bob were heading past in a hurry.

"Where are you off to?" I asked.

"I have found a shop that has these thick Tibetan-style tunics with the brass button over that you were on about, Bob said.

I joined them, but they were on a mission to get there before me. I had a stinking cold; I was last in line as we went past an apothecary. That's a chemist, I thought. I went in, and there were two monks poring over some papers. There was a bar the whole length of the shop. Dark Himalayan pine, I thought. The wall behind was drawers about a foot by a foot. Six or more high the entire ten metres or so behind the bar. The tall monk, who was behind the bar, stood up and asked me, "What do you want?"

I said I had a very bad cold and could I get contact 400 or something to dry it up.

He looked bemused. The other small monk was still poring over the documents.

"I only have Tibetan medicine," he said.

"Can you give me something for my cold?" I asked.

He took some large black balls about the size of a halfpenny gobstopper and others like aniseed balls. Told me to take the big one at night and the small one on during the day.

"How do I take them? With water?"

"Yes, with water."

"How much?" I asked.

"Ten rupees," he said.

I put them in my pocket, paid him and left.

I had lost Stornoway and Fat Bob. I walked back to the Hotel. As I came down the steps, I met BMC.

"This is quite a place, isn't it," he said.

"That guy was in here with his wee Indian, and they had a bit of hash. He is trying to sell to you, so he is coming back. I don't think they like tokers here at the hotel."

"I am going to ask Peter what he wants," I said. "He better not turn out to be the guy we are waiting for."

"Don't worry, the guy is Australian," I said.

I walked up to the cottage through pines and rhododendrons that went straight up to the sky. The cottage could have been in Scotland with a wee byre in it.

There is not so many like that in Scotland. The English are selling their tenement hovels and coming up here to buy all the cottages. They spend a grand on renovations and join the community councils, and they are the new middle class in their heads. All the country people are put in council schemes when the farmers sell their cottages to them.

Some change for these country people, but most of the older ones died of misery. Gone are the days when you kept the cottage after retirement.

When we arrived at Peter's, he welcomed us and invited us in to meet his daughter. His wife held up the baby. Bob started singing, "If you're happy in your nappy, clap your hands", and picked up the baby expertly.

"I was wondering what that big guy from Mrs Calasoes is wanting," I said. "He is offering us hash now. Have you said anything to him?"

"No," said Peter, be careful of him.

"We are, but he has a wee Indian watching us all the time."

We had some tea, and sure enough, he arrived. As he was coming up the path, Peter told me urgently that we should leave and talk somewhere else. He had friends of his wife's coming and did not want him coming there either. "You are welcome here any time," he added.

When I was about halfway down the hill, the wee Indian appeared. "Where are you going now? I want to show you some hashish! Come up to Peter's," he said.

"He has just had a baby," I replied. Let's leave them in peace. Let's see what you've got."

He produced a tola of good-looking hand-rubbed hash. We sat down on a fallen tree and rolled a joint. I smelled it, and it seemed fine. "Nice smell," I said. I smoked it but did not get very stoned. "This is not what I came all this way to get," I said. "It is shit."

"That's Chamba!" he replied. "It's the best."

"We will go to Manali. We know what good hashish is. Before you try to sell us what we don't want.

"I can pick up better than that at the shore head any day," BMC said disgustedly.

We went for a walk with him tagging along. "Look, we don't want it," I said.

"I went all the way to Chamba to get you the best," he kept on. "We are away for a walk," BMC said. "Stop following us about."

Passing the apothecary, I peeled off from the rest and went in. The two monks were in the same position as before, one squatting on a high stool and the large one at the other side of the counter.

"I tried to mix this with water, and it would not mix," I told them. "It floated on top, and I could not even dent them with my teeth. I will give you them back. Do not worry about the ten rupees. Give them to someone who knows something about Tibetan medicine," I said. I added by the time I mixed that with water, the cold would be gone.

The other smaller monk with glasses burst into loud and cheerful laughter at this revelation. At that moment, I recognised him: it was the Dalai Lama. I said goodbye to them and left.

Peter came down in the evening and told us his friend would be there in the morning.

"Can he come here tonight?" we asked.

"No, my wife would like to cook you a meal to celebrate your bringing me here at the right time. I walked in the door as she was giving birth, and that's a big deal, Dennis."

"OK," I agreed. "I will see you for dinner."

Next morning the hotel owner stopped me on my way out to see Peter's friend.

"Can you take five films to the west with you to develop for us?" he asked.

I said would love to but that I was not going directly back.

I pointed to a chap walking up the road. "See that guy there? He is a middle-class American. I would say he would be a sure bet to do this."

He was a bit angry and waved it aside. "We have been waiting for your aura for some time," he said. Not taking no for an answer, he handed me the films. I put them in my parka and zipped the pocket.

Peter's friend turned out to be an also-Peter. Aussie Pete, he had come through the mountains from Kashmir. I had neither the time nor the inclination to walk through the mountains, I told him. We wanted to leave by taxi. It would be one to Jammu, then a Kashmiri – the mountains there go over ten thousand feet, so you need a Kashmiri driver.

"Arrange it and haggle a good price and get them to come to the Green Hotel tomorrow morning," he said. "Ask the guy in the hotel to do it. He will get you a good price, you are in his hotel. I am going to sleep. Come up for me to my cottage when it is time to leave. It's that one." He pointed to it.

I went back and asked the hotel owner to arrange me a taxi with good tyres in the morning to Jammu.

We got up at the crack of dawn. I walked up the hill to the cottage with John and BMC.

Fat Bob came too.

We went to the cottage, and there were four girls there.

"Pete will be here shortly," said one.

"I will make you some chai."

Coming up the hill towards us was the Hooray Hendry. His Indian boy was saying to me that we must buy from him. He had gone to some trouble to get us good hash. He stayed about thirty yards down the hill. "I want a quarter of what you're carrying if you want to get out of this valley," he shouted.

"Nobody blackmails me!" shouted BMC. He then picked up a boulder and threw it at him. It went about ten yards down the steep hill, then bounced a long way down the hill. Stornoway chucked a smaller one: a better shot. He jumped to safety. I picked one up, and we stoned him until he had retreated entirely.

While this was going on, one of the girls pleaded to me: "We have to live here!"

"He is a bully," another of them said.

"OK, I'll turn the other cheek next time," I replied with a smile.

BMC made a fist. "He's getting that if I see him again!"

Our friend appeared, picked up his bag and came down to the hotel with us.

The taxi was waiting. We were putting our bags in the boot when the hotel people came out and stood us in a line and put prayer scarves round our necks, saying prayers. I nodded my thanks. I was quite taken with it, and I had not expected this ceremony. I've seen it on Everest expeditions, so I felt like Chris Bonington. Of course, we were carrying the spools.

The journey to Jammu was quite nice. Jammu seemed a bit down at the heel, but we did not see very much of it, to be fair. I went to buy some walnuts when the biggest rat I have ever seen came out of the sack I was about to pick my walnuts from and climbed up the vendor's canopy onto the roof. It was the size of a cat and slow-moving with no fear. I turned on my heel and gave the walnuts a miss. There was one stall where a vendor was squeezing sugar cane for the juice in a glass.

I thought I would try it and was surprised that it did not seem overly sweet. We got in the new taxi with a Kashmiri driver and headed up the mountains to the Vale of Kashmir. The pass coming into Srinagar was at ten thousand feet. We arrived at Dal Lake and stayed on a houseboat in Happy Valley.

Aussie Pete went off for an hour, then came back with a Kashmir twist. It was twisted in the ears of corn and still had a strip of straw caught in some of them. He told us this was the best quality twist. I warmed a bit and filled a pipe. The aroma was simply amazing. It slowly crept over you and filled the senses with well-being. We all smiled at each other. This was what we had come for.

So far, so good.

Peter said it was forty dollars a kilo and we could pay when we collected it the next day. This would sell for £1,000 a pound at home. It would go for three and a half times that in some of the better places in Europe. That was just where we were going to try to get to. We were ready to pay for it when the guy we were staying with stepped in and said, bring it here first, then pay!

I agreed this was the way I wanted it too. Pete had arrived. It was after dark; we paid the guy with him.

This happened seamlessly. It arrived in plastic sacks. The twists were about 150 to 170 mm long. I paid $2 800, and Aussie Pete took a sack to his room on the boat. I guess he made about twenty kilos from the deal. That was just fine by me. He went off to get it.

"I could have got you that," said the boat owner.

"OK, see you next time," I said. I told him I wanted to go shopping, so he took me out in a shikara. We went around warehouses of beautiful walnut furniture, carpets everywhere. There was jewellery and precious stones. There were furs, and I saw snow leopard skins, so I did not go any further along that route. I who always wanted a Russian wolf jacket, a poacher since my teens. Seeing snow leopard skins hanging there did something inside me.

The papier-mâché was amazing too: colourful, psychedelic even. The walnut furniture was truly great. I puzzled how I could haul the trees to the coast – Bombay, that would be. The trucks I saw driven by Sikhs mostly did not look like they would carry enough. My plan to try to ship some walnut from the Himalayas to Europe was interrupted.

Then we went to work on the hash. First, I had to make it smaller, Cutting them in half except for a few and bagging them in a plastic freezer bag, getting as much air out as possible. I took the houseboat owner aside and asked him to watch everything I did. We went to another room and added another sealed bag. They were about the size of a football. We changed our clothes and washed and had a swim in the lake before donning the change of clothes we had brought with us. I put our jeans and stuff in a bag and said to our host to give them to poor people at the prayers.

He smiled at that. I explained that it was done so that a dog would not smell it in our bag. We then taped them all round into balls. We filled the rucksacks with the sleeping bags round the outside for padding. All three were filled to the brim, then the cord tied tight padlocked and closed. We tied crampons on along with our ice axes, all looking a bit worn now.

We flew to Bombay, then on to Kuwait, sat around the airport for four hours then on to the Amsterdam flight. We were all a lot happier sitting in our respective seats. All except fat Bob, who was sitting sweating profusely as fat folk do. I went over to see him after BMC pointed it out to me.

"Are you OK?" I asked.

"Not really," he said.

Sweaty and shiny bright pink, he asked, "Remember the four fifty you gave me for the fines."

"Yeah?"

"Well, I never paid them."

"What happened to the £450?"

"I pissed it against the wall with George," he said. What a useless ratbag, I thought privately.

"OK," I said. "Just pick up my bag, and I will take yours. Don't worry anymore; stop worrying, go and wash and stop sweating. It's over for you. Just keep clear of us. I will take your bag."

At the arrivals, Fat Bob was in front of us all at the pass control. He handed his passport, and he got it handed back. He spoke to the immigration man, who took his passport back and looked in the computer. He told him to stand to the side while he controlled the rest of the people on the flight.

I thought he pointed the fines out to the controller we all passed through. At the baggage, I could see Fat Bob staring down at me from on high. My small rucksack came first, then John's. He immediately went through. Then BMC. Fat Bob's bag came last. I hoisted it on my shoulder, picked my bag up and walked out. Just like we were invisible.

We went to my car, drove into Amsterdam and checked into the Krasnapolsky Hotel in Dam square. We showered and slept for a few hours. I drove out to the countryside and stashed the hash in a wood. I checked us out and sent them back to the Torenzicht, for which I received groans. I telephoned George. "Hey, man, how goes it?" he asked.

I told him it had gone well.

"I have Bob here. He is looking for some money from you."

"What for?" I said.

"I carried the bag, not him."

I heard Fat Bob in the background priming him.

"Ah, man, he should get something," George pleaded on his behalf.

I replied, "He should be hiding his head in shame."

"He carried the bag through India," George argued.

"OK, then I have a thousand rupees. He can have that."

"Aw man, come on."

"I took the bag, not him. George, he was a bottle job, a fat liar. OK, ask him how much he is going to pay me. Come on, fat man, how much will you give me? I did the job. Sweating and shitting himself on the plane then told me he had wasted the money I gave him to pay his parking dues," I told George.

"Tell him to fuck off."

"Oh, man!" George groaned.

"I will think about it," I said with no commitment.

We headed home. I wanted a week's rest. Then I would see what to do with it. I did not like the idea of selling the goods in Holland or the UK.

About a week later, Fat Bob arrived at my door. "I need the money to get a car," he whined. "Can I leave my stuff here?"

"No, I don't want to know you, Bob. Look, get in the car."

He put his bag in the back seat, and I drove him to a garage. Bought him a car, threw his bag in the back, handed him fifty quid for petrol and said, "Don't call me; I'll call you."

"When?"

"Never!" I said and drove away.

I went back to Holland for work. I always think I'm better doing a bit of physical graft.

A couple of weeks later, after a straight seven days of twelve-hour shifts, I was knackered. I went for a couple of shawarmas.

I hate them normally, but the Dutch ones are amazing, with the bowl of pickles and the mayonnaise. I saw two people pass the window and rushed out. "Sherrie!" I called. She turned around, and her beau with her, and we were smiling at each other.

"Fancy meeting you here," I said and greeted him. They told me where they were staying. I would come along later.

"I am in the Torenzicht. A creature of habit," I said.

"Then I will come to you later," Tony said.

"I will be out till nine-thirty, so make it about ten tomorrow morning," I said.

"OK, see you later," They said, and then they left me to continue munching the kebabs.

I met Tony on the steps of the hotel. I called to him, and we slowly walked along the canal chatting, watching a car get lifted out of the canal by a small crane.

"Dirty water," he said. I agreed. We held our breath as long as we could.

"Have you got anything going here," he asked.

"Yeah, I am working with a team of welders," I said.

"What about a hash"? I have a friend who is wanting some delivered." I replied.

"How much?" I asked.

"Five grand, I believe."

"I can promise you this, Tony, mess him around, and you will be unhappy for a long time."

"I won't," he said.

We agreed to meet at the kebab place the next evening at eight.

"One thing Tony," I said, "be ready to start your journey immediately."

"Where to?"

"Tell you when he tells me, which will be when I see you next. Be ready to roll."

I asked off work a bit early, got back at six and had a little sleep before the alarm woke me at eight. I got up, washed and shaved, then went around to the kebab place. Tony and Sherrie were waiting there.

“What are you getting from this?” I asked her.

“Nothing, I am just enjoying the trip,” she answered.

Tony looked uncomfortable.

“OK, well, I don’t work like this, Tony. She gets half, or it’s not happening.”

“OK, but I would have given her something,” he said.

"Half is two and a half grand,” I said.

She smiled at me approvingly.

"Remember, smile and talk to each other when you are going through. Tell a joke, laugh and show your gums like you are enjoying a private moment. You are very happy to be here, kind of thing. No kissing the ground, be cool, don’t try to flatter them – it looks suspicious,” he said. They both smiled at this.

I would take a couple of holdalls to a place to wait.

"If anybody comes, act like lovers who have just had it off,” he said.

I drove a kilometre to the stash and went into the young wood. To my astonishment, in one of the stashes, the balls were above the ground. I looked around: nothing had been disturbed. They shone out in the moonlight, all very spooky. I filled the holdalls, reading the numbers as I went. Twenty-one one-kilo balls. There must have been rain to do this, I thought. The ground was super soft, and it was quite dry. The other places were undisturbed, so I didn’t go near them. I filled the bags, retreated and put the bags in the boot. “Here is the address in Bern,” I said. “He will give you the cash. Come back to me here, and we will sort out the money, OK?”

“Any problem, phone me on this number. It’s the Torenzicht. I will be there at eight sharp each evening. Keep trying if it’s engaged." I handed him a map with the route marked with some dots in red, others with black that meant nothing, but I didn’t want it to look like a direct route either.

"I expect you to phone me tomorrow unless you are broken down."

"Right, I am off."

"Hang on, here is the map. The red dots are the route to take; the other dots mean nothing. Bye for now."

I drove back – high on adrenaline since my spooky surprise in the wood.

It made my hair stand on end.

Finding somewhere nice to eat was not so easy. Amsterdam was the same, back now in familiar territory. My attention was taken up by a hooker with a Bouvier, a big chap with the devil ears. I don't like clipped ears, but it sure looks dramatic. I gently rubbed his curly black forehead, and he responded well.

"Is he for sale?" I asked jokingly.

"No, but you can pet this for fifty guilders," she replied.

I laughed, she smiled.

"I am looking for food," I said. "I am starving."

"Can't help you."

She went off, mincing along in hot pants and a T-shirt with that beautiful dog. He had a nice nature. So did she, for that matter.

The kebab place was open. I had my usual two with a can of cassis and turned in. Six in the morning was not far away, and I needed sleep after an eventful day.

Next day I finished at six and got back to the Torenzicht for eight. The phone rang. "Tony, for you, do you want it?" asked the hotelier. I took the phone. "Hi, how goes it?"

"We have done our part; he won't give the money."

“OK, come back here. I will sort you out. Don’t worry, I trust them.

There must be a good reason."

“He said it’s not what was supposed to happen,”

I smiled. "Don’t worry, see you soon.”

Picking up the cash was a carrot. It had gone exactly as planned; I did not really trust Tony out of my sight, so to speak. To be fair, he was untested. They arrived at eight, asked for me, and I paid them separately. Tony was a bit sour about it all. I wonder what his private thoughts really were.

Ike arrived from Bern a week later and squared me up.

“Your man wanted the goods back when I wouldn’t pay,” he said. “I told him to phone you. He borrowed a thousand German marks. I have taken it out already.”

"Was the girl with him?”

“I didn’t see a girl,” he said.

I nodded and smiled at my forethought on this one.

Seven

I spent the next two years working hard until I could take it no more. "Hi George, hoe gaat het met u, Meneer?" I asked George one day.

"Speak English; your Dutch is shit when you are sober," he said.

"I will never get better when you all revert to English as soon as I try. It's a conspiracy, so you can talk behind our backs and right in front our faces!" I told him.

"Are you still working with them?" he asked.

I told him I had resigned. He said he had thought I would have visited him more since I had been in Holland a long time.

"I worked and slept the whole time I have been here George," I said.

"But now, I will never weld again. I am broken; I will retire to Scotland. I can afford some small cottage somewhere."

I went out on the town with George. He had the ability to start a conversation with all the people in a bar, speaking in many languages: French, German, English, Arabic, Russian, and some more that I did not hear probably. "Can you speak Chinese?" I asked him, and he made an obscene gesture with his tongue in his cheek and his hands giving a blow job. "Me love you long time, Meneer," he said and laughed at his own joke, "ha, ha, ha."

He was greeted by many people as the bar filled up. Quite an eye-opener to get drunk with George.

I awoke on his couch. He was frying bacon and eggs. He greeted me with a "Goede morgen, Meneer," and went off in a spate of Dutch.

"Speak English, George; I can't understand Dutch," I said.

"No, you were quite fluent in the bar arguing with everybody. Frightened the shit out of English Sidney, called him a sash, Saha, what was it?"

"Sassenach!"

"Ja, he left the bar. Fucking sassenach, you called him. What does it mean?"

"It means 'southern' in Gaelic."

"It seemed more to me; you are a joker, Scotch."

"Scottish," I said. "I have a hangover and am leaving a bit later. Can I relax?"

"Eat. You will be better after this."

"George, this is too much for two people," I said. "Eat what you want."

We ate in silence – polished off the lot. A cup of coffee and a joint. "First smoke of hashish I had in eighteen months, George."

"I don't believe you," he said.

"It's true, though," I said.

"I will come and visit you in Scotland in the summer," he said, and I answered "that would be nice".

I arrived home, drove down to the harbour and along to the East Sands, then back. St Andrew's never changes much. I saw a chance to buy a couple of lobsters as a box came off one of the wee boats, into the car, and home to my aunties. It was still early, but people were moving now.

"Oh, you are back. It's been a while, said, my auntie.

"Would you like a lobster?" I asked.

"No, I have fish from the fishman, and I am having fish and chips for tea. I am not that fond of crabs, not like you."

We smiled. "I will have a wee sleep on the couch, then I will cook them when I get up."

"I am off," she said. "Mind and open a window. Leave it open if you go, for the cat."

I slept until two, longer than I meant to. I ate the lobsters with Ed, who was now working on a farm nearby. It was Sunday, his day off. I rolled a joint told him stories about Holland.

"Are you going back?" he asked.

"No, not for a while. I was in a job for a couple of years, twelve-hour shifts."

He asked how much you get for that, and I told him between fifteen hundred pounds and two grand a stint.

"A week?" exclaimed Ed.

"It doesn't work like that. We are up against the clock. They pay a big rent while we are working. The stints can be a week or less; they can be ten days. You don't know. The only thing that is sure is that it will be hard going."

We went over to Dundee, and I caught up with the news of the Village.

Erskine's was now Henderson's. Jock McLaren still had his dog. "We should have stayed in Australia," Ed said.

"I left you there. Why did you come back?"

"Ach, it was Zambezi's fault," Ed said. "He is in Canada now, and he will be doing OK after the education he got with us."

I spent an hour sitting on a dyke in the Village. Then I went into Cupar to find somewhere to live. There were a few places I liked. One took my fancy: it was not too expensive. A wee bit of land to plant a garden and some ruins. I bought it and started to tear all the old smelly carpets out. We took the windows out and took them back to the bare wood. I loved Woodmill. It was just what I wanted. I enquired about the adjoining sixty-five acres and would get it in a little over a year. They could not sell anything until then because of a sale on the stock exchange. It would all go on tax if he sold now. Next year, he said. I could wait, though.

My thoughts were to have a spring-calving herd of cows to produce a farmhouse cheddar. The big old mill building would be fine for keeping the cheeses till mature, in the manner of Cheddar Gorge. The walls were three-foot thick stone, three storeys, then I would build a modern high-tech purpose building. If the profits were as I surmised, it was a good plan, and I was quite confident. There would be grants to help me start up, I imagined.

I busied myself making the house right, doing the garden work and with visits to the coast. I needed to clear my head about my situation.

The phone rang. It was Tarquin.

I told him, "I went around by your cottage. There was new people."

"It was a short let," he said, "I am living down in Hampshire now."

"Where is that?"

"England."

"What are you doing?"

"Playing in the band. We have been doing gigs in Holland."

"Is it a jazz band?"

"No rock and roll, worst luck."

I asked where he was staying, and he said Hobbs Towers. "Sounds grand. I would like to visit you."

"Come on down."

"I miss your music, you and Steve. How is he?"

"He is well. Out shopping now."

"I might drop in. Have you an address?"

"Yes, it's Ayton Village. Phone when you get here and I will guide you in."

"OK, see you one day in the not-so-distant future."

"OK, may the force be with you."

"OK, goodbye the noo, Tarquin."

I told my friend, John, I had just been on the phone with Tarquin, so he asked where he was.

"Down in England," I said. "Let's visit them?"

I left the following day with Elaine. We reached Alton, and I rang from a phone box and was directed to the house. Fergus opened the door.

"Hi, are you here too?" I exclaimed.

"Yes, for a bit."

Fergus was an old friend, a great sculptor and artist. I always fancied a bit of his work.

"I hope you are working and not just lazing around," I said.

"I have not got a commission now, but I have just finished one that took me much longer than I thought."

"I liked the idea of the seven-foot demon climbing up to the roof of my house," I said.

He laughed. "Commission me then."

"OK, I will be in touch. And I will do the cooking."

"I don't doubt it. I love your cooking, Dennis."

"This is Elaine," I said, "the love of my life," and introduced her.

Later in the evening, Tarquin arrived with Steve, Rosie and Suzie. We ate some fish and chips they had brought; they were a bit less than hot. "There is one friend not here; you can have his room," they said.

Steve Maguire started to play his guitar, and he sounded a bit different. He switched to a keyboard; Tarquin came in with his Strat. That's the new one. Tarquin said. I could see that Tarquin and Steve were at odds with the tune. Tarquin looked like packing it in. I rolled a joint, and that got them going into Blues.

Next day we got up quite late, and they were all gone. "The girls are at college here," Sarah, Fergus's girlfriend, explained.

I asked if there was any food, and she answered there wasn't much, just some cereal. "I am going shopping," I said. "Back in an hour."

I left my car with them, and we took a lift home with John. We detected a sound from the gearbox, and I wanted it looked at before deciding whether it was serious or not before a long journey home.

I worked in the garden and did local stuff. Tony said he had heard the noise in my car but said it was not the gearbox: a rattle rather than a knock. He had borrowed it a couple of times; he said he thought it was the plate under all Saabs, something that just allowed a bit of a rattle but wasn't serious. I intended to pick it up before too long.

We came to pick up my car weeks later. Finding the battery flat, I went for a walk to see if I could locate the nearest garage. Nothing seemed apparent here in Ayton. However, I was advised Basingstoke was the nearest likely place. On the way back, there were three cars parked next door but outside their drives. This did not strike me as quite right. I looked inside, and under the seat, I saw a blue police radio, then I checked the next one. The same, and the third one equally menacing. I went into the house, and they were all there.

"Listen, what have you been up to?" I asked.

"Playing gigs in Holland," Steve said.

"Have you been up to a bit of smuggling too?"

"Only a little."

"Well, you are under surveillance. I am out of here in the morning. "They are just CBs. They are Everyday police radios. I can tell you that for nothing," Tarquin said, "you are paranoid."

"What have I got to be paranoid about?" I asked. "I cleaned up my act years ago."

We went to bed and slept a very uncomfortable night.

I said to Steve, "Listen, I don't say this lightly, but I am out of here tomorrow."

"Fat Bob asked for a lift with us," he told me, and I said no, to which Bob asked if someone could hire a car for him then. He really needed to see his mum, he said. She was ill, and he just had to get to Doncaster and back. Stornoway said no, but then Elaine said she would do it. Steve gave her a lift to Basingstoke, where she hired a car.

"She better not end up with a bill, fat man," I said.

"I only need it for a week till mine is fixed," Bob said.

"Why did you do that, Elaine?" I asked.

"Oh, he seemed stuck," she said.

"That's because he is stupid. Let's get out of here. I will come or else send someone for my car," I said as I left.

John, Elaine, and I headed north, home to Scotland in John's car.

I would try to stay put in Scotland. The farm project was high on my list of a permanent place to put my nomadic roots down. Getting the sixty-five acres adjoining me was the key. Waiting until it was secured was not really something I was good at, and I thought of how working another year welding would have been good for cash, but I did not enjoy it one bit. I could not see an opening. Forestry was a dead loss. The outlay in machinery would not justify a year, even if I sold it later. Too short a time to make any more than a break-even scenario as far as I could see.

No, it would not do. I thought of importing something like clothes from India. Suits, jeans, shirts, etcetera. Filling a container with carpets was another consideration. I did one trial at this previously; I had made a profit all right, but I felt I was lucky. My feet itched to go somewhere else.

Africa, perhaps, looking for an opportunity. Timber perhaps. Logistics bothered me: where there was nice timber at a good price, it was landlocked mostly. Rhodesia, for instance. I could get a boatload to Portugal. Then onwards to a market. A boatload of copper was another thought, but I doubted I could put the finance together even for Rhodesian copper via Malawi.

I found St Andrew's my favourite thinking spot. I went to cafés mostly, and I rarely went near pubs. I met two Rhodesian sisters, McLeod's. They had travelled to Portugal on a ship carrying illegal copper from Rhodesia due to the sanctions. They had found their way to Scotland to visit their grandfather's country. I wondered if the sanctions were still going.

I sat at the harbour in St Andrew's with a sandwich and a Coke, thinking what my next move would be. The copper stuck in my would-be entrepreneur's mind. I hired a boat from Danny and rowed out of the harbour for some exercise. It always helped me think. Hard graft does that too. It must be the peasant in me. I inspected a couple of crates full of crabs and lobsters floating in their boxes, turned, then headed back to the harbour. The tide had turned, and the rowing got harder.

"Where are you working now?" Danny asked once I had rowed in.

“Don’t use bad language,” I scolded.

He chuckled.

We had worked together one winter shovelling stones and sand into a concrete mixer at the local RAF base, an experience I did not intend to repeat. Super fitness was important, though. I thought spell woodcutting would do that too.

I would pick up the car, perhaps; Elaine would drive it back. I put it out of my mind.

We spent the night together in the Honeymoon Hotel, as Lorna’s house, where Elaine lived, was known by the locals.

We dropped in to see Tony at Sherrie’s farmhouse, but he was not there. We were having tea when the door went. It was the police.

“Elaine Macintyre,” a policeman said, “I have a warrant for your arrest.”

"What for?" she asked.

“It’s from Basingstoke police.”

They took her away. I was surprised and devastated. She has done nothing wrong in her life. What were they thinking? Fuck, she hired a car for that Fat Bob, I thought. He couldn’t pass himself off as a woman that was for sure. He must have told them she had hired it for him. What a rat!

I was very upset, hanging around waiting for word of her release. A week later, I was arrested by the local police and taken to the plane with a certain Sergeant Brian Steers, a real shithead who had been harassing me for years after hearing that I had been caught in Aus. I figured he was so stupid, I would just laugh at him. After all, that was about seven years before.

Steers gloated. “Ah, they will verbal you down there,” he said. “I’ve asked that Inspector Piper to fit you up. You are fucked.”

"You are sick; go and get help, you daft cunt," I said to him. Steers was beyond help, I thought. He was giggling and laughing hysterically about the English verbal evidence, where it only takes a couple of bent coppers to convict anybody.

"I wish we had the verbal here. You would have been jailed years ago," said Steers. "They know how to treat shits like you down there," he continued. I was taken onto the plane by a uniformed copper.

"Take the handcuffs off him," he was told by the stewardess. "I can't; he's dangerous."

"Take them off, or you can't come on board," she said.

"He must be scared that I'll roll a joint," I said to her. I got a big smile for that crack.

London airport and I was handed over to Detective Inspector Piper, a very small fat guy for a policeman, I thought, at about five foot two, I'd say. We arrived at Basingstoke police station. I was put in a cell. He came back with a mug of tea. I drank the tea. Half an hour later, he came with another detective constable, again very small in stature. "Why am I here?" I asked him.

"I want to ask you some questions."

"I want to know why I am here."

Piper was behind a desk with a chair at the other side. "Sit down and stop pacing about," he said.

"Some people have told me you are involved in selling hashish."

"Who?" I said.

"Quite a few people."

"Who?"

"Fergus Mercer."

"That's a lie. Fergus is a sculptor and a friend of mine. He would never tell a lie like that."

"He has given me a long statement about you. 'Dennis is the kingpin.'" He pointed to the middle of the page.

"That's lies."

"Why would he lie? He is not lying. You are lying. He says it here. 'Dennis is the kingpin.'"

"Let me see it then."

"Answer the question!"

I jumped over the desk, snatched the papers out of his hand and held him in the corner with my body. The other guy did not move from the door, despite Piper looking at him with a fearful expression. I handed the papers back to Piper, smiling and sat down. I had read the page.

"So, you are the liar," I said.

Piper rushed past his constable at the door, and then uniformed cops grabbed me and put me in a cell and slammed the door. A few hours later, some extremely large detectives from Southampton arrived. The door opened, and one of them said, "Get up."

"Come back later," I said. "I am sleepy."

"Get on your feet and follow me."

I slammed the door shut behind him. Two came in now.

"We want to ask you some questions."

"I don't want to answer them," I said. "Look, you have come to kick the shit out of me. Let's just get going."

"We don't do that," he said. "Come on, we will have a cup of tea. I have just driven up from Southampton."

"My dad was in Southampton during the war. Pompey and Southampton in the marines," I said.

I followed them into a room. There were two more giants.

"His dad was down our way during the war," he said. "Marines."

"What did he do in the war?"

"Sunk the Bismarck. He was on the Rodney," I said.

"Have you been in the army?"

"Aye, Scots guards," I said, referring to my distinguished military career. "Where did you train?"

"Pirbright," I said.

"I was at Pirbright," one said. "Coldstreams?" I asked. "Welsh guards," he said.

"You will be a good singer then," I said.

"We were hoping you would be a good singer," he said. "Well, you are out of luck," I said.

One of them wrote in his notebook questions of no real consequence. "Your car is in a garage at the house in Ayton."

"Yes, I left it there, I said and planned to recover it with a mechanic friend."

"What's wrong with it?"

"A bit of a rattle and a whine from the gearbox."

"Can it be driven?"

"Yes, but I want it checked before I attempt five hundred miles home in it."

"Is that why I am here? You got my name by running a car number?"

"You've got previous form," he said.

"I have had enough of this. I want a solicitor right now," I said and went mute for half an hour.

"Put him back in a cell," I heard someone say.

I was left for two days. This was the three slates all over again, I feared.

I was taken to court, then remanded to Winchester prison.

"Hello Steve, what are you doing here?" I said to Steve on seeing him in Winchester.

"Got nicked with six kilos of hash from Holland."

"I told you that you were under surveillance."

"Tarquin thought you were paranoid; he said they were CBs."

From what I could make out, Fat Bob got pulled in a car leaving the country with some kilos as well.

"The car Elaine had hired for him to go home to see his mum?"

"I think so."

"Fuck's sake, what a mess. This Inspector Piper is a can of worms, a lying bastard. Told me he is going to fit me up. Said Brian Steers doesn't like you, and I don't like you either. I am going to fit you up."

"Who is Brian Steers?"

"Oh, he is a cop from Kirkaldy; harassed me a couple of times because he had read, I had a record."

"What record?"

"Oh, I broke three slates," I said. Steve looked confused. "Oh, I was in jail for five years in Australia, as well."

"What was that like?"

"Sunny!" I replied.

"Sounds like I am up shit creek here, treated like the IRA terrorists that are blowing the shit out of them at the moment. They certainly don't like anybody from anywhere else."

It was getting my back up. I was doing Richard Hittleman's famous yoga routine that my friend Rose had sent me, and it was keeping my inner calm intact. Mostly, anyway. There were moments.

The Argentine war was going full blast. I saw Thatcher on TV, waving in her silks to the boys who would die for her, no doubt. After watching it on TV on the hour out of the cell, that vision with the silk summer dress and the handkerchief waving to the ships stayed with me. I was let out of the cell to go to see a movie: Finian's something. I came out of the cell and shouted full blast, "UP THE ARGIES!"

Five minutes later, four guards came in my cell, threw their hats on the bed and then I smiled and said, "Come on, then. Four little squaddies. You are too small for the army. Let's see what you've got."

I was doing a good impersonation of Bruce Lee at the back of the cell, kicking the wall a foot above their heads. They picked up their hats and left. I missed the movie.

I was let out for tea.

"How was *Finian's Wake,* then?" I asked Steve. "It was *Finian's Rainbow,*" he corrected. "It's on my list of things never to do again. Psychologically softening us up, I think."

A bit of this prison was full of IRA terrorists, he told me. They moved them around the country in the dispersal system. Category A prisoners, Steve added.

Twelve months I had been on remand and was at a court appearance before a judge from Liverpool. They were asking for another three months' remand. He said, "I have read the papers of this case, and I don't like what I see. I would not give any of these people more than nine months if I found them guilty." He emphasised the if.

I said to the others: John and Elaine, "If we plead guilty now, we are home tomorrow. The fact we are innocent doesn't matter; he sees what they are up to and is trying to help us." It took a few seconds to try to persuade the others to plead guilty when they were innocent: it just didn't happen.

They had to be put on trial in one month's time or released, the judge ruled.

Six weeks later, after thirteen months in all, they put us on trial.

I had opted for a barrister rather than a Queen's Counsel. "I will let you lead this without a QC," he said, "if you promise to fight tooth and nail."

"We are innocent," I said. "I know I have a few previous convictions, but that seems to mean you are meat for any bent copper's career."

"I will fight," he said.

"OK, you are senior counsel. I have seen you in the papers prosecuting.

I hope you can see it the way it is."

"I will fight, don't worry."

"I see you do the Telegraph crossword in three minutes," I said.

"I have practised," he laughed.

The judge was Sir John Sheldon, chief judge of the Western circuit. A hanging judge by all accounts. He started by throwing a childish tantrum straight away, waving his arms around. "I am here to do sentencing to reduce the backlog, not a trial," he said.

"This is a trial, my lord," the prosecutor, Mr De Navarro, said.

"I am not here to do a trial. What good will a trial do them I have made me mind up?"

"We are fucked. This cunt is senile," I said.

I waved at my barrister. He did not move until the judge stopped ranting.

"Object to him," I said.

"On what grounds?"

"Prejudice."

"You have never met him in your life."

"OK. I had a homosexual relationship with him," I said.

"I am not saying that," he said.

"Look, he is quite clearly senile."

"That's not so unusual," Mr Mitchell said, "He is 86."

As though that excused him.

It took quite them some time to calm him down, then they swore the jury in.

With Sheldon, we were going to be slaughtered, jury or not. We were charged with the import, export and supply of cannabis. It's a nurse with Valium they need for that old cunt, I thought.

"This is a farce," said John in my ear. Elaine looked bewildered. It was clear that we were going to be railroaded. We had to hope the jury would see what was going on.

They are famous the world over. Impose English law, then they control everything. Tyrants led by mad people that would be better exterminated if only the French revolution had been expanded. It was the right time for it, and the British monarchy and aristocracy was just as bad as the French, who had come up with the right cure in France.

They were terrified it would spread in this country. The First World War was their answer to ridding themselves of all the unhappy workers. They still don't admit any of their political ploys that involve mass extermination. We were in a bad situation here, and anything we could do or say would only make it worse.

They went through the police evidence where they had an expert witness who made sure that it was, in fact, cannabis resin they had on the table and said that from his vast experience in the field that it was the type from Morocco.

"That's a fucking lie for a start," Stornoway whispered to me. "Anybody who has smoked a joint could tell that the hash is Gold Lebanese. Cotton sacks half a kilo each."

"I wouldn't contradict them," I whispered back.

There was a car in the garage: a red car. They all said the same thing. It looked fast. It was registered in my name.

Each one of them said that. Trying to add mystery to the red car, which was, in fact, a brown car.

A Danish policeman came next; he told me off in a real bad light. He said that he had arrested me in Copenhagen, and someone else had let us go before he came back on duty again.

He told me what he would do to me with a machine gun, he said and held his hands up as though he had one pointed at the jury. He even cocked it. The jury looked shocked; mouths opened. I tried to attract the attention of the messenger, who gave me a dirty look and ignored me.

Psst! I hissed loudly. Everyone turned.

"Come here," I ordered him, and I handed him a piece of paper. "Give this to Mr Mitchell, and don't ignore me again, do your job." I met his eyes until he lowered his head. Mr Mitchell read it, turned to me, and smiled. He straightened his face, turned back, and asked his first question.

"Did Mr Anderson have a machine gun?" he asked most astonished.

"No."

"What?"

"You have lied to us!" Mr Mitchell said.

"He said what he would do to us with a machine gun." He blubbered. Was he joking?

"Come on," Sheldon interrupted to save the day, "he's an honest policeman doing his duty. Let's move on."

"Thank you, officer."

Oh, Sheldon liked a lying copper, all right.

I would have liked to have been able to question that Danish policeman further. This was sprung on me with no notice. He was lying. What had taken place was we were asking for a friend at Copenhagen airport, whom we were waiting for. He came and said he was not there. I said, "I saw you taking him away; why"?

He lost his cool, pushed me against a metal door and stuck his gun in my neck.

"Take it out of my face, or I will take it from you and beat the shit out of you, fucking twat!"

I was bending his arm so that the gun did not point at me. When a whole bunch of his fellows arrived, he said, "I am arresting you all."

Elaine, John and Duncan stood watching it all. There were four of us, and we were marched into a police station where a guy was lying on a bed in a cell behind several inches of glass. We did not look at him, and he gave no sign of recognition. We were put in cells and taken to court and interrogated in the middle of the night. We went in one after the other.

"You don't like the police, Mr Scottish man," one of the plainclothes policemen said.

"No, I don't, in fact." I could eat my breakfast, and I wouldn't miss a sip of tea. I gestured with an imaginary cup while gesturing, shooting them all with a machine gun.

He smiled, and that was it. Then it was my turn to explain myself to a judge.

They asked why we were there, and when we had all given the same story of meeting a friend, the lady judge said, "Well, they all give the same story; I can't argue with that. Release them." We left the court and Denmark at four in the morning.

Apparently, that bad attitude, lying twat must have got talking to them and got himself into this case with no evidence against us to give them. What he did have was a bad dislike of me and an attitude not befitting any kind of fairness.

The prosecutor asked him, "Are you familiar with hashish like this?"

"Yes, it's very common. It is Lebanese hashish," he said.

Six kilos of Lebanese hash that we had no idea where it came from, it sat there for all to see. Yet we were all asked to look at it, handle it, making our denial of ever having seen it before weakening simply by it being there. Of course, Steve had told us he had been busted with some from Amsterdam. Showing it to us and making us hold it up and look at it was all to make an impression on the jury.

Just standing in the dock is enough to convict anyone, I realised.

Especially with a swine like Sheldon in charge.

This dragged on day after day and seemed to be going nowhere when Piper went through the ritual of identifying the hashish again as Moroccan.

Then the questioning went to me. He was uncooperative but admitted the car at the address in Alton was his.

“What colour was it?”

“Red," he said.

"Mr Mitchel?”

“No questions, my lord.”

“I should think you should ask some questions," Sheldon said.

“He has made no allegations against my client, my lord.”

“Your client!" Sheldon snorted.

I was going to get it if found guilty.

Other police all tried to shit on me in some way, but with nothing to say. Mr Mitchell shot them down.

My bank manager, Mr Mackenzie, was sworn in. He referred to the judge as "your honour” in the Scottish manner.

The clerk of the court was on his feet. “You will call the trial judge ‘my lord’,” he commanded loudly. Sheldon smiled madly in approval.

“Your bank in Newburgh, it will be a small bank, is it?” Sheldon sneered.

“Yes, it’s a small bank where I live. I have an office in the back. I am the regional manager for Fife and Perthshire," he said.

“I see you gave him a ten-thousand-pound overdraft. Didn’t you check him out?" he scolded.

"Yes, and he was good for it, so I gave it to him."

"How did you check him out?"

"He invited me round to his house to see the carpets he was dealing in."

"Did you go?"

"Yes," Mackenzie answered.

"How many carpets were there?" asked Sheldon.

"They were hung all-round the walls, and there were piles on the floor."

"How high were the piles?"

"That high, your honour," he said and held his hand out over the side of the witness box, indicating about six feet.

Sheldon was visibly fuming. He did not come out of this exchange well. "You must call Sir John Sheldon 'my lord'," the clerk cried.

"I have only one lord, and it's not him!" Mr Mackenzie stated clearly. I felt proud of my countryman.

Sheldon, not managing to bully, hung his head and passed the matter back to the prosecutor, Mr De Navarro.

"Thank you, my lord, no questions." Clearly didn't want to tangle with an honest man with all his faculties and of his standing, a regional manager of the Royal Bank of Scotland.

Next came the accountant from the bank, whom I had never met. He snivelled and tried to help in any way he could but could merely say he did not like me. That was it.

Next was Detective Sergeant Brian Steers, a Scottish policeman, a man who had tried to harass me on a couple of occasions. He came and said, "I have known the accused for a number of years." As far as he was concerned, I was a dealer in hashish. Oh, Sir John liked him, shouting like a nutter in the witness box when put under pressure.

What he should have said that apart from a couple of harassments, fuelled by his small-minded view of my having a previous conviction in Aus, he knew nothing about me. His harassment was nothing other than an ailing career in hope. He would get a letter of commendation from Piper. Sergeant Steers would then be Inspector Steers on lies shortly. The hard life of a country policeman in Scotland seeking a pension hike.

They spooked the jury by telling them to watch out in case they were followed from the court. Sure, enough, it paid dividends when one woman thought she may have been followed home. She said she had a feeling. No, she was not approached. Someone else saw the same person on the bus two days running.

I was the first to give my own testimony. I told them that other than leaving my car there because of a knocking noise and coming to check it, I had done nothing there. I told that I had never seen the hashish on the table. I agreed that Fat Bob had asked Elaine to hire a car for him to drive to see his sick mother.

"Did she do this?"

"I don't know," I said.

"I left shortly after. I advised her to have nothing to do with him. He is not a friend of mine."

I agreed I had a carpet-selling business that I had been trying to get off the ground for some time. They showed a carpet a Persian silk carpet that I had brought from a Tibetan seller while in the MacLeod gang. I had bought many others in Turkey, Iran, Afghanistan, and many others through a Turkish dealer who shipped them to me in Holland. I would send him five thousand, and he would send them to his agent for me to pick up. I had a receipt book of the sales I had made.

Mr De Navarro said, “Here is a receipt to someone called Moron. Funny name to have.”

I asked to see it, and he handed me the book.

“Andrew Moran. It's Irish, Mr de Navarro. I remember him very well. You seem to have become less than honest," I said to him.

He blushed slightly.

Sheldon burst right in: “You are on trial here, not the prosecutor.”

“How can you administer justice with your foot in the scales?” I asked Sheldon coldly.

“Answer the questions the prosecutor puts to you," Sheldon said.

“Mr Anderson, you and Miss Macintyre arrived at Heathrow in August last year."

“Yes, I noticed you had picked the tickets up in my house. Please try not to pretend it’s a piece of high-tech police work. You know nothing more than the tickets exist. Unless you are trying to imply the hashish on the table may have circumnavigated the globe.”

"Is there something we should know?"

"Yes, it has been already stated that that hash has nothing to do with me. The only reason I am here is because of that nasty little policeman there.” I pointed to a brightly blushing Piper.

He got a fright when he lied to me. I snatched the papers, read them, handed them back to him and said, "I told you. You are the liar. ‘I’ll fit you up’ was his response. That is why I am here and why no one has said that the hash belongs to us. You can throw shit and hope that some it sticks.”

“Answer the questions!” roared Sheldon

"These are my answers. Do you want me to give your answers to the questions?"

"I'll send you downstairs for contempt of court in a minute."

"Carry on, Mr De Navarro."

After much looking at papers, he said, "No more questions."

Next came Elaine.

"You were on that trip to India with Mr Anderson?"

"Yes."

"You stayed in a hotel in London while Mr Anderson went to Scotland. Why did he go there?"

"He had an ear infection and didn't fancy an Indian hospital, so he went home."

"He could have gone to a London hospital, could he not? He went to a Scottish hospital. Then came back for you."

"Yes."

"Did Mr Anderson pay for the hotel?"

"Yes."

"Why would he do that?"

She put her hand on her hip and did a Mae West impersonation: "Gentleman wants to pay for my room? That's OK."

I was stunned. Why had she done that? He asked about lending Bob a hired car.

Her counsel objected that she was not charged with car offences. "It goes to a motive," said Sheldon.

She said he needed a car because of his ailing mother.

Antwerp was mentioned, and Fat Bob's QC was nudged awake.

"We are trying to agree whether Antwerp is in Holland or Belgium."

"It's in Belgium," he declared. "My regiment liberated them during the war," he said. They had all had their little laugh in joke. Sheldon looked pleased.

Bob's defender went back to sleep, and it droned on like this. The jury went out and came back with guilty on all counts.

"I'll hear mitigations from the guilty pleas," Sheldon said. And three other people came into the dock to join us.

Steve Maguire's counsel said, "My client pleads guilty and wants it made clear the hash is his, and he has no knowledge about these other people in the dock. These people have been found guilty by the jury." Sheldon cried.

"You can mitigate the blame," said Sheldon, his voice strained in a choking manner.

"My client will not have this, I am afraid."

The two girls, also pleading guilty, said the same.

The jury was putting their hands up, saying they had made a mistake. Sheldon looked like he was having heart failure. He turned to the jury white-faced and said, "This has been a long and difficult trial. You are all exempt from jury service for life!"

The dirty bastard, I thought. We came back for sentencing.

Sheldon was full of claret by the colour of his face – all that was missing was the black cap.

"Stand for sentencing."

I looked at the jury, who could not meet my eye.

"As far as I can see, you have been at this continually since your release from prison in Australia. I can't get your money, but I can send you to prison for a long time. Seven years!" he thundered. "Stanners, you are his trusty lieutenant. Four years! Macintyre. You were an important cog in the wheel. Three years! Steve Maguire: Two years!"

Rosie and Susie each got three months' time served on remand.

"Take them away," he said.

I hung on to Elaine until we were pulled away.

This was a bad outcome. Seven years was a long time, and I could not see the end of this tunnel; I lay in my cell thinking.

Fat Bob was next door to us. He got himself removed, and I could not get near him. Then he disappeared, off to some other better prison, no doubt. I had some questions for him to answer, but it was not to be. The gutless piece of shit.

I spent a few months in Winchester, then I was sent to Longlarten, an A-category top-security prison. I took up oil painting, got some books on technique and took to oils like a duck to water. I wanted to do figure painting, but the chances of getting a nude female model here was unlikely. I started with a seascape; next was a bunch of flowers: hollyhocks by Jan de Fries. I drew a grid, and by the time I had drawn the flowers, I was obsessed. Then came the Flat Ford mill. I had a little help from a fellow prisoner who put me right with glazes. He helped me a lot.

Johnnie Walker was making marquetry with Martin Brady, who ignored me when I asked.

"What is that?" I asked.

"It's the red fist of Ulster." Johnny said.

"What does it mean? I have not seen it before."

"He's a proddy," Martin hissed.

"No, I'm not," I said.

"What are you then?"

"A Buddhist," I said.

"He's a proddy. I can smell them. Where are you from, Angus?" Johnnie asked.

"Near Dundee," I said. "My name's Dennis."

There was the beginning of a friendship.

Johnnie called me Angus on account of my beard, and it stuck. I had a budgie called Joey that played football with ping pong balls. I worked in an engineering shop, welding. I sat my City and Guilds and got top marks. Painting became my thing, and I used wood from pallets and canvas that was made there.

There were a few good artists there, much better than I could ever aspire to. One made paintings of famous sea battles that I really liked. I took pottery classes and made a Turkish coffee pot with chillum in the top. It was taken by the teacher to get fired at the college. He got bust when he came back in. I was before the governor, who asked, "What is that?"

"It's a Turkish coffee pot," I said.

"Yes, it says that on it. You are not getting that in here," he said, "you can hand it out at the next visit."

After about a year, I had a visit from the junior barrister who told me my leave to appeal had not been granted.

I wasn't asking for leave to appeal. I was appealing!

"Look," he said, "Sir John Sheldon has died. I am not besmirching the good name of Sir John Sheldon, knighted by the Queen, for you." He turned on his heel and left the room before I recovered. The PO took me back to my cell.

"Was that your lawyer?" Johnnie Walker asked me.

"Yes."

"Is he any good?"

"No, I am appealing. He just said to me Sir John Fucking Sheldon Knighted by the Queen had died. He's not besmirching his good name for me. The cunt was senile. I'm telling you, like a baby in a pram, the way he carried on. What good will a jury do you if the judge had already made his mind up before the trial even got going?"

Once my humour returned, I was crossing over to the wings cooking kitchen.

"Come here, Angus," Johnnie said, "and I will show you something."

I followed him to his room in the spur. Longlarten was H blocks, same as the May's. He took out some pictures of himself with a big cheery smile. "These were taken when I was arrested, before questioning. This was after." He had only one tooth left.

"How did that happen?"

"We were a concrete crew on our way home for the break from our job in Birmingham, playing cards and having a drink on the train as you do. We were arrested and questioned.

"They stuck guns down my throat and all. Tried to make me sign a statement they had written for the Birmingham bombings.

"We took them to court and won the case for damages, for injuries and received ten thousand, eight thousand and seven thousand pounds compensation, respectively, for injuries received during questioning.

"I swear to you, I am completely innocent, Angus! Lord Denning, the master of the rolls, said about us that it was much better when we had the hanging – we would all have been hanged, then there would not be any of this fuss."

Johnnie Walker was one of the Birmingham Six who were also protesting their innocence.

Jesus and I thought I was hard done by. "Take them to the European court of human rights," he said. I was running, training for a marathon, and I had only a month left till the race. I was doing twelve-mile runs three days a week. It was only Saturday that I could try for practice for a long run. I got to eighteen miles and hit the wall. The Irish boy I was running with kept me going the last mile. On the day, a big Rastafarian from London's spaghetti siege was first, in two hours and ten minutes. We were the last survivors, coming in at four hours. I asked Rasta his time, and he told me. "Oh, you had an easy run. It took me four hours!" There was lots of support, with people shouting encouragement from the windows. It was like being in Ireland for a morning. Could have been the Dublin marathon.

One morning at seven, there was a rush heading for the TV room. Something had happened. I heard people asking: "Did they get Thatcher?" and "Shush."

The news reader said that the Brighton Hotel, where the Tory conference had been going on, had been bombed and showed smoke going up in the air. There was great cheering and dancing. I found myself cheering like Scotland had scored a goal.

I was painting one day, and the PO asked, "What's a rose like you doing among all these thorns? Did you upset someone or do something to get sent here?"

"I was a bit vocal when I was on remand."

"What was your case?

"Six kilos of hash that was not mine," I said.

He called me to his office and asked me where I would like to go. "I can send you to a semi-open prison," he said.

"The nearest to Scotland," I said. "Durham, maybe."

"Durham is worse than this. You get ghosted in the evenings from the dispersal system."

I ended up in Portland Bill, the most southerly part of England. I had figured I had about a year and a half, and they would have to let me go. Cannabis cases were let out after a third of the sentence, but with Leon Brittan as Home Secretary and Thatcher at the top, they stopped all parole for drug cases. The Tories always have to hang higher than all the rest. Parole was now only the last eight months and then only for surveillance purposes.

John got parole after two years. Elaine was refused.

I wrote to the Home Secretary and said that she was refused and that she was someone of previous good character who is refused. Yet the one who was deemed second in command got parole. "I urge you to check this out. She is from a good family and will never offend again," I wrote. I don't know if it helped, but she got parole. I felt relieved knowing that she was out.

A bit more painting, then one day, I was put in a van and shipped. I landed in the Vern on Portland Bill. So much for being near Scotland. The Vern was a strange place for me. There was a good running track, and my distance had come down to six miles, which was an easy run to keep my constitution working well. I had a painting from an auction catalogue that had a pair of lurchers lying on the ground in front of a garron with a deer saddle and a stag on its back beside a ruined cottage with heather thatch, a crack running down the wall, and a woman filling a very ornate whiskey glass. I loved this painting. It was about six feet by four, and the grey sky was right out of Landseer. For some reason, I could not bring myself to do the last little bit to finish it. A week longer in

Longlarten, and it would have been finished too. I think I was beginning to see light at the end of the tunnel.

I went into the dining room and looked for a table. I sat down at one with only one guy. The rest were full. I ate my tea of chips and something. After one year, I went to Leyhill to finish off. There was a horticultural course and a big market garden, an arboretum and a big house that was bought from the loot from the opium wars. This had been the estate of the Earl Ducie, a bought title. Finally, I was sent to Preston, from where I was allowed home. I had to get a job in a week or go back into Preston prison. I was in the hostel there, and time was running out on getting a job. I went into the prison after trying the council. No good.

There was a guy in there from a stove-enamelling plant. I said, "Are you needing any more guys? I am a wood cutter, but I can work anybody you have under the table."

"It's heavy lifting," he said.

"I am made for this," I said.

The warden tried to get me inside.

"Not him," he said,

"I want him". He said

He had lived and worked in Rhodesia.

I talked to him about Africa and mentioned a guy I had worked with in Australia, Neil Mackinnon. He had a safari outfit in Tanganyika when it became Tanzania. He had gone to the British consul and asked for a British passport through his grandfather, who had come from the Isle of Skye. "I'll give you a B-class passport," said the consul. He tried the Australian consul, and he had asked him what kind of passport he would get. The Australian consul said. "The same bloody passport as anybody else, mate, so I came here". He said. Neil also showed me how to cook a steak on a campfire with a stick like a willow bent over the fire with the weight of the steak: eland and kudu and sable. There is nothing like it.

After a couple of days, he came into the prison hostel and said to the warden, who did not like me, "Have you any more like him? I'll have a few more if I can."

We were working twelve-hour night shifts, and we had to hand our wages in at the gate, and it went into our property. We were allowed pocket money. The guards on the gate were mightily pissed off, moaning loudly about the wages we were earning. They seemed to be of the opinion we should be behind a door.

I went home for my first visit and was picked up at the station in Edinburgh. This was difficult for both of us. We made a brave face of it, and Ellie, as she was being called now and I were as much an entity as we had always been. This was not going to be easy for either of us. The next leave, I went to my house and went up to Perth to see a friend who had four salmon in his bath that he had caught the night before, so I bought three of them and took them back with me as we were allowed to bring back some food. I had promised the boss at work a fish as I had been telling tales of fishing. The two smaller ones I gave to the cook for the boys, and a twenty-two pounder I gave to the boss on the Monday. He was a right happy chap. Work went well there, and just before I left for my next leave, the cook told me, "Don't bring any back with you; he is going to ring the police; he thinks they are poached. I heard him talking in his office to another of his mates. He is dying to put a spoke in your wheel."

Next leave, I got two fish, and I picked up a permit from Lady Moncrief for £4.50. When I got back, I gave them to the cook, who put them in the fridge.

"Anderson, did you bring fish back?"

"Yes," I said.

He smiled. "I think you are poaching these fish." He put his hand meaningfully on the telephone.

“OK, before you embarrass yourself, here’s the permit.” I took it from my wallet, handed it to him and smiled.

“How many does this allow you to catch?”

"As many as you can,” I said.

I held my hand out, and he gave it back.

When the cook asked what happened, I told him he asked to see my permit, so I showed him it. I told the cook how to make salmon kedgeree for the next evening meal. We all dined well for about a week.

The work in the stove enamelling plant was hard. It was just after Chernobyl, and we were doing the bearers for Swedish generators to sit on in fallout shelters.

Time stops for no man.

Ellie picked me up at the gate and drove me home. Home was in a mess. There was a lot to do. Maggie and the kids had moved – she had a barman as a lover. The kids had a new dad that they knew better than me.

I had a bit of adjusting to do. I cleaned the place up with a friend, Anne, who helped. I filled a Hoover bag in the living room from the ceiling, and the light, dust and spider’s webs.

It took all that summer and most of the winter to get the place looking a bit better. I got the veggie patch done and planted in the spring. I tried to get a job in Holland on the docks, but none of the people I knew were there anymore. I spoke to one who was a foreman, and he asked me for my tickets. I didn’t have my City and Guilds with me since I was expecting the same gang to be there. He said there was nothing doing – he had a list of hopefuls. I tried George, but he could not reach any of them.

I went back to Scotland wishing I had not gone because I spent money I could have used for better things.

I went around to the bank and asked the manager, who was the accountant from the trial. I felt like dragging him off his seat and beating the shit out of him. I controlled myself and said, "Good morning; I would like to ask for an overdraft to renovate my property."

“You will be getting no overdraft from this bank,” he said. "You owe fifteen thousand pounds."

“No, I don’t,” I said, “I owe you nothing,” I bit my lip.

“Yes, you do; Stanners borrowed it. He has not paid a penny back.”

“Why did you lend him that?”

“His name is on the deeds.” He sat there with a disgusting square ring with a half-inch square of diamonds. Any smaller, they would be dust. He reminded me of flash Harry in St Trinian’s Carry-On films, and it was not just his hairline moustache on his lip; it was his whole bearing. A used car salesman.

I walked out of the bank.

When I saw John, I asked him about it.

“My names on the deed,” he said.

"Yes, but I paid it for you, and you didn’t come up with any money. The agreement was it would go back into my name. You owe me fifteen thousand pounds."

“Get out of my house before I kick the shit out of you!” He left with his girlfriend. Tuned up a fortnight later to collect his giro. This turned into a regular visit.

One friend came by and said, “Dennis, we are off to Spain, wind surfing; get yourself down to Tarifa. We will be there in two weeks. You will find us in the Rio Roja to get some sun and surf. This is a bad scene here.”

"OK, meet you there in a week then."

I went to Amsterdam and spoke to a friend about a kilo of hashish I had left with him. "I sold it," he said, "and put the money in my bank in case you came back."

He laughed. "I will get it tomorrow, but tonight we go out and have a nice meal and get drunk. You can stay here."

"What about your wife and the kid?" I asked him.

"Three kids now, but she lives with a woman now. The kids like it – they have two mums and a dad."

"When did this happen?"

"Officially, about a year ago, but we are all friends. I am living with a German girl. She is a super secretary. Spending a few days in Germany visiting her mother now, but it is a Dutch company she works for, so she will be back in two days' time."

"Where will we eat?" he asked. I fancied a shawarma, I told him. "We can do better than that," he said, "and it's on me; I am not going Dutch on you, so don't worry."

We ate steak followed by pears in red wine in a Dutch restaurant. The hangover I had when I woke about ten the next morning made me look at the bacon and eggs and smile. "Melk or sinaasappelsap?"

"Do you have melk?" I asked. He opened the fridge. "Hey man, is that kultuurmelk? May I have some?"

He gave me the carton and glass and said help yourself. I did, and my hangover abated with the last egg and bacon mouthful.

"Here's your geld."

I counted it.

"That's two thousand, no... just under three thousand pounds. Do you remember the lawyer in Germany you gave me to sell it to? Yes, well, that turned out quite lucrative. He is a good friend of mine now. I hope you don't need him back."

"No, that's the last thing I need. I am going straight; I have had enough," I said. "I was framed on that English case. I am going down to Spain to get some sun with two friends from Scotland."

I drove through Germany, Switzerland and France, crossed the border at Marseilles and was almost torn apart by some machine-gun-toting border police. They went over the car I had and the ten thousand guilders in my back pocket. My wallet was on the dash. To my great relief, I was told to go. I got in the car, and I must have driven twenty kilometres before I noticed that all the windows were still down and that it was getting very cool. In the morning, it was sunny and warm in the sun.

The tourists were not here yet, and it was strange to drive down all these miles and miles of empty places with palm trees and no people. I drove back onto the main drag when I saw a couple of hitchhikers. I couldn't believe my luck, someone to talk to. When I pulled up, I was greeted with the words "fuckie fuckie, suckie suckie". They were a Moroccan and a Spanish whore. "Sorry, I said I thought you were hitchhiking." They were quite pleasant despite my obvious embarrassment. I could only think of the AIDS epidemic that the world was dealing with. It must be hard to make a living for them, I thought.

At Tarifa, I met my friends and had three months there getting fit. They were windsurfing eight hours a day which was a lot. The windsurfing champions from Europe and Scandinavia were all there. I watched them do double loops and incredible jumps.

I tried surfing with a small wind surfing board, but no good. I ran along the beach in my bare feet. Mostly I took on the cooking. The fish market was great, and fish was high on my list of good things. One lot was a kilo of little square fish that could be grilled like sardines, the vendor assured me. They turned out to be delicious. Some had red stripes and some black. "Fuck this," Alan exploded, "we are not eating goldfish."

“They are really nice. Don’t judge until you have tried them," I said. I ended up eating most of them. Alan scoffed a couple of flan de huevos, which is caramel egg custard. He hoarded them.

It was a great time, and the girls were beautiful. Too bad they were all hanging on to the arms of the European and Scandinavian wind surfers. There was a lot of time on my own as Clifford and Alan were trying to up their game. I got to know a couple of the girls who would have a joint with this Yank who had made friends with Clifford and Alan before I got there and me. I was asked to be discreet and only smoke in the van. The Yank, however, rolled a spliff whenever he wanted.

We went up to town one day when the wind didn’t blow, which was unusual since Tarifa boasted 360 windy days a year.

I wanted to score a bit of hash since I had been smoking everybody else’s. We went to the main square, and there were a few anal-retentive guys standing there. I walked up to one, and he showed a nice-looking piece. He lit it with a lighter it so I could smell it, and it dripped like it was cut with candle wax. “No thanks," I said, and we made a beeline for the next guy, who showed a piece of dry old looking Moroccan but with no smell of anything except henna. “I can see Morocco from here,” I said, "and you are selling crap."

There was an arcade, a sort of gambling place that the guy from the campsite had warned them to steer clear of. There was a couple of right shifty-looking guys at the entrance.

“I think that’s the place to go,” I said.

“We are not going there," they said and went on walking.

I peeled off. I met one of the two we had seen a few moments before, so I asked him to tell me someone, I could buy a good piece of hashish from.

“I know someone, but he is not here," he said.

“Not one of these boys from the square,” I said. "Real hashish. I don’t want that dripping stuff.” He smiled. Don’t worry, I understand. Come tomorrow," he said.

“Well, did you get mugged?” Clifford said when I caught up with them. “No, but maybe tomorrow," I laughed.

Next day I did the shopping, then called into the den. I was greeted at the opening. The guy was there with his friend, a moustachioed Charles Bronson lookalike.

"How many kilos you want?" he asked.

"I want some to smoke here, but I will come and talk to you about kilos when I am leaving,” I lied.

He fished out a piece and a scale. It weighed 100 grams. I paid what he wanted and said, "See you in a couple of months when I am ready to go back."

I had a pipe with the Yank – the boys were out wave hopping. “Wow, this is what it’s all about,” said the Yank.

This pretty lady came over and joined us. She told us she had been up in the hills and had a bad time in a village with half a dozen young boys.

“What happened?” I asked.

“They tried to put me on the ground,” she said.

“What did you do?" I asked.

"I sprayed them,” and she pulled out a can of mace and gave it a wave. The Yank choked, laughing. “You fucking maced them.” He gasped. He could not believe what she had just shown us.

“That will teach them that German girls require respect.” She smiled.

We sat around smoking until I realised my cooking duties were imminently needed. I had swordfish, so it was easy.

I got to know most of the Barbie dolls during the days when we soaked up the sun walked on the beach. I sold them a couple of grams because they all could see we were smoking. They were cool. I had a feeling they had it in the evening when their boys came home from the water.

“I don’t want to continue this selling here. It’s not what I want to do,” I told the girl, whose name was Ingrid.

“I do,” she said. "Take me with you when you go back. I am low on cash to get home.”

“Ok," I said. “Come shopping tomorrow.”

We went into town, and the same guy was there. I asked him if he could get the chap to bring a bit more. “Give me the cash, and I will go to him. He does not like to come here. How much do you want?”

“Three hundred and fifty grams,” I said as I handed him the cash. He was back in the opening, waiting for us fifteen minutes later. We had gone for cake and were eating the delicious pastry, wiping the cream off my face. When I reached him, he waved his arms as though giving me directions and smoothly slipped it into my shirt and smiled.

It was getting hot, and time to head home for me, I decided. Ingrid paid me back very quickly. She always asked me to accompany her to score.

I said, “Ingrid, if they piss you about, just mace them."

She smiled and fluttered her eyelashes at me. I gave her a hug and told her I was leaving.

“Things are going quite well for me here,” she said. “I think I will hang on for the summer." She gave me her mum's address in Koln in case I wanted to meet up sometime.

I went through Spain – quite a marathon drive. Then I stopped in France, where both the food and the wine appealed to me, with every pore in my body. With a glass of wine and a Gauloise in hand, I felt very French. I have always loved the French and France. since the Auld Alliance was taught to me in school, I have always known them as our allies rather than England, the permanent enemy. I spent time there working in England, several winters when I was in my teens and early twenties. The view that we were inferior to them was a thing they took for granted. I was surprised at this, but it did not make me feel inferior. How could it? I saw them as ignorant, lesser people who displayed an arrogance that must have come from their schooling and pride of empire. I love the Pogues' song Navigator, which sings of the empire where the sun never sets, but it's late afternoon, and the railways there yet. We are the last colony.

Back to Holland, I went for a rest as I was worn out.

I stayed in the Marriot Hotel and pampered myself, went to see some of the boys and had a smoke and a few beers. I thought about trying a different yard for work in Rotterdam but changed my mind and headed home. I arrived home to find no one in. Doors open. John's brother Frank arrived.

"Is John around?" I asked.

"No, he came in, picked up his giro, then left for the North again," he said.

I went for a sleep, and when I came down to the living room, my parrot Billy was there, and when I picked up the phone it went 'ting', and Billy said in John's girlfriend's pissed-off tone, "Dennis is not in."

On their next visit down, I asked, "Were there any calls while I was away?"

Both said, "No, nobody called for you at all."

"That is a lie; the parrot is imitating you, saying I am not in." Things were not good between us.

John's friend Murdo strolled in.

"Do you mind knocking when you come here?" I said.

"I came to see John."

"You just walked into my kitchen."

"It's John's house," he argued.

"It's my house. Don't come here anymore!"

John left and lives in Dingwall. He looked at Frank, who was John's brother, but a normal kind of a guy.

"I think you'd better leave," he said to Murdo, who was out of sorts and getting near to being thrown out by me. He got in his taxi and left. I heard on the grapevine that he had been stopped and searched with his taxi and bust with a gun, A pistol of some sort. That he had said, "You get all sorts late at night, and this was for protection to wave in their face." He was charged with possessing a firearm, a pistol without a permit. This carried an automatic five-year sentence. He wasn't even on bail.

I did not want him in my house. He and John were at it; I was trying to go straight. I was fed up with jail after being fitted up in England.

A guy I knew from the remand in Winchester arrived in a BMW. I greeted him. He came in with me, and I made coffee in the kitchen.

"Is this your first visit to Scotland?" I asked.

"No, I came up a year ago; I did not realise they would keep you to the last minute."

"Yes, and a month of days all round for being angry."

"I have been bringing the Leb."

"Have you got some now?"

"No, I came to pick up cash."

"Well, if I were you, I wouldn't come back. I've gone straight, and they are under surveillance."

"He is paranoid," said John, who had arrived just before him.

"I am not. See these trees? See the two cars? That's the police. I have not long come back from Spain."

"Have you my cash?" he said to John.

"No, I will go up to Murdo."

"Go with him. I wouldn't let him out of your sight till you get your money. Go the other way and look out for them following you."

"Thanks, Dennis," he said.

"Let me know if you change your mind."

"I will probably do another stint welding if I can find the boys I work with. Great to see you doing so well," I said, "I like your car."

John and Murdo came back later. Murdo was raging. "Does he know everyone?" He spat at John.

"Fuck off," I said, "I told you not to come back here."

Murdo left.

"What did you do that for?" asked John. "Anyway, you should have told him you're a wanker I said. Somebody from the pub told me about one of your bold runs, so you are not keeping it cool. You are an alcoholic, and so are your friends."

"Who? You should know unless you blab to everyone. The thing that pisses me off is that it was me that did that run. You did nothing but get a share from me. You got out of the nick three years before me, and I got sent a tenner once. You are a cunt; you don't have friends, only boozer buddies."

"You have stabbed me in the back by putting me in debt. I am trying to go straight, and you are at it, right under my nose," I said, "I trusted you. I am going straight because, for sure, the police, with their small-minded bastards like Steers who will be wanting me in jail. You saw that cunt Steers in the trial. A dirty, lying bastard. He has a bee in his bonnet about me. Doing business in Holland doesn't matter either, not if you live here. So, it's straight and narrow for me. I am always happier when I am working. I suppose it will have to be the woods again. I can't borrow from the bank because of you."

He got in his car and went, only coming to pick up his giro. I was thinking of selling my parrot and anything else to boost my stake. I would need about ten grand. When I mentioned selling Billy, they were all horrified. Friends came around one night, and we had a smoke. Billy liked getting stoned on the reek when we were having a joint. He would dance and talk away like anything, getting his head and neck scratched, then dancing from one to the other, whoever had the joint or pipe. Then he would go to his cage, which was always open, and go to sleep. "He is having a whitey when he does that, one eye opened and observing," said Rosie.

That was that, Billy was off the selling list.

I had a party that lasted three days. Day one got going, and about a dozen people turned up. The next day many more appeared. It was Saturday, and we cooked a twenty-pound salmon in the barbecue. I boiled some brown rice and made a kedgeree with a lump off the tail end on one side. I let it cool and put it in the fridge. The next time I saw the fish, it was cleaned, with the head and tail on each end of the bones. I put it on the compost and buried it with a couple of spades full of soil.

The summer went on. It was September. Ernest and his wife arrived. He had phoned me and asked if they could pitch their tent.

"No problem," I said.

"Could we be near the house for water?" he asked.

"Aye, you can cook in the kitchen if you feel like it," I said.

Ernest had been in Spain and made about seventy grand selling timeshare. He now had a share portfolio that he was keeping of Far Eastern and other shares.

"I am waiting until it reaches the magic one hundred grand," he said. "Then we will build a house."

One day they were going down to the midlands and left some of their stuff in the shed. I had been thinking about stuff I had read, I said as they were getting in the car. "Ernest, you know you were saying you had a share portfolio. Well. I used to read the Financial Times and other papers. There were articles about one of these banking crises being imminent, where the bank guys jump out the windows of skyscrapers and stuff. I've read a good few of them, and they said it would be in the next year or so. I know you will be thinking, what the fuck do I know about that, but I did follow these articles, and if, in case they are right, why don't you put your money in gold for the next six months? This thing in the Gulf looks like it might blow up into something that will push the gold up. They have sent six minesweepers out there. Try it, then if nothing happens, get your shares back and stick with it. If I am right, you will be safe."

I watched the car go down the road, and Ernest was saying something full-on, animated with great flashes of teeth that looked like I was seen as a madman with my prophecy.

I smiled, a little self-conscious. I had elaborated on my thoughts.

I was in Dundee visiting my brother, who spent a bit trying to get me to join his church.

I would say I was religious in my own way, smoking pot and living the hippie life. "It is better than being a slave. Living with like-minded people," I said.

"They all smoke hash," he said.

"So what? It should be legalised anyway."

"The law says otherwise."

"Well, the law is wrong on this one. It's all put up by the cotton trade because hemp is a far superior fibre."

"What about getting high?"

"What about it?"

"What's this? Mum was telling me about you are going to university."

"Since I broke up with Lindsay, I am going for custody of my kids. Halliburton has given me a year on full pay to get myself sorted. I have sat the entrance to university, and I am going to study law. I figure if I go back to school, I will be doing the same as them."

"That's a good idea. You can forget about practising law. It will never happen."

"Why?"

"It's all a closed shop. Barristers and QCs are closed shop. You get called to the bar. It's all jobs for the boys."

"Remember that guy in Dundee? Couldn't get a job, so he started up the claimant's union. That was a smart move and very good for the folk on the brew."

"A real socialist. When they find out you're a Mormon, they will run you out of town like the Ku Klux Klan in America," I chided.

"Come on, I will take you for an Indian." We went down to Gunga Din for a curry.

"Is that toothless alcoholic still hanging around?" he asked. "He reminds me of Catweasil."

"I persuaded him to get a set of teeth for the court," he said. He now has a girlfriend and a smile. I am trying to evict him at the moment. He comes once a week for his giro and to spy on me. His brother is staying there, but I like him. He is a nice guy.

The curry arrived. After a couple of mouthfuls, I realised that this was a great curry. He beamed his approval.

I finished the food, stayed the night with him, and we talked until late. He gave me a lift home as my car needed testing. I left it in a garage in Dundee.

I arrived, and John and Fee were there with an air of expectancy. "There has been a guy phoning for you," Frank said. "Been driving from the south of England."

Ed was visiting me, chopping firewood in the barn. They had about two tons cut and were stacking it against the wall. You will be owing us forty pounds by tonight," he said.

"That sounds good if you finish that lot," I said.

"Phone!" Frank shouted to me. I went in and picked up.

"Hi, I've been trying to get you for a couple of days; where are you?"

"In Auchmity." He said

"Where in Auchtermuchty?"

"There is a pub called the Boar."

"The Boar's Head. OK, I will be there in a few minutes, I said. "Can you give me a lift?" I asked Tom.

"Yes, but I can't be long. I have something to do at home," he said.

We drove around to the pub. I got out and walked in. It was deserted. I said, "hallo, hallo." Nobody there except a rough-looking guy playing pool. "What's this?" I said to him. "The pub with no beer?" He started to talk. I got in Tom's car.

"Let's go."

We nearly ran into another car as we left the car park. They followed us down onto the road back home. I saw my sister and her friend walking toward us.

"There's Rosie," I said, "pull up." We stopped, and the car behind stopped. "Are you the guy who has been phoning me?" I asked. There was another car on this straight bit of road, and it had stopped. Looking conspicuous. I got in the car that was a police car, I figured. I wasn't that bothered since I had nothing to hide.

Arriving at the house, I stopped and asked the driver, "Have you any hash on you?"

"Yeah, I have eleven keys of bush."

"Well, just stay in your car and get the fuck away from here. Follow that road to the end and turn right, then go home," I said.

They went, and Tom went the other way on his way home. "They have turned into your shed," said Frank.

"What?" I ran up to them. He started hauling two bags with bush out of his car. The shutters on the window had spaces. A car drew up, and they were going into the other end of the old byre where the firewood was being chopped.

"Who is that?" he said.

"The police," I said. They were not coming our way until the guy with him, his minder, got white with fear and started walking to the door.

"Stop," I whispered, holding my hands up.

"I am getting away from that," he said. He walked out as the last detective was going into the other shed. He looked our way and stopped.

"What have we got here?" he said and came back. I felt that sinking feeling.

I was never charged or even questioned, but I could hear it all going on the whole night though with everybody else.

They must have charged me in my absence, and I answered, “Nothing to say.” Which is about what would have been done had it happened anyway. Three months on remand.

The remand was antiquated, slopping out, a week or so, and the place blew up, and a prison guard was taken, hostage. The first I knew about it was when John and I had smoked a joint. We were listening to doors being opened. Suddenly ours was opened, and a hooded figure put his head in and told us, “You are free!”

We looked out, and all the beds and anything moveable was getting slung over the rails onto the floor in front of the gates. The toilets were smashed, and the canteen raided. We settled down to play Bella at the far end. A few days went by. “Take some of this tobacco,” my Bella partner Willie said. “It's time to go. The place was emptying fast, and we were put in another wing. There were mattresses on the floor and about eight to a cell in what were normally four-man cells. I was lying face down in the cell. The others were reading and talking in low voices. I woke suddenly and said, “The police are coming”.

"You are too late,” an old man said. They all burst out laughing. I eventually shared the moment of hilarity. It was the emergency dream in Karl Gustave Jung’s basic psychology

At a visit, Tracy and Carry, her friend, came to visit me. On the way back, a young chap who looked about sixteen said, “My aunty knows you. She said to say John Cameron, and you would know her.” I knew John and remembered her from a few years previous.

“She says ask him to look at your papers and tell you what to do.”

“Ask your solicitor," I said. “I have my own trial in a couple of days, and my lawyer is coming tomorrow, so my head is full of my own stuff.”

He had been asking everybody to read it for him and tell him what he should do. I wondered if he couldn’t read. My door was opened. There he was with the papers in his hands. “OK, I will read it, and I will give it to you back after tea in an hour and a half."

I drank my tea. I had seen this in The Sun – they were going to crucify this young chap. I read the papers. It was accusing him of having sat on the Aberdeen train, befriending old ladies and stealing their purses and chequebooks. His sister had been caught with a chequebook and card, shopping in a store in Dundee. There was an accusation of drugging them by putting a Mickey Finn in their coffees. There was no evidence of this. No forensic, nothing. The Sun was going on about it. He would be lucky to get a jury in Dundee that had not seen the headlines. The door was unlocked, and he was there. "I have read the papers, and there is no forensic evidence," I said. One person thought her mother was a bit high when she saw her. That's normal enough.

"They are hoping to get you in the dock. If you plead guilty to the stealing the chequebook, but when they talk about slipping a Mickey Finn into the coffee or administering a poison, you deny it – there is no evidence, so get the waterworks going and never mind giving it the big one for friends in the gallery. Because if they find you guilty on that, you won't know them by the time you get out. It's serious. That is the same advice a solicitor would give you. So good luck, tell your aunty I am asking for her."

Macfarlane, the solicitor, arrived and Mr Macaulay, QC. I asked to see what was being said about me. "No, we prefer it to be fresh in court," they said. "Then your answers will be better." He waved his gold Rolex in my face. I ignored it, a gaudy thing that looked just the same as the fakes.

This was a guy so full of himself I thought there is no room for anyone else. He said there is no real point of going through it all, as we will only have to do it in the court. Our case was last, and the prosecutor was the Solicitor General, Peter Frazer MP, a Tory who was not doing very well on any of his cases. One where there was no evidence, only a councillor and his wife went for a walk along the cliffs at Arbroath or Stonehaven, and his wife tumbled off the cliff to her death. He was a councillor, and the only evidence that it may have been a murder was that he had a woman from Thailand that he was shagging in a flat in Dundee. He was given leave to appeal, he talked to anyone that would listen in the prison before he left on bail.

Then there was the young chap who broke down several times. The trial had to stop till he composed himself. He got two years for stealing the chequebook. Next was us.

"They are offering a deal," said Macaulay. "They will give you nine years if you plead guilty or thirteen years if you are found guilty," he said.

"What kind of lawyer are you?" I asked. "I came here to fight, not to lie down. I'm fucking innocent!"

"I've looked at your record. You are just out of jail."

Macaulay didn't do innocent, apparently, a complete anal retentive.

Three slates all over again, I thought.

The trial started, and we listened to the forensic so that it was, in fact, marijuana we had here. Then the police evidence, in which one policeman said he saw me carrying a bag of grass from the car. This incriminated me, though; it was a lie.

"Where exactly were you when you could see this," Judge Prosser asked. "It must be over a good distance."

"I had binoculars," he said.

"Show me on the map exactly where you were."

Peter Frazer carried a map over to him, and he said "there" and marked it carefully.

The Judge Lord Prosser held his hand out. Looked at the map. "Are you sure?" he asked the policeman.

"Yes, we are trained to know our position exactly."

"Well, there is a hill there; you could not see the car from there or Mr Anderson for that matter."

Peter Frazer was thrown. He dismissed him with an angry face. "You will ignore that witness," he said to the jury.

The man from England gave his evidence: a long story of me being responsible and pointing the finger at me for everything. He said that he was only a courier.

His friend said he knew nothing of it and had been asked if he fancied a trip to Scotland. He knew nothing of the drugs.

I was talking to my solicitor, and the rest were going down the stairs to their lunch. MacFarlane and Macaulay were saying he told a different story to the one he gave the prosecutor. They were excited. "I will put Mr MacFarlane in the witness box," said Macaulay. I was grabbed suddenly from behind by the police. The judge had just gone. The jury came running back, the few who had gone through the door. "Get off me," I shouted, but I was kept in the neck grip, wrestling to get free, swearing until I was down the stairs. This had been put on for the jury by the police. Probably because the police witness had blown it for them. This was them throwing a dead cat on the table, so to speak. After lunch, it was the defence case.

My brother Tom was called next. He gave his occupation as a law student. He told of our meal in the Gunga Din and him giving me a lift over. He went around to Auchtermuchty to see who this person was that I did not know who had planned to visit me.

"It was not you in the car; it was one of the other residents." The prosecutor said.

"It was me in my car," he said.

This established, they asked him, what was Dennis doing when you arrived back from Dundee? "Feeding the hens," he said, "then we got told there was a visitor that could not find their way by directions. We went to get them."

"What happened then?"

"I dropped Dennis back at his house. I had taken longer than I had expected with the extra journey, so I waved goodbye and left for home. Back to Dundee."

Next came Ed.

"Who fed the hens?" Ed was asked.

"What?"

"Who fed the hens when you were chopping wood?"

"Er… Tom, no Dennis, it was Dennis; they are his hens," he sputtered.

"Why were you there?"

"I was helping him with his garden, and we were chopping logs from a tree we had felled earlier in the year."

Next it was me. I wondered why my defence was sitting with red faces down at the table. Macaulay got up and said, "Mr Anderson was just out of jail in England for drug offences and was trying to go straight. He has agreed the jury should know this." Then he sat down.

What they had said is that we should mention your imprisonment in such a way to let the jury see why the police were trying to fit you up. The fact that he has told a different story makes it all the easier to stop this from going to a jury, I thought – the main and only witness is telling a different story than he told the prosecutor.

Instead, Macaulay served it up like another indictment.

I was in the witness box, reeling. Macfarlane and Macaulay were sitting with their heads down, faces red, looking very guilty. The judge said that his statement had surprised him; he did not think his advice to his client was very good. If I had had an axe, it would have be in his head. I glared at them, or rather the tops of their heads.

Peter Frazer went on to question me about what it is like to be out of prison. "It takes a while to get on your feet again," I said. To be dealing drugs again. He came back with.

"No, I mean socially, being in an all-male environment."

"Even speaking to women is difficult for a time when you come out."

"How do you feel now?"

"Just fine, Mr Frazer."

"This chap who brought the drugs up to you has told us the whole story."

"A pack of utter lies," I said.

"He spilt the beans."

"Mr Frazer," I said, "we saw you talking to him during the lunch break, trying to get your story right."

"Why would I do that?" He reeled back, aghast.

"You are a Tory MP. To put a feather in your political cap, Mr Frazer. That's why you get up in the morning. You have a policeman who can see through hills. You are relying on your friend Macaulay to stick a knife in my back. You are well aware that I am innocent, Mr Frazer!"

I mentioned the police evidence told of a party where hash was being smoked and that it lasted several days earlier in the summer. How could anyone with a telescope know whether hash was being smoked or not? Peter Frazer got back into his stride, and the entire court was certain that I had been smoking hash there.

"Of course, all this should not really concern me because if you will refer to the police evidence, I was not present at that party."

He had just proved something and had it taken away from him, as it was stated earlier. I noticed the judge had got what had been done, and he was smiling.

I was exhausted. I had spent the whole afternoon in the witness box. I looked out to the gallery, and Ellie was there with Robyn in her tum. She came down and hugged me. Another long jail sentence, as another example to others, was my fear.

The jury came back and found me unanimously guilty. I wondered where they had got that flock of sheep.

They had asked for the defence witnesses to be put out of the canteen to spook the jury. I asked who else was in this canteen: the police and everybody. They spooked the jury, had them thinking they were being followed. One of them had said they saw someone on their bus. It turned out to be Tom, my brother. He was questioned. He had indeed been on the downfield bus to his home in Cox Street.

"I am satisfied, said Lord Prosser. There is nothing wrong here."

We were being sentenced, and I looked at the jury.

Hrmm...

I jolted my head round. I put my hand on my heart, ready for the shock.

Lord Prosser said, "I am extremely disturbed in this case; I am not sending a man of his obvious intelligence for a long and mindless sentence. I regret that I have guidelines in this case. I sentence you to five years."

The minder got six months, all backdated, and the guy who testified against me had hoped through his cooperation to get a lighter sentence and to be allowed to serve his time in England for his safety. He got five years with no previous convictions.

All the other lawyers came down and said they thought that I would have been found not guilty. They all shook hands with me and said I had made a great job of prosecuting the prosecutor.

Macfarlane and Macaulay never came to see me at all. I wish they had, for I would have punched their lights out, and they knew it.

Back to Perth, and this time put in the observation cells in case I would commit suicide.

I was innocent, I told the Governor when he interviewed me. He said, "Well if you fly with the crows, you get shot with the crows."

"I like crows," I said, "I used to have a pet jackdaw."

"I want out of here," I said, "I am not going to top myself. I do want a book to read, however. Can you do something?"

"Get him out of this; he is not a risk. Give him the newspapers." He smiled and said the paper said, "pack of utter lies". I smiled at this too. I should have appealed, but I was fed up, and I had little rest. I set about leather work. Bought a hide. Had to deal with Macfarlane as he was selling my house and was more an advocate for Stanners to steal from me. I argued that the fifteen grand that he had borrowed from the bank would have to come off before I considered selling. Macfarlane got me the worst price imaginable. It was hard not to mention the knife in the back he had given me in court. His advice was, "don't appeal; we got you quite a light sentence." I was taken aback, which does not happen often. I had to bite my tongue. I put my head down and worked with my leather. Clifford's girlfriend wanted to get a pair of leather knickers. I wanted to measure her up, but the visiting room was not really the place. "Get some nice gloving leather," I told her. "Get me some, and I will make them."

The conditions were abysmal, much worse than England. Victorian conditions. If it was not so cold, it would be full of disease. Not a healthy environment at all. The food was very poor. The tatties were mashed and looked like the grey death. Full of dark, ominous bits. The porridge was the most edible. If we had got enough milk, which we did not, it would be perfect. The wages for work were shocking. Visiting committees were a joke.

A Tory joke: Like the parole board. The same do-gooders that came to ask you if you were sorry for what you had done if you wanted to apply for parole. "No, I can't get it because Margaret Thatcher said no parole to any anyone with a drug conviction."

“Don’t you want to get out?”

“I don’t want to grovel for something I have already been told I can’t get. You work for monsters,” I said. “I must go, I am very busy,” I got up and left.

“I would like to make a brew,” I said to Henry Sanchez. “Let’s see if we can get one of them white ten-litre containers.”

“I will get the one in the passmen cupboard. It must be clean.”

I said, “Wullie Cadds. See that guy that brings the chips in from the kitchen?”

“Aye, the cook.”

“Aye, could you get me some yeast for a brew?”

“Too much bother. Here have a bit o’ hash.”

“Thanks, but I still want to make a brew.”

“I’ll see what I can do,” he said.

Next day a block of yeast appeared along with a big bag of raisins and a tattie for starch. We collected sugar. When we had all the ingredients together, not a long time, we went to it. After a week, I was asked, "How’s your brew going?”

“Didn’t work,” I lied, “too cold.”

“Aye, you have to know what you are doing, alright.”

It was bubbling away against the pipe for heat in my cell. The Diddler was going to Noranside.

I would miss him.

“That is it, ready Hendry, get ready to cool it down with cold water.”

We poured it off into two smaller bins. Stood them in running water.

This was a very dodgy moment.

Wullie Cadder was on the guitar, singing the rock and Proud Mary. Everybody came in with a mug. I filled them indiscriminately. The whole landing was soon pissed. “Put that in the toilet,” I said to Hendry.

“No, well, it’s not staying here.”

“I’ll keep it." He grabbed the remaining half of the brew and hid it in his cell. Two Colombians were put next door to Hendry, who was next door to me. They were done with eighteen kilos of coke and were appealing; Hendry came from Peru and spoke Spanish, so he was their interpreter. Hendry introduced me to them, and we had a good drink. The next day the prison was much more relaxed; people kept smiling at me.

“You put alcohol in that?”

“No, it was a three-week brew.” The IRA had taught me well.

The milky, yeasty brews I had seen here were a waste of time. All it did was ferment in your stomach. It was awful. This was about the same as Sherrie. It pleased me no end to have blown their minds.

I said to Wullie one day, “I think I will try for that Noranside.”

“Nobody from this camp gets Noranside,” he laughed, “you are wasting your time.”

“I think I will put in for it anyway.”

“Try it; you never know," said Wullie, smiling knowingly, “The Diddler got it. He is finishing seventeen years,” Cads said. “Try it; you never know.”

I went down to the office, asking, "Can I put in for Noranside?

“You have not been here long enough. Another six months before you can get it," was the answer.

“Can I put in now, and if I have to wait, so be it?”

“Aye, all right, you are quite well behaved. You have not kept up your brewing career.” He laughed. “Personally, I would give everybody a couple of pints to cheer them up.”

I filled in the form.

Back at the landing, I put in for it, but he told me to try in six months.

He handed me the joint he had just lit, and it was forgotten.

Tam came in and sat down. He started talking about his appeal. Wullie said, “Tam shut up. You’re guilty.”

“I am innocent,” Tam protested.

"The jury found you guilty, and the appeal court upheld it. Get on with your sentence.”

“What court were you in?”

“Sherriff and jury.”

“Wullie, o fer fuck sake, he’s another one. ‘It wasn’t me, mister, honest.’” Tam ignored Wullie and said, “A sheriff-sheriff.”

“Go and look at your papers and tell me what kind of sheriff. There are a lot of different kinds of sheriffs.”

Next day Tam came along with papers in his hand. “That kind of sheriff,” he said.

I looked at it. Appointed sheriff. “Who appointed him?” I asked him. “How the fuck should I know?”

“Well, I know. Peter Frazer, the Lord Advocate or whichever one was there at the time. How long since your appeal?”

“A year,” said Tam.

“Right, put in a new appeal in just write a page saying you are appealing against the decision. They will send you one of these labels saying your case has been sympathetically considered and refused. That is the first thing everyone gets. Keep that. Write to the court of human rights in Strasbourg and complain that the prosecution is choosing their own judges, and you will win.”

Couple of days and we were smoking a joint at lunchtime. A guard came in. “No screws in here," he was told.

"I have a message. The PO has asked for him to go to the office.” I got up and went.

The PO said, “What makes you a farmer?”

“What do you mean?” I asked.

“Are you a real farmer?”

“Aye,” I said.

“What makes you a farmer?”

“Eh, I’ve got a farm?” Stretching it, but I am well capable of running a farm, I thought.

He came back an hour later. “Don’t go to work tomorrow. Get your kit together. You are going to Noranside.”

I walked upstairs dizzy as well as stoned.

“You made it big, man,” Wullie said. “You will be able to help the Diddler to deliver the papers.” They all laughed at that one.

I was told, “Nine o’clock down here with your kit.”

Cads had come in with a joint at seven. By nine, I was floating. I went to the reception, got my baggage and boarded a minibus with other people. I decided to be mute due to being stoned.

On arrival, we were given our rooms and told to put our stuff there. I lay on the bed looking out the window for an hour. The door burst open. A guard came in and asked what I was doing there.

“I put my kit here and made myself comfortable, waiting for the next thing,” I said.

"You have missed the induction. We thought you had done a runner.”

“Sorry, misunderstanding; I thought I had to wait here.”

“Come on,” he said, and we joined the others. The Governor JC Stewart was smiling.

“Right, that’s it, no drugs here, or you are fired straight back to Perth,” and he emphasised the point by pulling his imaginary six guns and firing at us. “Walk around and get to know the place here. You are Anderson?”

I nodded.

“My office at nine tomorrow.”

It was great to walk around. The Diddler found me and showed me around.

“Cads said to say hi," I said, "he tells me you are the paper boy.”

“Aye, but it’s a cushy number.”

I went down to the farmyard after being sent on from the office. In the shed, a guy told me, “I walked in the shed, and there was a squad forking tatties into a dresser. They were fifteen foot high, half of them turning to slush.”

This was a big shed, and they were stacked to the back. No wonder the tatties in Perth were a horrible grey mess. “That’s a disgrace,” I said. Even in the days when they stacked them like that, they built wooden boards so they could breathe. They are alive. I was appalled at the waste.

"What can we do about it?" Stewart asked me.

"Tattie boxes is your answer."

A PO there was blushing a bit – I guessed he oversaw the farm.

He said, "I have asked for boxes. They won't spend the money."

"You would pay for them with the savings from the first crop," I said, "how many tons do you get?"

"About two hundred and forty ton on average," he replied.

"Well, if it was me, I would fell some of these beautiful blue-skin larches and saw them up in that sawmill. You are not short of manpower."

"These trees will be coming down for a building," the Governor said.

"Can you do all that?" Stewart asked me. I nodded.

"Give him everything he needs and get going."

Next day we went up to the trees, six of us. The PO was the only one with chainsaw trousers and wellies. He fell some small scrub trees out of the way. He was older and struggling. "Can I show you something?" I said. I took the big felling saw, a Stihl, and snedded the five trees he had felled in quick time, considering the size of the saw. His chainsaw trousers and boots that were too big for me by a good few sizes.

Then I laid five big, beautiful boat-skin larches down in a fan. We crosscut the first two: they were big. "Have we something to lift them with?" I asked. "No? Then we will roll them onto a flat trailer with planks and wedges so it can't roll back."

I cut them into the size for boxes and double the side dimension. That would give us better planks than the scaffold boards we were about to use. We had a go-to roll the first one up. It stopped at the top of the planks. "Listen up, we must do this together," I told the men. "Like one, as though we were robbing a bank, and it had to be done when it gets going, keep it going, and you," I said to the firsts one, "put the wedges in if we must stop."

"OK."

"Aye, come on then. One two three!"

It was rolled up with ease. I saw the chests puffing out at the accomplishment.

The saw was the next problem. It went with an old belt pulley from a tractor.

"When did you last use this?" I asked.

"Never in my time here."

"Right, I need a file, grease it, and I will sharpen the blade."

We got the rust off it and cut a few wee sticks to clean the blade, then a smear of oil. It was a Yankee saw with a large blade, four foot in diameter. We cut through the first log, and there was a good 5 inches still to go. I jumped up on top and let fly with a six-inch felling axe from days gone by, and with a few well-aimed strokes, it cleaved in half. I got nails from the joiner's shop and told them we would need a lot more.

"I will get a drawing made for you," he said. Then two hours later, he came back and said, "Make a box, and we will draw it from there."

We did. Then it was inspected, and we decided to change the design slightly to have the ends inside and the long planks going to the end for the forks.

"We could do with the forks to lift the logs," I said.

"It's not all-terrain," he said.

We had two hundred and forty tattie boxes finished by the time the tatties were halfway being lifted.

I made a couple of doors, then fences with a man from Leven. He was keeping fit like me, a miner with no mine. He could bash the posts in. We took turns, and after a few posts, I said, "Have you tried the fencer's swing?"

We had post-gripping tongs and swatted about.

"Watch this: bash, bash till it's got a good hold." Then I measured the swing with my hands stretched and feet in place and with measured swings swinging round in a circle, starting from sitting on top the post. It wheeled round, and the post was smashed into the ground with ease. He picked it up with no bother. When we were finished, they had another fence.

We were loading neeps onto a trailer one cold afternoon. This heavyweight who spent a lot of time in the gym said to me, "I know you are not a grass because you are a pal of Wullie Cadder, and they would not have it. Why do you work like that for them?"

"I don't," I said. "I do it for me. You go to the gym and keep fit. I do, too, if I am not working, but it's like football training. This gives you stamina."

That was it, the neeps became a competition, it was Glasgow against the Teuchters. The work on the farm accelerated.

It was spring: April Fool's Day, and I was sent to work in the tattie shed for a couple of days. Stewart came in, and I was watching him. He went to a box across the shed for me and lifted some tatties in perfect condition. They were four boxes high with straw on the top. He smiled and nodded to me.

I was called to his office next day. "I want you to go to work in the old folk's home in Kirrie to give them a hand with their garden," he said.

The bit of land the lady in charge wanted made into a vegetable garden was an acre of cocksfoot – very rough grass.

I had an assistant, or rather, I was his assistant. He was deaf and dumb. He gave me a paper with his language, so I learned that as I went along, and we chatted away all day. There was a nursery in Kirriemuir with a big chap with a red beard and long hair. I asked him if he would go down and plough the acre, and I would pay him. He agreed to do it on Saturday when no one was there. I phoned my lawyer, and he sent the cash I required. It was done Monday morning; I told the deaf and dumb gardener what I had done. He took me for a pint. This became a habit. We were warned about the old folks: sometimes, they would offer a nip. That was OK, but we couldn't get drunk, or the guns came out, and we were shot back to jail.

I got some Kelso onion seeds and had them planted before New Year in all the windows I could. We planted them out eight inches apart when they were the size of spring onions. The garden was going well when mid-summer arrived, and one of the chaps got released and pissed in Kirrimuir then came to visit. We went to the park with Abbey and a couple of others. We had a bottle of malt and vodka and then went down to the chippie for lunch.

The ambulance came. They said, "Come on, the chief is asking for you."

They sat me in the kitchen and poured black coffee into me.

I sat down, and he said, "You have been drinking. I can smell it."

"I had a nip a few minutes ago," I said.

"I can smell it strongly."

"It was whiskey; it does smell," I said.

I was having difficulty sitting on the seat, and I wanted to slide off.

"I think you are drunk."

"No. I have not had any more than you gave me when I did your garden."

"What is annoying me is they are all covering up for you," he said.

I slurped the tepid coffee and swirled it round my mouth, trying to extinguish the fumes. Getting off the bus, I was sent to my room. Abbey gave me a knowing smile. He was just as pissed as I was but had not been interrogated, so he didn't get caught. I never did find out what it was the chief wanted to see me for.

Next day I was back on the farm, so it was not all bad except that I didn't know any of the workers anymore. The Diddler was still there and due to be released.

I was working on the farm a few months later when I was sent to prune the roses outside the offices. I know nothing about pruning roses, I said to the farmer PO.

"Oh, it's easy. Here are my secateurs. You just snip the heads off the ones that are done."

I was feeling stupid doing something that seemed unnecessary when JC Stewart came out.

"You are coming up for parole for your last eight months," he said. "I am going to talk to the parole board to try to get you it. I could do with a wing of Andersons."

"I don't think my mum would like that," I said.

He was in his car and gone.

The result came back: the parole board had decided they would give me five months because of my hard work.

Ten days later, the Home Office bastards overruled it, taking it away again. Regarding the work, they said, "He is a farmer; that's what they do. That was rich." Everybody else had called me a drug runner or a hippie.

I was in the office getting this news when I was asked, "What are you going to do now?"

"Just keep my head down and work, and it will soon be over eight months. That is just time for shite and a shave, and I will be home and getting on with my life," I answered.

JC Stewart said, "Right, I am not sending you back to Perth. In fact, away back to the old folk's home. They are still going on about you every time I see them." They were all smiling.

Me too.

I stood with a wee tear in the corner of my eye; a couple of days later, I had got a message from my sister at breakfast time that there had been a death: my sister had asked them to tell me that Brutus had died in the night. I went back to my room numb. They were thinking I had done a runner. The farmer came in. "You've been posted missing," he said.

"My dog died in the night, and they told me at breakfast," I said.

"I understand," he said. "Just stay here till you are ready. We lost our dog two years ago, and I and the wife and still have a tear when we talk about him. Take the day off; I will sort it."

I thought about it. These are nice folk, part of a rotten antiquated system. J C Stewart was on a tightrope because many wanted it closed. Especially the Tories who wanted the Victorian standards of a hundred years ago when folk would be hanged or transported for stealing a cake or a rabbit.

Back at the old folks' home, they told me the onions were like footballs, and it seems like they had a good crop all round. I had planted a herbaceous border. I asked, had this not grown? I was told, "Oh, I think all of them went to Forfar with your friend. It's good you are back here again – he was getting a bit crabby. He gave us all the paper to learn his language, but you are the only one that did it."

"It's having time to do it, I think," I said.

I was getting excited to be free again. The visits home were getting easier to deal with, especially when Clifford came.

Then I was picked up and out. It was great free again, but I didn't have a house to go home to this time/

I looked around for something that I could work on. Eventually, there was one piece of land with some buildings with planning. It was hard to read the sign. It was old and had been defaced so that I could not find the name, but I could just make out a Perth number.

I asked around Perth, and an old man said, "It's them over there. They used to be what you are looking for."

I went in and asked. The receptionist said, "Mr So and so, I have a customer asking about the Denmylne property."

"Can I get a prospectus?" I asked him.

"No, the bids are all in," he said, and he turned me round by the elbow and steered me out the door. "You are too late," he said.

I was angry. "What kind of way is that to sell something," I said.

I went back and walked around the place, pissed on every corner and decided somebody was getting screwed here, and it was not going to be me. I took a trip into Cupar and asked MacFarlane, "Do you know the Whitefords? They are from our neck of the woods on the coast."

"Yes, well, they have a property, Denmylne, that I want to bid for."

"Yes, but that would be Leiper Dunlop."

"Do you know him?"

"Yes."

"Do you have his phone number?"

"Yes, I think so."

"Well, phone him and offer him the asking price and tell him I need to know in twenty-four hours because there is another place of interest."

He went off, and I sat waiting. He came back and said, "He has accepted your offer; you have one month to find the money."

I thanked him and walked out an excited man.

I had most of it but was ten grand short. I regretted some of the spending I had done. But then this girl that I was sweet on was wearing Jean-Paul Gaultier clothes that made her cute. I had bought them in a moment of madness. Did I regret that? Well, no, I didn't. But where would I get the cash now? Then I thought a month's welding would bring in enough. I got the plane to Holland.

"George, where are the boys?" I asked him when I got there, "I need to work."

"I think they are in Spain. I heard something."

"Where can I get ten grand?"

"Try asking the bank."

"I don't know. I don't like banks; they don't like me."

"Ask Bert or Hans; they may lend to you."

I asked them, and they gave me thirty thousand guilders. I was dumfoundered. I still needed the boys when they would come back. I needed to work. Rotterdam was a different place, but they were still on a long holiday. I could have tried with a team myself, but I was part of this established team, and I longed for them to come back. To try to have a go and fail would be fatal. There was a lot of expertise that came with them, so I put that idea aside. The other folk worked on a different system, more like employees than a piece work crew. They would never put in enough hours to be a crack squad to get the job done ASAP. George would let me know the minute they were back. He told me they were building a place to holiday in Portugal and that they were running out of money. So, I guessed it would be soon. I did not have this loan forever.

I arrived back and bought the bit of land. My neighbours were not happy: their little game had not worked.

Fuck them then, I thought.

I bought my piece of land and went about seeing what I could do with it. The first obvious thing would be to renovate the buildings – a heavy job, but I was only forty-six. I thought of selling some, but I would see about government grants. My brother Tom was now a practising solicitor for Muir Myles and Lafferty in Cupar.

I went to see my local councillor, who was also an architect, Crab Nairn.

"I am wanting to get plans drawn," I told him. "Can you give me a price for renovating six houses from my steading?"

"I believe the best renovation grant is £7, 500," I said.

"Yes, but it's a change of purpose you will get, so it's £5, 000 – that's what you will get times six."

I had got it wrong I wondered if I should go for another stint in Holland. "I will come back in a week when I have discussed it with my brother," I said.

A lot of thinking happened the next week. One morning it was early, and the sun was shining. I lay in the sun looking over where they had ploughed and were sowing barley and a good timothy hay mix. Man, it was great to be free, and summer was coming fast.

I spoke to Tom, telling him of what happened. "What are you going to do with them?" he asked. "Rent them out to get an income. I am 46, and I won't get much of a pension."

"If you are going to rent them out, there is a Scottish homes grant. It's for people providing rented accommodation." Tom explained it to me.

"Will you chum me when I go to see the architect?" I asked. "How much is he wanting for the drawings?"

He said he would do them for three thousand. I shook on that since it sounded doable even from my poor pocket.

On the next visit, Tom came with me and introduced himself as a solicitor and my brother.

"We are thinking about a Scottish homes grant," he said.

"I have never done anything like that. I will take advice." Crab said.

He phoned us to come, and at the next visit to Crab Nairn's, he had a whiz kid from St Andrew's who had worked with Scottish homes.

"I am a quantity surveyor," he said, "and I will calculate this to the last screw and light bulb. Then I will approach Scottish homes. There is no point in us going anywhere unless they still have money to spend, but I am pretty sure they have," he told us.

We said in a week's time we would meet again. We arrived, and the whiz kid arrived ten minutes later.

"Yes, we can get it," he said, "and it will be £246,000."

Crab swallowed and said, as he stifled a little choking, "My fee will be ten thousand pounds."

I held my hand out and shook his. We left, and in Tom's car, he exhaled and said, "Well, that was a stroke of luck. You will not be able to sell them or do anything but rent them for five years."

"That's fine by me. I have no intention of selling them."

One day when I was sitting at the back of the court, watching Tom represent a client, the sheriff's clerk noticed me and started getting flustered going through papers, then came up to me when the next case was being called. "Are you up here today?" She asked. "I have not got your name on the roll."

"No, even I am simply a member of the public, come to watch the wheels of justice at work," I said. I got up and left. I was pissed that someone with a long memory could really upset me by assuming the worst on sight.

When I saw Tom next, he said, "You are banned from coming to court when I am there."

"Why?" I asked.

"Because you put me off!"

"OK, I can live with that, but I wondered what kind of lawyer you are."

"I defend my client with all my wits because that's what I am supposed to do. Now your friend Macfarlane, what a neep. He thinks I became a solicitor and that you sent me here to steal his business away from him. An act of revenge for what he did to you in Dundee. Can you believe it? The law society told me he tried to get me disbarred, told them I had a drug conviction."

"What?" I asked.

"Aye, that was your bit of hash I took the blame for when I was sixteen and stupid. A ten-pound fine. He had written to the law society when I was at university and told them of it. They wrote to tell me about him. It was to tell me I had an enemy in Mr Macfarlane." I had informed them of it while at University.

"How do you feel about him?" I asked.

"I think he's a twat," said Tom, "he tried to get John Muir to sack me as well."

"Does that not make you mad?"

"No, but he is a twat."

He was in the Caribbean, and some guy held him up and got his wallet. His wife ran after the guy and beat the shit out of the guy with her handbag. I read it in the paper.

"I don't hold grudges much either," I said, "but I hate his guts. He made me guilty by not informing the court that the grass was lying. They all knew it.

Everyone except the jury."

I partially blamed my Harris tweed suit for that conviction. It itched like buggery as it had now become summer.

To think it stood for good Scottish clothing, but to a Dundee jury, it was not a good move looking like a Teuchter, so to speak.

Too bad they had not listened to Lord Prosser, who had said that even if someone had carried a bag, he would not be guilty of position if he were a porter. "In this case, Mr Anderson was that porter," were his words.

The jury were either led by a stupid loudmouth with too much to say, or they were all deaf, dumb and stupid.

Anyway, I told someone how to win a case in Strasbourg concerning appointed sheriffs. It takes ages to come up, but MacFarlane got three days from Peter Frazer, I think. "I read that he won the case in one of the couriers you sent me and that all the appointed sheriffs were out now, and so were those they had sent to jail."

"Ask your guy in the law society. I told Macfarlane to go to Ladbrokes in Cupar and put a grand on a horse called Rhythm and Reason. I would have got thirteen to one if he had done as instructed, but no, he asked the Law society if it was proper for him to do so because I was in jail. He told me this himself when he let me know that I had got eleven to one. Two grand missing when you think about it. He didn't take it, though, because it was in the paper that a Cupar man had won over £10,000 on the national. It would have been £13,000 if he had done as instructed."

"I thought you didn't gamble," Tom said.

"Normally, I don't, but I did the same on Kahyasi that year, too, in the derby."

Sometimes you see something obvious like the stamina of Rhythm and Reason, who fell and did the splits and still won the race. Sheikh Muhammad had fallen out with the snobbery of the British racing scene. Here he was back again with Kahyasi and Luca Camani in this first derby in years. You knew; you just knew. I liked his humour. The bookies knew that means a lot of earnings to them when the favourite is false.

I went out with a local lassie for a few months. Bought a Rhodesian Ridgeback pup. He was shaping up well in his obedience, walking at heel with one word. I had a one-to-one with him. If I stood up, I could tell him not to move with one move of my finger. He was five months old.

I went out with him one evening, and he was growling and telling me we were being watched. I followed his line of sight. He concentrated and growled at the spot. I went back in and asked, "Do you think you have peeping Toms here up on the hill?"

"I wouldn't be surprised," she said, "you get all sorts in Newburgh."

I got my black widow catapult and a few half-inch steel balls. There was a tree, a thick, easy target where I thought they were.

Whack! Another whack. Movement erupted, and a few minutes later, three cars came down the hill. There were two young drivers. They didn't look at me, but I pegged all three as policemen. So, I was under a surveillance.

I felt that since I was going straight and had been since before the last frame up, this was a bit close to the bone.

I awoke next morning to a knock at the door. The local policeman, PC Tattie, was there. "Excuse me, Dennis, the police are at the door. There are forty armed police surrounding you here. I have been sent in to get the dog because I am a dog handler."

"That's him sleeping on the chair; he is just a pup."

"They are a bit worried about him."

In came a pair from Edinburgh. "We have a warrant for your extradition to Norway," they said.

I couldn't imagine why. I was taken to Edinburgh locked up in Sauchton jail.

That evening, I had a visit from Mr Macfarlane, the same solicitor that had kept quiet about evidence that would have released me. "Why didn't you call me?" he asked.

I could not believe the audacity of this prat who had knifed me in the back in the trial in Dundee. How stupid must he think I am?

I suppose I should have let him know it in no uncertain terms, but the selling of my house got in the way. I wasn't happy about the price that Macfarlane got me. The fact that I had to deal with him further made me broke.

I just looked at him open-mouthed. "I have contacted Tom's firm," I said. That was it: the door closed again.

Mr Lafferty arrived and asked what was happening. "No idea; it's right out of the blue," I told him.

"Well, we will just have to wait and see what they say. I will see you in the morning when they will have to tell us what is going on."

Next day I was remanded for ten days for an extradition hearing. I went for the hearing with Lord Wheatly. We argued the case, and I was the first in Scotland to be extradited under Maggie Thatcher's new extradition laws to show other people how easy extradition should be. She could not get her terrorists. So, Britain would dish out anybody to anybody for the asking. Most countries like the USA, Holland and many other countries would not send their citizens anywhere.

They had argued no evidence. I saw three slates all over again.

When we went in, it was all over. My QC, Mr Turnbull, said, "If you want to submit to the warrant and take the chance that Scandinavia is more enlightened like you said earlier, then do it now."

"I don't want a trial here after the last one," I said.

"They will offer you a trial here, but I agree with you they will just fit you up again." Said the QC. Now Lord Turnbull a Judge.

"You were there in Dundee defending one of the others, weren't you?"

"Yes, I wish I had been defending you in Dundee."

"I know we have fought hard here, but can you ask them to put it in writing that I have submitted voluntarily?"

"My Lord, may I submit that my client wishes to submit to the warrant voluntarily."

Sherriff Wheatly grinned at the audacity of my QC.

"My next words were going to be that he is going to Norway, but if you think that may help him, so be it."

"Could you write that into the judgement?"

He looked over his glasses and said to the stenographer, "Write it in that he submitted to the warrant voluntarily."

The woman from the Lord Advocate's office said in ringing tones, "If you waive your rights, Mr Anderson, you can have a trial in your own country."

"If I have any rights, I'll hang onto them; thank you, I will go to Scandinavia; I believe they may be quite enlightened there. In fact, I would go to Russia before I would trust you lot." I was taken away.

I thanked John Muir and Mr Turnbull, who had come through with me to say goodbye. I think seeing someone jump in the fire to take their chances, rather than meekly get the usual ill-treatment that Thatcher had injected into an already second-rate justice system, blew their minds. It's a monarchy, of course, so it's all about the boys in this country. All through the English system, with which they are poisoning the Scottish system, bringing in laws like verbal evidence. Many cheap bastards in the police force love it; a wee lie and someone goes to jail and is often ruined by this. Thinking about Steers and Piper, Greedy for their pensions through promotions that a lie can bring. I also think about the difference this makes in the people of a country. In Holland, I always found the Dutch honest and hardworking people, easygoing. Governments are the parent figure, and not all of them molest their people, but a lot of them do, especially so in Britain. We will see how Norway stands in this, I thought.

I was collected two days later by a couple of detectives who took me to Aberdeen to be transferred to the Norwegian cops, who had a drink with me on the plane over. In fact, I arrived quite pissed. They put me in a cell in the bottom, which looked like a drunk tank. They brought me a sandwich and a mug of coffee. "We will come back and question you tomorrow."

"You'd better find me a better place to sleep."

"Tomorrow."

"Right fucking now!" I said.

"I will see what I can do," he said.

I was then taken to the top of this multistorey building. The top two storeys were where Kristiansand's remand prison was. I was put in a room with a TV and stereo radio cassette. So far, so good, I thought.

It was explained to the very good-looking Norwegian female guard that I was to be kept on forbudt, which means 'forbidden'. Here, however, it meant no talking, forbidden everything. I was left on this wing, and nobody came near me except the guards who opened the door. As they handed my food in, I asked many questions. "No talking, no talking," were the answers I got. Then I was taken down to the police station immediately below, introduced to the investigating officers, Inspector Geir Hanson and his companion Birger Tvet.

"We want you to answer some questions," they said. "I have nothing to say."

"We are police; you must answer our questions."

"I am innocent, and on advice from my solicitor, Mr John Muir, I do not need to answer any of your questions, but you do need to tell me what I have done and show proof."

"This is Norway. You are in now, and you will tell us what you know about this case."

"Fine, I know absolutely nothing," I said. "I want a lawyer."

Next day I was introduced to a lawyer. This guy was a mile away from anyone I would choose to defend me. "How long have you been a lawyer?" I asked him.

"Ten years," he answered.

"How many people have you got a 'not guilty' verdict for?"

"In Norway, the police don't arrest people who are not guilty."

"You are a police lawyer? Official police lawyer?"

"Yes."

"How long were you in the police before you became a lawyer?"

"I was in the police for several years."

"I am not wanting a policeman as a lawyer," I said.

"I want you to tell me your involvement."

"I am innocent. Look, go away."

"It's no good being difficult. That will get you nowhere. I am your lawyer."

"What the fuck is wrong with them? They are like sheep, or I am like a sheep being driven into the slaughterhouse?"

I decided to put them on forbudt and would not talk to them. I would not talk about the case. Anything else was fine about their family life. The weather, the news, anything except the case.

I woke up at three in the middle of the night.

"We want to question you," they said.

"I am busy," I said.

"What do you mean busy?"

"No night-time appointments. Come back at a decent hour."

"You must come with me."

I got up, and there was Hanson and Birger Tvet waiting for me, sweating and looking like they had run a marathon.

"Listen, getting woken up in the middle of the night by Hansel and Greta here is a waste of my beauty sleep," I said.

They took me down in the elevator. Hanson stood up to his full height of one point four metres, at a guess.

"We are pissed off with you now," he said. "We have been out busting people; we are busy and fed up with you."

"Come on then, you wee shite!" I leapt to my feet. "I will throw you through that window!"

Tvet stood up. I adjusted a little to face them both with a smile on my face.

"You go back to your cell, now," he shouted.

Next day they came and told me, "We are sending you to Åna fengselet."

"How long can this forbudt last?" I asked another prisoner that I had seen come out of the toilet. "Two to three years, max."

"No talking!"

"Ignore them," I said.

"We are human beings; we are social animals."

"You can't talk to him; he is on forbudt."

The Norwegian smiled at me. "I apologise for my countryman," he said in good English as he was taken away.

"He at least looks like a Viking," I said.

"He is a Hell's Angel," he answered.

I was let out for a shower, but no one else was there. I would dance around, especially if the guards were beautiful women.

"I am a social animal. A human being," I would say.

"Please go in, or I will call for help," the guard would say.

"OK, but please smile."

She looked at the other woman, who smiled back and said, "We don't like it either that they keep people on forbudt, but it's the job." I saw genuine regret on her face. That moment stayed with me for a long time as I thought about things in the cell.

I was transported to prison. It was the same thing, but I got better exercise for one hour a day, and although I was on forbudt in a remand wing, it was not so bad. After a couple of months, I was taken with no explanation to a small airport. I was beginning to think they were releasing me. I was sitting in a small police division of this very small airport. A plane arrived, a wee Fokker Friendship plane from Aberdeen. Then I saw Hanson and his buddy. They looked hungover, very hungover.

"We have been to Newburg," they said.

"Newburgh," I corrected.

"Did you get many statements?" I asked, smiling.

Hanson hissed, "Yes, they were queuing up to give us statements."

I laughed.

"The police in Scotland do not like you."

"No, I am sure you will have found a few trying to get into the case, especially if you were buying the beer. You look like a couple of alcoholics. If you want me to answer your questions, get me off this fucking forbudt."

"Answer some questions now."

"No. When I am among the normal prisoners."

"You can stay and rot," he said.

They went, and I went back to Åna fengselet.

I was moved back to Kristiansand, to the forbudt wing once again.

"How did you Like Åna?" a guard asked.

"Shhh! No talking!" I said.

Hansel and Greta came next morning and said, "We want you to answer some questions."

"Shh, no talking," I said. "I am still on forbudt. I want to go back to Åna. The girls there were very pretty."

"We are going to put you next door to the people awaiting trial." They closed the cell door.

An hour later I was told to come to get my stuff, that I was going next door and that forbudt was over for me. I followed the guard next door, as simple as that. The forbudt wing was one large room with cells, toilet and shower block. Very modern, but where the prisoners were only let out one at a time and no talking. Six months had gone by, and I had still not been told why I was accused or by whom.

The cleaner guy gave me the things I needed. We could mix freely, and we would exercise on the roof. There was a big guy over the other side, and he smiled at me. I walked over to him and said, "Do you speak English?"

"Yes," he replied, "I used to live in Leeds."

"I need a good lawyer," I said, "do you know one?"

"My lawyer is a good lawyer. I can give you his details," he said.

I said, "There is a TV show where a lawyer there is very clever and not afraid to argue with the police."

"Yes," answered the man, "he is Tor Erling Staff."

"I would like him. He is an honest man, I think."

He smiled. "Go and ask them to let you phone him."

I did, and this was granted. He pointed to the phone on the wall.

I phoned his office, and they said that Mr Staff would be in touch.

I was taken down to the police office and asked, "What can you tell us about this case?"

"Nothing. I am innocent, and you may not like me, but I think you are aware of this by now. Why do you think I am a guilty person?"

"Your lawyer thinks you are guilty," Hanson said.

"Who, Staff?" I exclaimed

"Staff is your lawyer?" asked Hanson.

"Yes," I said.

"I mean your lawyer in Scotland, Macfarlane. He told the police in Cupar that he thought you may be involved when we were asking them to inform Wilsons's wife."

I was shattered by this revelation. All I knew till then was that I was being accused of being involved with two other people: Patrick Wilson and Brian Boyes, of smuggling hashish into Norway.

"You extradited me because my lawyer, Macfarlane, told you he thought this?"

"Yes," said Hanson. "If your lawyer thinks you are part of this, then what else can we think?"

"You mean you fucking took the word of a greedy conniving solicitor, trying to get in on another high court case off my back! You extradited me for that. That is totally illegal," I ranted. "The bastard came to ask if he could represent me too," I said unhappily. I was reeling with the outrage that had been done. They took it as all in a day's work.

"We are going back to Scotland," he said.

"Well, don't bother with me until your hangovers are clear. I want no more lies and threats from you. Mr Staff has asked me not to talk to you. You can put me back. I have a lot to think about."

They took me back up to the prison levels. On the way back, there were three lady detectives in an office with a large basket of green grapes. I turned into the office. "Can I have some?" I asked.

"Have them all," one of them said. I was filling my arms with them when Hanson's head came in. I walked to the elevator, and they were helping themselves to grapes on the way up. I did not like it, but three kilos of grapes would give everybody some. I went to my room with them, put them on my bed, went to the kitchen for a big bowl and gorged myself. I shared with any of the others that wanted them.

I lay on my bed thinking of Macfarlane's audacity. A low-life piece of shit, after what he did to me in Dundee. Here he is again, trying to get himself another high court case. There is an old saying, "show me a lawyer, and I'll show you a thief". Like everybody everywhere, some are good, and some are bad. Betrayers of trust are the worst kind of human being. You would think evolution would thin them out. Councillors in the council are often like that, especially the Liberal and Tories I have had the misfortune to run into. They seem to be always judgemental where I am concerned.

I had a meal with some people in the wing who invited the two Arabs there and me. It was a tasty meal, but then there was a great flash, and a guy had hit me on the side of the head with a cast iron frying pan. He did not like me and had made it obvious with his pouting attitude. He was shouting about eating with stinking foreigners. I got up and was out my door as soon as it opened the next morning. I went to the tea urn, but it was lukewarm. I needed boiling water.

"I have some tea in my room if you want a drink," said one of the others.

"No, thank you. I am going to cook that rat like a lobster," I said.

The young chap immediately went and told him – he went up to the guard and went next door to the forbudt on protection. Guido, he was called. I could have thrown him a good distance. My ploy was better. Wullie Cadder and a good few of the inmates in Scotland would have destroyed him for that. I smiled at the thought of it.

I was reading a science fiction book. Hanson came and took me down.

I sat down in their office. Hansen asked the questions, and Tvet typed it all in Norwegian. Sometimes they had an interpreter, but not this time.

"Where were you on July 31st?" he asked.

"I was at an agricultural show in Perth with at least twenty farmers who can prove this."

They asked my whereabouts on another day.

I reeled off where I was and told them it could easily be proved. They were fishing for a day. I couldn't remember what I had been doing, I surmised.

"Where were you on the 7th of August?"

I thought for a while. I made my eye flicker, and along with a twitch and my face, I jumped up and shouted at them, "Do you know where you were every fucking day of your lives?" It was eight fucking months ago." They looked at each other and smiled.

They had another interview about ten days later. They told me that police in Scotland had seen me get on a plane on the 7th of August from Aberdeen. That was a lie. Well, I bet there was not even one Anderson on the plane. They said, "You have been known to use other names. They don't know what name you were using."

Who did he think I was, 007?

They also said that someone, an honest citizen in Kristiansand, had seen me waiting at the time the car came through on August 7th, looking nervous, a face they could never forget. Hanson talked, and Tvet typed it all. Two policemen saw me hanging round at the same place waiting for a car coming through, they said.

A couple of weeks later, I was taken to court.

Staff had said that I should tell them I plead not guilty to the allegations. I wanted to do much more, I thought.

I resigned myself to sit it out.

I went to court and was met by a young man from Staff's office. I did not feel so alone. He sat next to me and translated what was happening.

It was the end of the investigation. I was given a date for trial; it would be thirteen months. I had put up with this, like a piece of flotsam carried along on the current, helpless. The people seemed normal, but I think they had no idea what normal is. I said to him that they boast of a 100% conviction rate and that everybody goes to jail. I wanted to know if that was true.

"It's about right," my translator said.

I stood up. "Excuse me, Judge," I said, "am I right in thinking the investigations are finished?"

"Yes, you go to trial now," he said.

"Then I would like an investigation into these policemen. I want you to let me go and put them in jail where they belong. They are lying, and so are others."

"Can you prove this?"

"Yes, or else I would not be saying so."

A couple of weeks later, I was on the top level, playing football. There were just glass sides and steel girders between us and the sky. I was taken down to have this hearing against the police in a room hastily prepared for the hearing. There was an electrician who came in with a ladder and stuck a listening device in the ceiling. He apologised and said he was late because of some other job.

This was made a courtroom with a dock, etcetera. There was a lensman (a country policeman), an advocate (lawyer) and a judge on the bench, the interpreter on the floor between us. I said, "Before we go any further, they are listening to us; that is a listening device." I pointed at the ceiling. "That was put there a few minutes ago." They ignored what I said. The judge said my allegations were serious.

"They have threatened a witness, Wilsons's wife, trying to get her to make a statement against me, and said they would have her children put in care. It's serious, alright."

"How do you know this?"

"My brother is a lawyer, and I was speaking to him regarding my property. I gave him the right of an attorney to act on my behalf and pay my taxes and other legal things. He told me she had come to him and told him this."

I told them that on that day, the 7th of August that I was apparently seen by the Scottish police in Aberdeen flying to Norway in the morning. Then I was supposedly waiting the same day in Kristiansand for a car full of hashish and seen by an honest citizen, "a face he could never forget".

Two Norwegian police officers also saw me there, and they were suspicious, but apparently, I got away somehow. All very damming. Except for the fact that on this exact day, I was in the head office of the bank of Scotland in Dundee, surrounded by witnesses that could prove this. I was signing mortgage papers and visited two law practices immediately after the bank. There would be a drove of witnesses of good character to prove this.

They adjourned for a week.

The judge read from a letter from the statsadvokat or public prosecutor – in America, he would be the DA.

I would take all this evidence out of the case; would that satisfy him? No, it fucking wouldn't, and I wanted these policemen jailed. I also demanded to be released. Any other country in the world would have released me. Instead, this bunch of idiots kept going, safe in the knowledge that they had a 100% conviction rate for anyone arrested by police for any crime at all. Bastards – real fucking bastards.

I was back one week later, and there was a lot of fussing about.

They had a statement from Hanson, which said they had visited Wilsons' wife and played with the children, and she invited them in for a cup of tea. They had spent an hour and a half there. I asked to see this but could only have the interpreter translate it.

"Wait a minute," I declared, "they would have had to have Scottish police with them."

"Yes, they did."

"Then they must have written what happened."

"They don't say anything," the judge said. "Let me see it." He handed it to the interpreter.

"I can read English better than you can," I said, "let me see it."

She handed the Scottish police statement to me. The other copy was handed on to the judge, who was getting pissed by his expression.

"They say nothing at all," he said angrily.

I read the other. "You are right," I said, "not much. However, it does say here that they went to her house, she was uncooperative, interview terminated after 3 minutes." It would take that long to be read her rights.

Fuck me, Roger Banister couldn't play with children and have a cup of tea in three minutes. And they had said one and a half hours: an amiable visit where they played with the children.

"Your police are dirty lying bastards," I said. "Interpret that to them. They are perverting the course of justice."

"I can't say pervert to them."

"Why not? It's a legal phrase," I said.

She was blushing.

"That's all for now, I will show more proof in the trial." I sat down. "This is nothing but a whitewash," I said.

Staff came to visit me a week before the trial. He had a big folder. "Here is a copy of the evidence for you to look through," he said. "I have a week to get familiar with the case. Tell me what really happened."

"I do not know what really happened. Have you never represented a client who was innocent before?" I asked him.

“I need to know so that I can defend you.”

“I am innocent,” I said.

“I have another client. He was not pleased. Read through this, and he handed me a folder.”

“The gentleman from Tanzania, is it?”

“At least,” said Staff.

I sat down on the steps outside and read through the folder of documents: a lot of stuff from my bank. No mortgage agreement or other things like references from my employers. I wondered if they had taken only stuff to try to make me look guilty. Left the rest or dumped it. Now that was a worry.

“Staff,” I said, “they have only put stuff in to make me look guilty and left the stuff that shows me to be innocent.”

“What’s the point if you won’t tell me everything that happened?” Staff said, clearly miffed and packing his stuff to go.

“I will see you in the court,” he said.

“Mr Staff, I will ask my brother to send anything they did not want to take from my bank.”

“What do you mean?” asked Staff.

“They only took selected stuff to make me look guilty.”

“Send it to my office then,” he agreed.

Back in prison again, I asked to phone my lawyer. I phoned and got Tom. “Listen, use a power of attorney,” I told him, “and get the documents about my job in Holland and the documents that’s the mortgage agreement and anything else that shows me to be in the bank on that day. Get something about my appointment time because that is exactly where and when they don’t want me to be there.”

"Are they lugging into this?"

"Aye, but they cannae get our accents. I keep getting told that I am supposed to speak English on the phone. Send it to Staff's office and write 'urgent' on it. It will be touch and go."

"I won't hang about," Tom said.

I rang Staff's office and said that Mr Staff had asked me to get a letter with papers from Scotland brought to him urgently when it arrives, as it will be touch and go for my trial.

The actual situation was ludicrous. Staff was not talking to me. He had taken the huff since our last decision because of my record and the fact that I was so in the dark about what had happened.

Basically, I had been kidnapped by a bent solicitor's imagination and two foreign policemen under the guise of extradition, coming into a foreign country and abusing me on a faint notion that I might be involved, put into their heads by gossip from a bent solicitor. That and Margaret Thatcher failing completely to protect her citizens, all because she couldn't get her terrorists. She was trying to show how easy extradition could be. Nobody would send IRA prisoners to England because they would not get a fair trial. I thought of Johnnie Walker and the Birmingham Six. Also, the Guildford Four, who were on the roof for an awfully long time while I was in Longlarten.

The six months in isolation were quite a blow to me, never mind that it took thirteen months to go to court. One thing that kept me strong on forbudt was that someone passed me a book in English: Papillon. It made my prison set-up, with heating, TV, and ghetto blaster, seem not so bad. Nevertheless, it was a mind-bending experience.

The fact was that the statsadvokat took all the evidence of them lying out, whether I liked it or not, and was still proceeding without any evidence. This made me think of Sheldon, also of Nazi Germany. More injustice on the way, it seemed.

Mr Wilson and Mr Boyes, neither of whom made any allegations against me at all, stood in the dock beside their lawyers with me.

Boyes went first and agreed that he had been in a car along with Patrick and had come to Norway to accompany Patrick for a trip. He said that he knew nothing about the hashish in the car hidden in an LPG tank – some thirty-seven kilos. Patrick, who was driving, had crashed into the concrete kerbs on being waved through. So, they changed their minds and invited them into the shed to search the vehicle. They had searched the car for five hours, they said, and Mr Boyes and Mr Wilson were looking extremely nervous now.

"Did you know Mr Anderson?" the prosecutor asked him.

Boyes said, "Yes, but I did not really know him very well. His friends and mine were not socially alike. Mine were well-to-do people; he was not really socially acceptable among my friends."

"You mean you are of a better class of society?" asked Staff.

"Yes," he declared.

I smiled at this, and I looked at Staff, who was still not speaking to me for wasting his time, in his opinion.

"Mr Anderson had a Mercedes car, did he not?"

"Yes, a very nice car."

It went on like this, of how he was a friend of Menzies Campbell, MP and that he handed out his leaflets.

Then came Patrick, who pleaded guilty and said no more other than he knew both of us from the village.

He was cross-examined by the advokat — much the same stuff. Then, it was my turn.

The prosecutor, Mr Andreasen, started with,

"Anderson! Where does the name come from?" Andreasen asked fiercely. "Norwegian Vikings, who settled most of the north of Scotland and the isles," I answered. "Mr Andreasen, when the Viking thing broke up, they became Scottish. In Ross-shire, there were many MacGillie Andreas there.

They became a sept of clan Ross, which is a Norwegian name. My ancestors were Vikings like yours unless yours were bide at homes."

There was a laugh from the jury.

"Enough," said Andreasen. "Do you know Wilson and Boyes?"

I answered, "It's a small town of two thousand people. Everyone knows everyone, and usually what colour of underwear you are wearing."

Laugh again from the jury. A good sense of humour is a plus in my book. I could tell they understood me.

"Did you work in Holland in the past year?" asked Andreasen.

"No, but I worked in a shipyard in Rotterdam from the previous year, I think."

"Were you in Holland in August last year?"

"No."

"You had a Mercedes car?" he asked me.

"Is that a crime in Norway?" I asked.

"They are a luxury car."

"Mine wasn't. It was second-hand, but I liked it."

"Did Mr Boyes ever drive your car?"

In fact, he had. I wondered where they had gotten this from.

"Yes, he borrowed it twice. He had a rusty old Cortina and was going to view a house and asked if he could borrow it to put on a better appearance. On another occasion, it was a job. He must have found the car socially acceptable," I added.

The jury liked that one and laughed. That was good. I thought that their English was very good.

They had a lunch break.

Staff caught up with me at the lift. I could see the excitement on his face. "I told you to be brief. You haven't, but you are very clever."

I asked him if they could let me into the exercise area at lunchtime. I needed some air. Staff had phoned them. I had my lunch and kicked a ball against a wall for half an hour. Time to go back, and I was cross-examined by the other two advocates.

After a few questions from Boyes's lawyer, I saw a young man come down the aisle and hand Staff a long brown envelope with British stamps. He whispered to Staff, who took the envelope, opened it drew out the papers. He flipped through them he beamed a smile up at me.

"Good, now I can do something with these," he said gleefully. I felt better now that Staff was enjoying himself. It was all the stuff about my mortgage that they had approved, several contacts with my employers, including phone calls to the agent who paid me, as well as other stuff that the police did not bring because they only wanted to paint a guilty picture. Two years' wages was just an amount of money, without the explanation of the Dutch work and company information documents, etcetera. I was asked some more questions.

The Mercedes was driven around the court by all the lawyers. I asked for a drink of water after my ball play. I was thirsty. I had a long drink and nearly fainted managed to put it down as I slumped into the chair. Then it was back to Andreasen. "I think he has had enough," he said.

In Norway one has to prove ones innocence then comes the police to try to disprove what you have said and state their case as an afterthought. Instead of me answering their case first. They come last so you don't really know what you are defending because you have not heard what they are saying.

I had been re-examined by the other two defence lawyers.

Next, it was the two policemen. The first was Hanson. Staff doing what Staff does best took him apart. Hanson had tears in his eyes. Tvet was angry and bit back: a mistake. The lagman (trial judge) tried to help him but to no avail.

Staff gave a good performance. I gathered he didn't like bent policemen either.

The interpreter, who was talking beside me, failed a bit, getting carried away listening. I nudged him back on track.

There was a summing up by all of them, then we had to wait for the verdict.

We were sent back to the wing. Staff came to see me. "Why is it taking so long?" I asked him.

"They are having a hard time getting the jury to convict you," he said, smiling.

I came back to hear the verdict.

"Guilty, all three. Pat Wilson: two years and Brian Boyes three years, and me with no evidence and the police caught lying their heads off, I was given six and a half years!

"Lagman! I want to appeal," I said.

"There is no appeal against guilt in Norway," he said, looking down his nose at me.

"No, have you ever heard of the European court of Human Rights in

Strasbourg?"

He stood up, laughing, and said, "Not in Norway!"

"Well, keep listening because you will," I said.

"Not in Norway," he repeated, smiling at my stupidity.

They really needed to weed out these Nazis from their legal system and get rid of this police state. They are the money; that's the trouble.

I was moved to Åna fengselet once again. I settled in, going to work in the snekker, which was a furniture shop with all the kind of machinery I like to play with. I was making tables and chairs, corner cupboards, and boules like the French use for bowling; you have six balls and a wee red one you throw to put the peg in – a Francis Drake type. The balls were birch, and I filled up boxes of them: hundreds.

I wrote an application to the European Court of Human Rights. About a couple of months later, I repeated it and mentioned my previous letter. I was hauled up before the deputy governor, who said, "You can't say things like that about the country. It's insulting."

"You are not supposed to read any letter to the Court of Human Rights," I told him. He tore the letters up and binned them. "Go and behave yourself!"

I looked for the next guy going home. I gave him a letter and asked him to post it to my brother. I asked him to put it in his shoe so that he could get it out the jail and forward it to my brother. "They are stopping my mail to Strasbourg," I said.

Then I heard from Strasbourg, but I still did not trust the prison authorities to post my mail if they did not like what I said.

I researched them. I wanted to know how a legal system could be this fucked up. One guard was an ex-Marine bilingual, and he helped me with translations from Norwegian to English.

Another older guard, Harald, I had good conversations with. He had been to Scotland for the war and used to speak with a Highland accent to me and also a Glasgow accent. I asked him why the legal system is such a joke. "Your prisons are very modern, and the education system here is good. But the legal system is totally crazy. Where did it come from?"

"They made it up," he said, "by taking some from France, some from Russia and some from other countries."

Forbudt, I read, came from Okhrana, the Czar's secret police. The KGB inherited it and put it to good use. The courts are very strange too.

Harald was in the merchant navy and knew a lot about naval history. During the war, he told me, Norway had the largest tanker fleet in the world and a lot of shipping. There was hardly a convoy during the war that did not have Norwegian ships in it. When these heroes came back after the war, the quislings, who had been under the Nazis, formed the legal system and the police. They were the beneficiaries of the slave labour, which had built gun emplacements, tunnels and underground things like U-boat pens, as well as heavy water plants for the H-bomb.

"They became rich during the war," said Harald.

"Yes, but it would be occupation money. Worthless after the war?"

"No," Harald said, "they were clever; they put their money into insurance, they lost nothing. The loyal police, mostly in Oslo and the east, they all ran away to Sweden and formed regiments to take back Norway from the Germans."

The Allies did not come from the north, as we know now that they came from France. At that time, the North had anti-tank blocks. (Hitler's teeth, the Norwegians called them). The Wehrmacht were the crack German troops there to hold Norway against the Allies if they came that way. It was feared that they may fight on after peace was signed. Luckily they were glad it was all over too.

When the king came back from Britain, the police and legal system were all quislings. King Haakon VII decided to have an attitude of forgiveness. They shot quisling but should have shot a lot more than they did. The legal system was left because they needed them and the police with them.

These sailors that came back on their ships from the convoys were asked if they were working. They had just signed off after years of running the gauntlet. So the answer was, "No, I have just signed off." They were arrested for vagrancy put in Åna for three years. Many Norwegians were conscripted into the army to fight the winter war against the Finns, who fought the Germans on one side and the Russians on the other side.

I was stunned to hear these things and went to look all this up to check, and wow, it's real.

Søren Nielsen was the guy assigned to me from Strasbourg. He was Danish, and I wondered about that, them being of a committee of nations with Norway in Scandinavia.

His first letter to me was that a Dane had appealed against his sentence, and his appeal was refused. He advised me that I should give up.

I pointed out to him that I was appealing against conviction, not against sentence.

All his letters were aimed to get rid of me. I continued with my appeal, but I did not trust him anymore, having been screwed by those people in jobs for the boys before. I didn't trust any of them. One of Søren Nielsen's letters said, "We in our ivory towers find it extremely difficult to relate to someone in your position or see their point of view."

I dug my heels in and pushed. Sensitive letters were smuggled out and posted from another town by a lady to whom I am extremely grateful, Ingor Gudall, who was a social worker, the head of the department. I asked her to see some evidence with me. I had written to the statsadvokat, who ignored me.

Then I wrote to the høyesterett (high court) to have sight of the documentary evidence from the case. Boyes had told me he had complained to the high court, and they had sent to Kristiansand for the documents, so I wrote to Sofi Solheim, the secretary of the høyesterett, for sight of the documents. I wondered how they had got the jury to find me guilty. I asked Ingor Gudall to accompany me when the lensman brought them from the high court on the way to Kristiansand. I knew her to be a completely honest and honourable person. When they arrived, I called her to accompany me as a witness. I opened the evidence book. There it was on the top. Must have been the last thing on the case, which it was not. It must have been after the case, as it was not mentioned in the trial. I asked if I could get a photocopy but was refused. I asked if someone could take me to the toilet. I said, "Did you read the first document?"

"Yes, it said your fingerprint was on a piece of hash. Take note of the number on the document." Then I said, "I am going to ask for a copy of this again. Do you want to look at it again? Because you will never see this document again."

"I am not senile," She said, "it is only one line."

"They will send similar docs to confuse you, but not this one."

"They have shown this to the jury to get them to convict me after the trial," I said.

The result of the long couple of years work in Strasbourg was that the twenty-five judges found unanimously in my favour. Norway had contravened my human rights. I did not get a fair trial. The first thing that I asked for was that they let their population know that they were fully signed-up members of the European court of human rights – that they had signed up to all the protocols, unlike England, who had signed the articles but had not signed the protocols, that is, until Scotland signed the lot and put human rights into Scottish law. England signed the protocols to keep up with the neighbours.

My first demand was that they announce it in the newspapers. They called it retts (law) review, as though it was something they had done. No mention of the Scottish scumbag that had brought some enlightenment into a bad legal system.

I was watching the news one morning, and I could see angry people talking, but I couldn't understand much of it.

"Harald, what are these lawyers talking about?" I asked.

"Human rights. They sound just like you," he said, laughing.

I must have opened a right can of worms here, I thought. The government is pretty good, but the legal system can shelve their laws if they don't want to change them. It is good that the government is apart from the legal system, but not in this case.

I had a conversation on the telephone with Søren Nielsen, asking why he had refused me compensation. One other signature he had got disqualified me for compensation, which is all he needed. His friend co-signed.

Compensation is different in every Country. In Norway is 300,000 kroner per year for four and a half years, which makes £1,350,000. Plus, my building enterprise that was scuppered for £240,000 plus compound interest.

I was not released one day early. Søren Nielsen, you are a twisted bastard and should not be in that position to get one of your friends to disqualify me and jeer at me the way you did, I thought. That did not reflect the unanimous decision of twenty-five judges.

When I asked him what went wrong with my compensation claim, he said, "There is no appeal against my decision."

At that moment, it came through loud and clear to me he was Norway's man.

"I am going to get you, Søren," I said. I have been threatened before, he replied.

"I'll bet you have. I am going to get you," I said, "would you like to know what I am going to do?"

"Yes, I am very interested in what you are going to do," he said.

"I am going to write a book, to learn how to write a book, then I am coming for you."

With that, I hung the phone up on him.

I enjoyed my time working in snekker 2, making furniture and doing woodwork. The time flew by, but I needed to learn how to use a computer. I then asked to go to the education department to learn how to use the CAD programme. It was CAD 12, a DOS programme. I did a drawing of a cow shed. I was learning how to use the computer most of the time. When I asked how to do something, my teacher said, "how did you do that?" It was lifting the drainage system out of the building I had drawn, then making an adjustment and putting it back with a few clicks. The teacher said, "I had no idea you could do that; you know as much as me!"

They then gave me a computer and allowed me to sit in the library to write my book, which I was doing every opportunity I got. I was together with a German and a Polish chap who had smuggled diamonds from Russia. The German was in for a car loaded with two hundred kilos of contraband at Kristiansand. Five years was reasonable. I thought of that judge that I had; what a jumped-up piece of shit. He was a quisling Nazi for sure.

Ingor Gudall came to visit me. "I am surprised to see you are still here," She said.

"I won the case, but that is all," I said, "where did you go to?" I asked.

"I went back to my old job with the United Nations High Commission for Refugees, this time in Sarajevo and Bosnia. I could not work here after what I saw with you. They tell us not to believe them when they say they are innocent."

I was asking for extra telephone time when I met Ingor, and I noticed her wall had photos of Afghani children playing. These are Afghani kids," I said.

"Yes, have you been there?" she asked.

I said I had. She told me of her work with the United Nations High Commission for Refugees, teaching women to work. In this life, you meet some very special people, and this lady was amazing.

I started a book in anger with the intent of getting even with Søren Nielsen. I wrote a fantasy story about the Celts, who were being attacked in Ireland by their neighbours who set sail for Scotland: Dalriada, to be precise. A storm blew them way off course in their skin boats, with all their dogs and horses. While most of the passengers were bailing water, a mage on board was praying to one of the lesser gods that he had something going with. He waved his hand in answer and revealed these lands to them. They happened to be on a different plane, of course and were washed up on the beaches in swamped boats, with some dogs and horses and five hundred people of the Scotti. It turned out to be an enormous land of plenty, with an enchanted forest that kept them penned in. There were forest spirits, the scagsra that would appear to woodchoppers as beautiful women. When they embraced them, they could feel the bark on their backs. They disappeared, and no one knew where they had gone – trapped inside a tree for a hundred years.

A thousand years had passed. They had built castles, and still, they had not settled all the land there. There were feuds, of course, and for Celts, this was normal. That was the foreword to the book that turned out to be 150 000-word fairy tale.

When I wrote something I was really pleased with, I would dance around my cell, then go back to writing and trying to improve the grammar. Writing this was the single most exciting thing I had done in my life. So, the time went by faster than I would have thought.

It took me fourteen months in all to write. I also learned to use a computer and type.

At Christmas, I was asked by the dentist's assistant if I would like to spend Christmas with her and her family.

This was allowed, but the governor was worried I wouldn't come back. I had about eight months left. It was great, a snowy winter wonderland. I met her son, who let me hear The Red Hand of Ulster, Luka Bloom, Pink Floyd and other good music. Then she had asked me if I would like to watch

Braveheart. This was amazing. I loved it and had tears in my eyes several times.

We went out for a walk in this winter wonderland. There was a duck pond where only the centre was still water – the ducks kept this open.

All too soon, it was time to go back. Anna drove me to the door.

Next time Harald was on duty, he said, "Ah, you came back. I would have lost money on a bet if I had been here." He laughed as he made this revelation. I don't think he was serious. "Would you like to come out to the supermarket?" he asked.

"Can I?"

"Why not? You came back. That is the rule."

"Yes, but it was a special thing," the Chief had said.

"He is special, all right. He should have the same rule as all the rest," declared Harald.

"He is foreign," another said.

"He came back as he promised to do," Harald said. He went off and came back. "Yes, he can go; I spoke with the Governor."

Walking and talking with Harald was good. I enjoyed meeting his friend too. They had been in the merchant navy with him. He used to tell me you have never fished for cod till you have done it while serving on a flying boat. Tales of the coastguard days were many with Harald.

I was moved up to the top flat where all the good boys go. Every other kind of sport was played, every opportunity I could get.

The last eight months were spent cross-country skiing on a fitness course, which I loved.

Mariana was good in English. I think she had lived in America and gone to school there for a time. She read a bit of my book and came in one day to work with her hair tied up in a warlock style, straight up a foot in the air, like some of the female warriors in my book. I could have hugged and kissed her. Of course, I couldn't, but I truly loved that woman. We played doubles together in tennis a few times, burst a few bubbles too. We went for walks in the hills.

We spent time walking around the grounds, which were on a mountainside with wooded hills. A Vietnamese friend and I caught a red-breasted minnow in a burn, put him in the fish tank, and watched him make a nest in a jar. After about three weeks, he was so red it was bright like an electric eel. Poor wee chap. We put him back in the stream where we got him. The tropical fish didn't like him – he chased them away from his nest, waiting for his love to appear. I have seen many of them in my childhood, but never so bright; they glowed. The tropical fish kept clear. He would not let them near his territory. We ate Vietnamese food and Indian and pizza when I cooked. I soon learned Vietnamese cooking and how to debone a chicken and chop it all up into small pieces because the dark meat from the legs and wings makes the whole taste much better.

They also thought, like me, that skinny chickens that have run around the yard are far superior to the Frankenstein chickens of the west. I told them of the chickens in Kashmir that looked like the Road Runner, as BMC had said when he saw it. "Aw lad, we are not eating the Road Runner, are we?" he had quipped.

I picked cross-country skiing up very quickly. I had to, or I would have been out. Still, I was referred to as the Eagle, after our British Olympian Eddie the Eagle. There were fourteen of us, so I had the best of instruction. One chap, fifty feet straight above me, shouted, "Scottish, stand there!" I couldn't do otherwise. He jumped off an almost vertical cliff and, with a couple of turns and twists, landed right beside me. How the hell? "Telemark skiing," he said. I was gobsmacked. The instructor told him they are cross-country skis. "Don't do it again," he warned him.

The time to leave came, and I said goodbye to my friends. The guards too. The headmaster said to me when they shook hands, "You are the very best student we have ever had here."

"I wish my mother could hear you," I said. I left to be taken to the airport at Stavanger.

This was not like any other prison system or any other leaving. My head was in good shape, and I was ready for getting on with my life. I needed to see what awaited me. I thought of going to Holland and living there. I needed open-mindedness. I would speak to Tom and see what he thought about it. I arrived at Aberdeen, loaded with all the books I had read. I gave the whole lot of them to Rosie.

"Tom, this is the whole of the papers from the case in the Court of Human Rights, Anderson versus Norway, 1994," I said.

"Where the full 25 judges found in my favour. I am pissed with Norway for not compensating me or even freeing me, and a rat called Søren Nielsen, Norway's man in Strasbourg. It is he who cheated me out of compensation for four and a half years of my life. Keep it in a safe place. I'll never forget the smug tone of his answer that there would be no appeal against my decision. Someone was helping Norway to ignore its agreement to abide by The European Court of Human Rights rules and protocols that they had signed up to keep and not implemented."

"Who is Søren Nielsen?" asked Tom.

"He was the one who was putting the case to them on my behalf. We did not get on; I couldn't do anything about him. I tried, but he got everything sent from Norway to Strasbourg went on his desk. I was unhappy about the Dane," I continued. "He answered all my complaints about him handling my case being a member of a committee of nations – Scandinavia – where there is a clear bias. Denmark and Norway, being full of Nazis since the occupation, they got on very well with Søren Nielsen."

"I phoned him a few weeks after the judgement," I added. "About his handling of my compensation claim, and said there would be no appeal against my decision! All he needed was one person to co-sign his decision. The way he jeered at me, all-powerful, was soul destroying, I can tell you."

"Never mind, you look like you have come from Hawaii," said Tom.

"Sunbeds," I answered.

"What kind of prison was that you were in?"

"One that would reduce the crime rate of this country by half if they could use their brains instead of institutional violence. This country is a monarchy and full of great men: figureheads and no brains."

I stayed in a cottage for a while, then moved to another when Ellie and I got together again. I had given up. I could go no longer hoping she would come to me. We had never discussed it once. Then suddenly, she was there, and my heart sang with joy.

After four years in Frank's cottage, I counted the rent, which was not dear, and realised I would be far better getting a mortgage and building a house. Ellie had an operation which did not go well.

Mr Mole said," Give it a year or so to give it a chance, and we will do something else than to fix it." Unfortunately, he would not see her or do anything when we went back but instead sent her away. His words had meant nothing. He wanted space so he could not be blamed, I thought.

I would go and see councillor Arbuckle about the sewer that had disappeared to ask if he would support me in this. I knew he hated my guts; after a day, I had gone up to the community council and was backed up strongly when I put forward that they should build a gym and make a park out on the waterfront, where the council wanted to build houses. I proposed a gym and a park for the football team and the village.

"Where will the money come from?" I was asked.

"The EU will pay for half of it," I said and gave them my copy of the EU grants from the Scottish office (the Nazi party in Scotland).

"Where did you get this?" an accusing voice asked me.

"I sent for it," I said.

"Can I borrow it?" he asked.

"Yes, if you bring it back to me. I got it for myself for an idea I have." The booklet was never returned.

"It's the council's land," said a man in Wellies.

"They can do what they want with it."

"It's the village's land. Give them one row of houses, one and a half storey, so folk could still have a view and get the builder to pay for the gym with a five aside football in it for the team in the winter. You can't do that!"

"Why not?" I said.

"Everybody else does. Every town this size in Europe has a gym. It's a royal borough, same as St Andrew's, though Fife Council tries to hide that," I pointed out.

James the Fourth granted it. A lot of history here. Wallace spent three days celebrating at the Abbey after the defeat of Pembroke and the English army that pursued him here. Arriving with five hundred men, mostly from Galloway, they raised two thousand locals and ambushed Pembroke and defeated him. They spent three days eating every cattle beast in the area. The army swelled to five thousand, and he went on to free Scotland of its garrisons of English from all the castles, then invaded England. This was the turning point where the worm turned. I always felt the plaque that commemorates this should be a statue at least, doing justice to the importance of the battle of Black Earn side.

Arbuckle opposed every move I made. Especially if planning was involved.

I went to see him and said, "Andrew, what would you do if you were in my position, released after a frame-up? What would you do?"

His answer was a blank stare and a reddening complexion. I answered my own question. "Put my right foot forward and get on with my life?"

"Yes," he agreed but was looking bewildered.

He was the councillor I met at the meetings, and because they had read about me in the papers, I supposed, he cried me down at every given opportunity and opposed my planning applications for a house vigorously. He was able to influence the planners and others in the council. This guy served as chair of the planning committee, replacing his friend Francis Melville who had become provost (mayor) of Fife.

Conflict of interest doesn't seem to affect these people – buying and selling and developing the properties when he could.

He would have known about the Scottish Homes grant of £246,000 that we had got the nod for, as Crab Nairn was the previous councillor before Arbuckle. This opportunity was never put in place due to my being kidnapped by the Norwegian police. This severely damaged my business at the time.

When I asked Andrew about the sewer that was to go through a piece my land, he said there was no sewer that he had not heard about it.

It was a sewer paid for by the EU under the Tay purification. One leg had been mysteriously rubbed out. He knew nothing about it, of course. I said I was going to take up a petition.

"I will help you with it," he said.

I took up the petition, and everybody on the course of this burn that had a reed bed that did not work. It stank, so everyone wanted something done about it. The only one who did not sign it was Tommy, who said he would ask his friend Andrew, the councillor.

I also asked the councillor, Mr Arbuckle, to sign it. He said it was too long – it needed to be more concise. I think he meant the bit about him in it. He said it was too long; he said they wouldn't read it.

"Oh, they have read it all right; they have all signed it, too," I said. I showed him the bunch of signed papers. I had given him a blank to sign, but he folded it over and said he would write a letter.

The local paper did well with an article on the front page, then four more articles. It wouldn't go away.

Soon after the article, the water board handed the entire Quango, of which Fife council was a partner, back to the government, who gave it to Seepa, the environmental body, and told them to set up a new water board. They set up Scottish Water and Scottish Water Solutions.

We waited to get the water board, and when they came to the community council, I gave them the whole story in writing and a few copies for their upper management. They had been set up for two years, and nothing had been done. I asked questions like, "Where's the money from the EU gone?" I also said if I did not see actual work done on it by the end of the year – three months away – I would go to the EU.

Work started, and they got it in. It should have gone right down to take in Craig Mill and the rest of the houses in Burnside. They came as far as me with the sewer to shut me up, I assume, and did not put the rest of it in, even though it had been paid for by the EU.

I set up a wood business here, which is something I have a passion for. What triggered this was a friend of mine, Ed the Yank, said to me, "Dennis, could you accompany me to Cupar? I am buying some pitch pine boards from the office of a building being demolished. You could tell me if they are pitch pine or not?"

I agreed. Next day we went into the site that was being demolished.

There was a lot of ten-metre joists by three inches by twelve inches.

The guy showed Ed's wood. I looked at it and agreed it looked good to me. He saw me looking at the timber.

"How much will you pay for these beams and joists?" he asked.

"How many would I need to take to get them for a tenner each?" I said.

His head jerked round. "All of them, everything," he said; I held out my hand.

It came to £4,500. I said I would come on Saturday; I had the six-wheeler plant lorry stop on the outskirts of town at seven-thirty on the Saturday morning. I would phone him from there to come soon as all was ready for him to drive in.

I went along in my car and spoke to the man.

"See that Irish guy," he said said. "He's the boss. Can you give me £500 for him?"

"Ask him if I can load them with that manitou there then," he asked the Paddy, pointing at the manitou, and he nodded to indicate it was fine.

I gave him the money, and they all went off for the weekend. Tommy was left to lock up after us. I phoned the driver, and he came around with the lorry. They had all gone off.

"Do you have a key, Tommy?" I asked.

"No, and the forklift is locked."

"Do you have a key?" I asked the lorry driver

He smiled and came out with a large ring with twenty or so keys on it, opened it, jumped in and loaded his six-wheel plant lorry. We came back and forwards until we had put five loads in the yard in all my buildings and courtyards. I went back on Monday following to buy some Belfast sinks from Tommy. When his brother arrived with others in tow to buy some of the wood, he was shocked.

"Where is the wood?" he asked.

"You sold it all to him." Tommy smirked and said, "He loaded it with that forklift, and it's all gone."

I smiled. "My wood, you mean."

"No, there was some I wanted to keep. There were a few deals that would have gone if they could."

Tommy was greatly amused at this. I was aware of all the tricks and loved the game.

That was me back in the timber business again. I loved the work. It was hard and made me feel free.

My next deal was pitch pine from Clydebank, enormous beams from the same people. We turned most of this into flooring – beautiful, expensive flooring. The Lusitania must have leaned against some of these beams. They were a hundred and sixty years old, and the timbers were as good as the day they were felled. I enjoyed this work.

One of these beams yielded up a Viking spearhead. The trees came from the Canadian American border when they built John Brown's in Clydebank. In the sawmill at Scone, I was called because they had found some nails in the wood.

"I thought you had a metal detector," the large Aberdonian foreman roared down the phone at me. I had told him about it, but I couldn't get one, so I had one sent from America, and I was running out of sawmills because of nails.

"I have," I said.

"Well, the batteries must be needing to be changed." It was lying in the car seat next to me, unopened.

"I am on my way up to you," I said, and he replied that I had better be quick because if they were not finished by four thirty, they would not be getting done for a month.

I arrived quick smart in the yard with a lumber wizard. There were six beams ready to be cut into a size I could handle. I went to work: "beep, beep," then one went "Beeeeeeeeeep! Beeeeeeeeep!"

"That's a bolt," Sean said.

I rolled the beam. "No hole. I can't see where it goes in."

The beam was ten metres long, and it was smack in the middle. I marked the sides of where it should be by the beeps, took a chainsaw and cut down a slot on either side. I put a three-inch chisel on the bottom of the slot and began hammering it in. A piece flew off the top, and looking up at us was an arrowhead: A perfect leaf shape.

I cut the slots much deeper and took out a large chunk of wood with the arrowhead in it. More of the top came off, exposing it to be about four inches long. The foreman came over.

"Look at this; I've found an arrowhead," I said.

He replied, "Well if that's an arrowhead, I wouldn't like to see the size of a bow that fired that."

I had a vision at that moment of a hunter throwing a spear, and it snagged a sapling, and the shaft kept going. The thing was at the centre of the tree. This had grown to be a monster to have cut two 14" x 14" beams from it. I put the spear in a Tupperware sandwich box in my car and then finished checking the beams. On the way home, I took it to the archaeologists that were doing a major dig in Perth.

They said, "This is an important discovery you have here. You are doing the right thing by keeping it in a Tupperware container. When did you find it?"

"About an hour ago," I told him.

"You need some crystals to keep the moisture out," he said and provided some.

"It's probably iron, protected by the tree resin. I wish I could do something, but I am a guest here. You should take it to the local guy." He told me I would find him at the museum.

I walked round to the museum and found he was on holiday till Monday.

I returned on Monday and told him I had a spearhead. He looked at it and asked how I knew it was a spearhead and that I could have made it myself. He either had a hangover or had a terrible holiday.

"I'll tell you what," I said.

"What?" he asked.

"Get stuffed." With that, we left.

So much for the local archaeologist. He must have had a really bad holiday.

I did try the Fife archaeologist, who said, "Bring it to me. It's a treasure trove."

I didn't after hearing first-hand of his handling of a guy with an axe head, three thousand years old. He asked how much he would get for it to fund a film script he had written. He offered £350. My friend, Trotsky's pal, told him he would rather put it back where he had found it. A photographer got in touch with him and asked about it. When he showed him it, the police struck and took it away. I said that I would not do it, that I had put it in my bank. So, if he wanted to make legal moves, I would defend it because it came from a Canadian American tree and therefore was not a treasure trove.

The funny thing about the axe head is it was a beautiful green stone ceremonial axe head, never used. They came from Ireland, and they were traded here and elsewhere three thousand years ago. There were two of them, not one. Trotsky showed me the other one a few days before he died. He thought I would like the addition to the story. It was a thing of great beauty, a shiny, luminous blue-green.

The British Museum said the spear was a Viking spear of circa 1200 in the newspaper article on it.

I gave it to an American lady called Shirl Binney to take with her to Texas to get it dendrochronologically dated. She bumped me, so I have never seen it since. I reckon this would have been the oldest American iron artefact due to the preserving qualities of the tree resin. She just never brought it back.

While building a fence for him In the Village, I made friends with Evelin, and we would often enjoy coffee and a joint together. I told Evelin about the book that I had written in Norway, and he asked to read it. I told him he would have to print it out, and he said he could do that on his friend's computer. I gave him two floppy disks and told him it would need two reams of paper.

Later that day, Evelin's friend Catherine screeched to a halt at the top of the village. "Evelin has just called me, she said, "very excited about your book. 'Come quick, he said on the phone, this is major. It's like a cross between Tolkien and Terry Pratchett,' he had told her.'"

I was quite taken with this because I had had different reactions. One large Norwegian asked me to read it. His English wasn't that fluent. I asked him if he could read English, and he replied, "Yes, I am speaking English to you now." I was quite pleased that he wanted to read it, so I printed out four chapters from the beginning. I handed them to him, and they were returned next morning with a thump on the table. "I think you are a homosexual," he declared. I smiled. "I don't believe you can read that," I said. "Come on, read a page aloud, you primitive, piss off."

He left, and I never saw him again.

I sold my buildings, which was a farm steading with outline planning. I moved onto the land and asked for planning for a house. Arbuckle and the council opposed this. Made it quite clear that I would be getting nothing and poisoning every possible remedy.

I was busy sawing timber with a mobile mill, where I drove to estates and milled their timber there. The planers sent an enforcement officer to my small farm. I was amused at first. The only enforcer I had heard of was one called

Charles Bronson. He said I needed planning permission for a sawmill.

"I don't have a sawmill I said.

He said, "That's a sawmill."

"No," I said.

"That is a piece of mobile plant parked on my own land. You need planning permission for your caravan too". He said.

"Who sent you here?" I asked.

"The planning department."

"Does the planer have a name?"

"The head planner. Alister Hamilton."

"Well, you see the four wheels that this sits on." No answer.

"Well, when they say sawmill, you say wheels, now fuck off."

"You need planning," he said.

"Get off my land!" I spoke pointedly.

He got in his car and locked the doors. We left him there. I was furious.

We had our lunch, my wife and I, and went down, yoked the sawmill, and then drove to the next job.

We went to the committee to ask for planning permission for the house to be built. Every contact with the planners, trying to get them to do the right thing, they said send in three more copies of your drawings, even when we had made no mention of any change. They were out to break us.

This was costing us a fortune.

We went to the committee meeting, and our case was first. They said they were opposed, and the committee all agreed to oppose. That was it, finished in seconds, all done in less than a minute. We were asked to leave as there were a lot of people needing seats.

The Traveller site was granted planning permission on agricultural land at the same meeting to have six caravans. That was fine, apparently.

What was not fine was that I had no objections but had seventeen people saying it was a good thing and no objectors whatsoever, where the entire county was against the Traveller site. I am glad they got it since it was their land. Andrew Arbuckle, to his credit, supported them admirably.

He obviously had no beef with them for some reason.

The main reason they had been able to take it to the planning meeting was that because there were seventeen letters of support. They could pretend there were objectors. There were no objectors

It was getting near the end of time to put in an appeal. We had a visit from Alison Waite, our planner from the council, who had said from the first day that she would not support this application. She said it would be a nice place to have a house, but no.

This time, she said: Pull your application and put in a new one, and I will support you. I felt dubious of this change of heart. I couldn't think of the huge amount of money she had cost me. She went on to say, I will grant the barn you have built, and the cabin you have built, and the sawmill.

"The caravan too?"

"Yes," she answered, "just pull this one, and I will support you."

"I will wait and see if this happens," I said, looking as gullible as I could.

Two weeks before the date to lodge the appeal, the documents arrived, all stamped with planning permission. I phoned my planner, Andrew McCafferty. He asked me what I wanted to do.

"Leave it till the last minute and lodge the appeal."

"Right, I will lodge two copies at the two places at the same time. That should guard against an accident."

A while went by, and the recorder came, and so did all seventeen supporters.

Plus, Madame McCall, who was supporting me.

"Who is from the Council?" the recorder asked. Andrew McCafferty took the initiative and spoke. "No one, they have not come; there is no one from the council here."

"Who are all these people?"

"They are the supporters. There are no objectors to this application, except the council, of course."

"I will give them another thirty seconds," he said, and he pulled out his pocket watch. Then we were off, and we walked round the farm and answered all the questions he asked.

Sometime later, we received the news that the application had succeeded. The cost had been heavy on us, and it was going to take a long time to build a new business as well as finding the money to replace the costs of the council's horrible behaviour. I thought of the song, I've travelled round the world, met all kinds of men. Some will rob you with a six-gun, some with a fountain pen. The one good thing was the conditions the roads department had tried to have imposed; closing two four-hundred-year-old gates did not apply. Getting the sheep across the road would be easy as it always was, instead of impossible as the roads department on behalf of the nearby quarry. They tried to make things difficult and worthless by closing all our entrances. The quarry flooded us by digging a two-foot pipe out of the ground and replacing it with a one-foot pipe. The first time there was a spate in the burn, the pipe took away everything as it came out high up. All the soil that was built up since the Ice age was washed away until there was a twenty-foot drop and kept going so until the railway was being undermined. I was worried that the London train would land in our field because the wall was bursting and falling. I asked the community council to write a letter to them. They said in their letter that they thought I was only asking them to come so that I could charge them for crossing my land.

I know this because the rail track guys told me so because they were let in and shown immediately. The engineers thought it was in imminent danger, and the trains were made to slow down until they fixed it with a thousand tons of rock and a thousand tons of sand, which I gave them.

The council saw work being done and sent the enforcer out to cease all excavations.

"You can't start yet," they said.

The foreman of the job looked at me in disbelief and said. "You said they would do this." The foreman gasped.

He said to him, "We are rail track; we don't need planning permission." The enforcer reddened and hastily ran to his car and left.

Every hand is against you where the council are concerned. They will harass you until you die because of what someone read in the papers. If you are innocent, then it makes it very stressful to put up with all the shit that is thrown your way. The three slates all over again; it never ends.

Being of strong stuff, of course, one just keeps moving and working hard.

Cutting timber and building my house with Ellie, my wife, who is the best cook in the world, it makes it all easy to bear.

My daughter has been a great help to me, especially these last three years.

She has taken over the sawmill. She told me, "Go and write your book."

So, I have. I hope you like it. I would like to embarrass Norway into compensating me for my losses; systems built on state corruption are no good to man nor beast. The people in Norge, well, that's a whole different thing. I love the people of Norway; they are a shining example of humanity. Their legal system, well, that needs to be brought into the 21st century. A lot of the wealthy people there are the quislings Nazis who like control. They have the power of the legal system and the Police. That's the way of it in Kristiansand's.

I don't know if the Strasbourg ruling changed that much in terms of the rett review (law review), as they called it. I hope it did.

They seem to think that silence on the ruling that I did not get a fair trial should be kept secret, especially when it is benefitting their own citizens so much. They now must appeal a judgement against them, at least. Anderson against Norway. Fifteen judges all found in my favour unanimously. They were talking about a special prison to house foreigners when I left so that Norway could enjoy a police state hidden to outsiders. I hope the judgement made it better though I have doubts about police and courts who claim a 100% conviction rate.

The English courts are bad, but even if they don't claim 100% conviction rate. There are still many lying, unscrupulous people in the police and legal system who will stop at nothing and use gossip and Chinese whispers that are just like the witch trials. Same ideology. Promotion at the cost of a wee lie gives them great financial gains in pay and pension hikes. It does get a little better one hopes.

Printed in Great Britain
by Amazon

16991788R00162